Mind Scripts:

How the Stories We Tell Shape the Life We Live

Alice Reed Murphy

For permission requests, please contact the publisher: Alice Reed Murphy at amurphy.jolcc@gmail.com or www.jolcc.com

ISBN: 9798282939903

This book is a work of nonfiction. The names, characters, businesses, organizations, places, events, and incidents are either the product of the author's imagination or used in a factual manner. Any resemblance to actual persons, living or dead, or actual events is purely coincidental. In cases where real events or client stories are mentioned, identifying details have been modified to ensure confidentiality.

Cover Design: Alice Reed Murphy

First Edition: June 2025

Printed in the United States of America

This book is dedicated to my incredible clients, whose courage, resilience, and willingness to embrace growth continually inspire me. To my family, whose love, support, and unwavering belief in me have been a constant source of strength. And to my friends, who challenge me to think deeper, dream bigger, and live with authenticity. You all are the heartbeat behind this work, and your presence in my life fills me with gratitude and purpose.

Table of Contents

Note to the Reader

Dear Reader,

As you journey through the pages of this book, I want to extend to you a message of encouragement, love, and hope. This book is born from the desire to help you understand the power of the stories you tell yourself and how those stories shape the life you live. It is my heartfelt intention to guide you toward a greater sense of awareness, empowerment, and positive change.

However, it is important to remember that this book is not a substitute for professional help. We all navigate unique experiences, emotions, and challenges, and healing often requires personalized support. If you find that you need guidance beyond these pages, I encourage you to seek the assistance of a licensed professional who can support your journey with care and expertise.

Moreover, the insights and exercises shared here are not one-size-fits-all. Just as our stories are unique, so too are the paths we take to heal and grow. Take what resonates with you and leave behind what does not. Your journey is uniquely yours, and it deserves to be approached with compassion and grace.

Thank you for allowing me to be a part of your journey. I hope this book inspires you to explore your inner world with curiosity, to challenge limiting beliefs with courage, and to craft new, empowering narratives with intention. You hold the pen to your story—write it with love and purpose.

With warmth and support,
Alice Reed Murphy

"Within each of us is a sacred story waiting to be told, remembered, rewritten, and reclaimed. When we choose words aligned with love, truth, and possibility, we awaken the power to heal, transform, and create a life that reflects the soul's deepest wisdom."

— Alice Reed Murphy

Preface

We are all storytellers.

From the moment we begin to form thoughts, we begin to narrate. We create meaning from our experiences, we draw conclusions about who we are, and we explain our world to ourselves and others—sometimes with great accuracy, sometimes through distorted filters formed by fear, trauma, societal expectations, or old wounds. These narratives, while often unconscious, become the invisible scripts that drive our behaviors, shape our relationships, and ultimately define the life we live.

I have always been fascinated by the way people speak—not just what they say, but how they say it, and what those words reveal about what they believe. Through my years in counseling and working with individuals and families navigating anxiety, depression, trauma, and self-doubt, I noticed a common thread: the internal language people used to describe themselves often held more power over them than the actual circumstances of their lives.

That power—both to limit and to liberate—became the seed of this book.

Mind Scripts was born from the desire to help people become aware of the language they use and the beliefs they carry, and more importantly, to teach them how to *rewrite* those scripts. Too often, we repeat stories we have inherited from childhood, culture, or past pain—stories that no longer serve us, yet continue to dictate our choices and our sense of self-worth.

This book is not just about words; it is about awakening. It is about realizing that you are not the story you were told, nor are you bound to the story you've always told yourself. You are the narrator. You are the editor. And yes, you are the author of what comes next.

As you journey through these chapters, you will explore the psychology of belief systems, the neuroscience of thought, the influence of emotion, and the power of faith and hope. You will see how even small changes in your language can ripple into profound transformations in your behavior, your relationships, and your inner peace.

You will also find parts of my own journey woven throughout. Like you, I have had to confront old scripts. I have had to challenge assumptions, unlearn patterns, and find the courage to rewrite my own story with greater compassion, truth, and intention. I have come to believe that language is one of the most sacred tools we have—capable of wounding or healing, confining or setting free.

Whether you are reading this book because you're in a season of transition, looking for clarity, or simply curious about how thoughts shape your world, I invite you to read with openness. Highlight what speaks to you. Pause to reflect. Do the exercises. Come back to the stories. And most of all, be kind to yourself as you learn to listen differently—to your inner voice, your heart, and the new story that is waiting to be told.

This is your life. Let's write something beautiful.

With gratitude and hope,
Alice Reed Murphy

Ready to Go Deeper?

Transform Insight into Action with the Companion Journal

You've taken the first step by exploring the stories that shape your life. Now it's time to **put pen to paper and begin the process of rewriting your script** — one reflection at a time.

Introducing the companion guide:

Rewriting Your Script: *A Guided Companion Journal to Mind Scripts* **by Alice Reed Murphy**

Designed as a powerful extension of this book, this journal offers:

- ❖ **Bonus reflection prompts** aligned with each chapter
- ❖ **Lined pages** for free writing and deep self-exploration
- ❖ **Visualization space** to draw, sketch, or map your thoughts
- ❖ **Inspiring quotes** to encourage and ground your growth
- ❖ **A clean**, minimalist design that creates space to think and feel

"Awareness is the first step, but transformation happens when you begin to engage."

Whether you're journaling daily or working through a chapter each week, this tool will help you **clarify your inner voice, uncover limiting scripts, and rewrite your story with intention.**

Available on Amazon – just search for:

Rewriting Your Script: *A Guided Companion Journal to Mind Scripts* **by Alice Reed Murphy**

or visit: www.jolcc.com

Mind Scripts: *How the Stories We Tell Shape the Life We Live*

Introduction: *What Are Mind Scripts?*

We are all living by a script—sometimes written by our past, sometimes borrowed from others, and often so deeply embedded that we do not even realize we're following it.

These "mind scripts" are the internal stories we tell ourselves every day. They guide our choices, shape our relationships, influence our emotions, and determine how we respond to life's challenges. They are the silent authors behind our habits, behaviors, and even our sense of identity. And the most fascinating—and empowering—truth? We can rewrite them.

You might recognize a few of these scripts:

- "I always mess things up."
- "I'm not lovable unless I'm perfect."
- "Nothing ever works out for me."
- "I have to do it all or I'm failing."
- "I'm not good enough."

Sound familiar? These scripts can play quietly in the background, like elevator music for the soul—always on, always influencing, always setting the emotional tone. But what if you could press pause, listen closely, and decide to change the tune?

A Moment That Changed Everything

I remember sitting in my car one afternoon after a long day. I had just finished a counseling session—not as the therapist, but as the client. I had gone in expecting a solution, a fix for the emotional despair I could not seem to shake. But instead, my counselor looked at me and asked, *"Whose voice is that in your head telling you you're not good enough?"*

At first, I was defensive. *"It's mine,"* I said. But the truth was, it was not. It was a mix of past teachers, well-meaning family members, and old cultural messages about success and worth. I was living out a script I had not consciously chosen—and that moment changed everything for me.

That single question sparked a journey. I began to listen more closely to the words I said to myself. I started paying attention to the tone I used when I spoke to others. I noticed how much of my life was being shaped by silent assumptions and unspoken beliefs.

And as I challenged those thoughts and rewrote those scripts, something powerful happened: I began to feel free.

This book is the result of that transformation—my own, and the many I have had the honor of witnessing in others. It is a guide for anyone ready to reclaim their mind, their language, and their life.

This is not about toxic positivity or pretending life is perfect. It is about reclaiming the pen and becoming the conscious author of your experience. Whether your story has been filled with pain, doubt, or just plain confusion, there is always room to revise, reframe, and rewrite.

By the end of this journey, you will have a deeper understanding of the hidden scripts running your life—and a roadmap to rewrite them in ways that align with who you truly are and the future you want to create.

Are you ready to transform your life? Let's begin.

Chapter 1

Scripted from the Start: *How Early Narratives Shape Our Identity*

"The most powerful stories are the ones we don't even realize we're telling."
— Brené Brown

Before we ever had the language to describe who we are, the world began to tell us. From the moment we entered life, we were handed roles, expectations, labels, and beliefs. And slowly but surely, those external messages became our internal monologue—our *mind scripts*.

These "mind scripts" are the internal stories we tell ourselves every day. They guide our choices, shape our relationships, influence our emotions, and determine how we respond to life's challenges. They are the silent authors behind our habits, behaviors, and even our sense of identity. And the most fascinating—and empowering—truth? We can rewrite them.

In this chapter, we examine how the earliest narratives of our lives—shaped by family, culture, environment, and early experiences—form the foundation of our internal script. From birth, we are influenced by messages about who we are, what is expected of us, and how the world works. These unspoken and often unconscious scripts begin to write our sense of identity, worth, and potential before we even have the language to question them.

We will explore how these early-life messages—both direct and indirect—embed themselves in our thinking and become the blueprint for how we navigate relationships, emotions, and goals. You will learn how family roles, cultural expectations, and formative experiences contribute to beliefs that may empower or limit us as we grow.

By bringing these foundational scripts into awareness, we gain the opportunity to evaluate which parts of the story still serve us—and which are ready to be rewritten. This chapter invites you to reflect on the origin of your personal narrative and begin the journey of conscious authorship.

The Early Narratives That Shape Us

Most people are not aware of the scripts they are living by. That is because these scripts feel like truth. They are not always loud or obvious. They show up in how we respond to feedback, what we believe we deserve, how we pursue love, and whether we step into opportunity or shrink from it.

As children, we absorb more than we are taught. We soak up the tone in a parent's voice, the look in a teacher's eyes, the silence after a mistake. We learn what earns praise and what earns punishment. We observe who gets affection and who gets ignored. Our developing minds work overtime, trying to make sense of it all—and in doing so, we start writing the first chapters of our internal story.

These internal scripts often form in childhood, through a blend of family interactions, cultural norms, and our interpretation of repeated emotional experiences. As young minds, we do not have the critical thinking skills to question what we are taught. So, we absorb—deeply.

Some early scripts may look like:

- "I have to be strong, or people won't respect me."
- "Being vulnerable is dangerous."
- "I'm only valuable when I'm helping others."
- "People like me don't get ahead."

Other examples include:

- A child who only received attention when they performed well in school may carry the script: **"My worth is in my achievements."**
- A child who was constantly compared to a sibling may internalize: **"I'm never enough."**
- A teen who was bullied for their appearance might form: **"If I don't look perfect— I won't be accepted."**

These scripts become our internal rules for living, whether they are helpful or not.

Science Spotlight: Attachment, Identity, and Memory

John Bowlby's attachment theory (1969) and Mary Ainsworth's observational studies (1978) emphasize how early emotional bonds create the foundation for how we understand love, trust, and safety. Children with secure attachments tend to internalize scripts of worthiness and connection. But when attachment is inconsistent or lacking, children may form negative scripts that echo into adulthood—scripts like *"I'm too much,"* *"I have to earn love,"* or *"I can't rely on anyone"* (Ainsworth et al., 1978).

From a neuroscience perspective, early emotional experiences do not just create thoughts; they literally shape the brain. Repeated patterns of neglect, pressure, or criticism get encoded into neural pathways and become the "default settings" for how we interpret life. The amygdala, hippocampus, and prefrontal cortex work together to store emotional memory, assess threats, and make sense of social cues (Siegel, 2012). This means that a child who frequently feels criticized may neurologically rehearse defensiveness and shame, building a script that can last a lifetime unless disrupted.

How Scripts Become Habits

Once a script is written, our brain works to reinforce it. This is known as *confirmation bias*—we filter out anything that contradicts our belief, and we seek out what supports it. If you believe you are "not smart enough," you will dismiss praise and obsess over every mistake. If you believe "people always leave," you may sabotage connections to protect yourself from pain. And the more those beliefs seem to be "proven," the deeper they root.

This concept is often illustrated by the cognitive triangle, which shows how our thoughts, emotions, and behaviors are closely interconnected and influence one another (Beck, 1976). A thought like "I'm not capable" leads to feelings of anxiety, which may cause us to procrastinate or avoid challenges— thereby reinforcing the belief. This loop keeps the script alive, often without our awareness. Remember, you are creating your future with every thought you have.

The Role of Language in Shaping Scripts

Language is one of the most powerful tools of the mind—and a major vehicle for scripting. The words others use to describe us, and the words we hear ourselves say, create grooves in our psyche. Children are especially susceptible to this. A single label repeated enough— *"lazy," "dramatic," "bossy," "too sensitive," "you'll never amount to anything," "you're stupid,"*—can become a script we unknowingly grow into.

According to sociolinguistic research, repeated verbal messages influence a child's self-concept and behavioral patterns (Snow, 1999). The internal repetition of those words, even into adulthood, becomes a kind of *autopilot narration* that can shape major life decisions.

"I can't lead."
"I can't do anything right."
"I don't do emotions."

Those are not just thoughts. They are echoes of a script rehearsed long before you were conscious of it.

A Moment in Awareness: Michael's Moment

Michael, a high-performing college student, came into therapy with anxiety and a deep fear of failure. He could not explain it—he had always been *"the smart one"* in his family. But every exam triggered a near-panic attack.

When we peeled back the layers, a powerful script emerged:

"If I fail, I'll let everyone down."

This was not just his own belief. His family, struggling through generations of poverty, had invested all their hopes in him. That pressure, paired with praise only when he succeeded, had embedded a belief that his value was tied to achievement. The fear of failure was not just academic—it felt existential.

Unfulfilled: Jasmine's Story

"Let's look at a client story—Jasmine"—who came to me feeling deeply unfulfilled in her career. She was successful on paper, had a steady income, and even had the admiration of others. But she felt like she was living someone else's life.

When we explored her internal narrative, we uncovered a script that had shaped her every decision:
"Good girls don't take risks."

That belief had been subtly passed down through generations of women in her family—encouraging safety, rule-following, and not stirring the waters. Jasmine was not just dealing with a career crisis—she was trying to rewrite a generational script that told her who she was *allowed* to be.

Generational & Cultural Scripts

Our mind scripts are not just personal—they're often *inherited*. We carry the weight of generational beliefs, sometimes without ever speaking them out loud.

Some cultures script silence in response to struggle, viewing emotional expression as weakness. Others script overachievement as the only path to value. Even within the same family, siblings can inherit different scripts based on birth order, gender roles, or parental expectations. These inherited beliefs often remain unchallenged until we see the dissonance between what we want—and what we are unconsciously acting out.

That is the power of awareness. When you recognize the script, you reclaim the pen.

Reflection Questions: Starting Your Journey of Awareness

If you are ready to dig into your own scripts, here are some questions to start with:

1. What did I learn about success, failure, and love growing up?
2. Whose approval did I work hardest for, and what did I believe I had to do to earn it?

3. What phrases or messages do I hear in my head when I make a mistake?
4. What role did I play in my family (the fixer, the quiet one, the achiever)? How has that shaped my identity?

Your earliest scripts are not your final story. They are just the first draft.

I want to take a moment to explore this topic because, coming from a large family, I have seen firsthand how birth order shapes our roles. As the oldest girl—even though I was the third born—I still carried the responsibilities and expectations often placed on a firstborn. The birth order dynamic remained just as powerful.

Birth Order and Differing Scripts: How Siblings Inherit Unique Narratives

Even within the same family, no two children grow up in the exact same environment. While they may share the same parents, household, and community, siblings often develop very different internal scripts—shaped not only by personal experiences but by birth order, family dynamics, and the roles they are assigned (or assume) within the family system.

Birth order has long been studied in psychology for its influence on personality development, behavior, and self-concept. According to Alfred Adler (1956), one of the earliest psychologists to explore this concept, a child's position in the family influences how they perceive themselves in relation to others—and this perception can form the foundation of lifelong beliefs and internal narratives. *More on the birth order in a later chapter.*

Firstborns: The Responsible Achievers

Firstborns are often socialized to be leaders, caretakers, and overachievers. They may inherit scripts like:

- *"I have to be perfect."*
- *"It's my job to set the example."*
- *"I must always be in control."*

Because they are typically given more responsibility early on, firstborns may carry a heightened sense of duty or pressure to succeed. These scripts, if left unexamined, can lead to stress, people-pleasing, or difficulty asking for help (Sulloway, 1996).

Middle Children: The Peacemakers or the Forgotten

Middle children are often described as adaptable and diplomatic, but also prone to feeling overlooked. They may carry scripts such as:

- *"I have to keep the peace."*
- *"I don't really matter."*
- *"I'm the glue holding everyone together."*

Middle children sometimes struggle with identity, particularly if they are sandwiched between a high-achieving older sibling and a more doted-on youngest sibling. Their internal dialogue may reflect a deep need to stand out or feel significant (Eckstein, 2000).

Youngest Children: The Free Spirits or the Overlooked

The youngest sibling may be seen as the "baby" of the family— often more indulged, but sometimes not taken seriously. They might internalize messages like:

- *"Someone will always rescue me."*
- *"I need to be fun or entertaining to be noticed."*
- *"I can't make decisions on my own."*

While they may develop creativity and charm, they can also grow up with scripts that undermine their confidence or autonomy, especially if older siblings overshadowed them (Stewart & Campbell, 1991).

Only Children: The Lone Stars

Only children often receive undivided attention and adult-level expectations. Their internal scripts might include:

- *"I have to do it alone."*
- *"I must be the best."*
- *"I don't know how to relate to others easily."*

Though often mature and self-directed, only children may also struggle with pressure to excel or challenges with sharing control and intimacy in relationships (Falbo & Polit, 1986).

How Scripts Are Passed Down Differently in Families

Even when parents do not intend to treat their children differently, they inevitably do—because each child is born into a different version of the family. The firstborn enters a world of two adults learning to parent. By the time the second or third child arrives, dynamics have shifted. Parents might be more relaxed or more stressed, more financially stable or more distracted.

This evolving environment impacts what kind of attention, praise, discipline, or emotional support each child receives—thereby shaping the beliefs they form about themselves and their role in the world.

In therapy, it is not uncommon to see adult siblings who remember their childhoods completely differently. One may recall an overly critical parent, while the other remembers encouragement and warmth. Both experiences can be true, filtered through birth order, temperament, and interpretation.

Rewriting Birth Order Scripts

The good news is that birth order scripts, like all mind scripts, are not destiny. Once we become aware of the narratives we carry—whether it is the "hero," "mediator," or "rebel" story—we can begin to challenge them.

- Firstborns can learn to embrace imperfection and delegate.
- Middle children can practice asserting their needs.
- Youngest siblings can build independence and self-trust.
- Only children can foster collaboration and community.

Healing begins with recognition. When we understand that the roles we played were responses to our environment—not definitions of our worth—we gain the power to rewrite those roles into more authentic, empowered identities.

Key Takeaways

1. **We inherit our stories before we write them.**

   Before we had the language to define ourselves, we were absorbing powerful messages from family, culture, and early experiences. These messages became our mind scripts— internalized beliefs about who we are and how the world works.

2. **Mind scripts are often invisible but impactful.**

   These internal narratives feel like truth because they are deeply embedded. They influence how we see ourselves, how we behave, what we pursue, and what we avoid— often without our awareness.

3. **Early scripts are formed through experience and emotion.**

   Childhood moments of praise, punishment, silence, or comparison help form beliefs about worth, safety, love, and belonging. These scripts do not always come from what was said—but from what was felt, seen, or lacked.

4. **Science confirms the power of early narratives.**

   Attachment theory and neuroscience both show that early emotional bonds and repeated experiences literally shape the brain, forming the lens through which we view life— and ourselves.

5. **Scripts get reinforced through habit.**

   Once a belief is formed, we look for evidence to confirm it and behave in ways that keep it alive. This cognitive loop keeps outdated or harmful narratives running on autopilot.

6. **Language plays a key role in shaping identity.**

   The words we hear (and repeat internally) create our self-concept. Labels like "lazy," "dramatic," or "not enough" become mental refrains that script our actions and limit our potential.

7. **Birth order and family roles deepen our scripts.**

   Even within the same household, siblings can inherit vastly different narratives based on their position in the family and the roles they were assigned or assumed. These roles shape long-term beliefs about identity and worth.

8. **Scripts are often generational and cultural.**

   Many internal beliefs are passed down subtly through family dynamics and cultural norms—reinforcing silence, perfectionism, or self-sacrifice without ever being named.

9. **Awareness is the first step toward rewriting.**

    When we bring unconscious scripts into the light, we gain the power to question, challenge, and revise them. Our earliest stories may have shaped us—but they do not have to define us.

10. **You hold the pen now.**

    The chapter invites you to become the conscious author of your own narrative. Recognizing that your scripts were written for you opens the door to rewriting them by you.

By actively engaging in these exercises, you can begin to identify, challenge, and rewrite the scripts that were given to you early in life, ultimately creating a more empowering narrative for your future.

Reflection Questions: What Role Did You Play?

Take a moment to reflect on the following:

1. What birth order position did you hold in your family?
2. What were the unspoken expectations of you?
3. What scripts did you inherit based on that role?
4. How have those scripts shaped your relationships, career, or self-worth?
5. Which of these scripts are ready to be rewritten?

Your story is still being written. And your awareness of your script is the first step toward freedom.

✦ Chapter Summary

In Chapter 1, we explore the origins of our personal narratives, examining how we inherit stories long before we actively write them. Our early life scripts are shaped by our family dynamics, cultural influences, and significant experiences from childhood. These narratives are often formed without conscious awareness, yet they profoundly impact how we view ourselves and the world around us. As we uncover the science behind how these early scripts are developed, we come to understand the lasting effects they can have on our identity, emotional responses, and behavior. The chapter emphasizes the importance of recognizing these inherited scripts as the first step toward rewriting them. Through awareness and reflection, we can begin to take control of our narrative and start the process of conscious transformation, ultimately empowering us to rewrite the story of our lives.

Chapter 2

The Voices in Our Head: *Understanding Our Inner Voices*

"Change your language, and you change your thoughts. Change your thoughts, and you change your life." – Louise Hay

Chapter 1, we discover how early life experiences shape the scripts that guide our thoughts, behaviors, and beliefs. These scripts, however, are rarely silent. They manifest as a constant inner dialogue—a stream of thoughts and self-talk that plays in our minds. Often, these voices are not entirely our own; they echo emotional experiences, inherited beliefs, and cultural messages we have absorbed over time.

In this chapter, we will examine these internal voices and their powerful influence over our emotions, decisions, and self-perception. Some voices uplift and guide, while others criticize, doubt, or sabotage. You will learn to identify where these voices come from—whether parents, teachers, peers, or societal norms—and understand how they shape the story you tell yourself.

Drawing from cognitive psychology and self-awareness practices, this chapter will help you recognize and reframe unhelpful internal dialogue. As you quiet your inner critic and strengthen your inner guide, you will begin to cultivate a more compassionate and empowering voice—one that supports healing, confidence, and growth.

Where Do These Voices Come From?

The voices in our minds often originate from those closest to us during our formative years—caregivers, teachers, religious leaders, and peers. Through everyday interactions, we absorb their words, tones, expectations, and even unspoken messages. Over time, these external influences become internalized narratives, shaping how we see ourselves and interpret the world.

Our inner voice is rarely ours alone at first. It's built through our relationships with those who influenced or disciplined us, such as:

- Parents or caregivers
- Teachers and coaches
- Religious or cultural leaders
- Peer groups

Psychologist Richard Schwartz's *Internal Family Systems (IFS)* theory (1995) proposes that our inner world is made up of various "parts" or subpersonalities—each with a distinct voice and role. Some of these parts protect us from harm, some push us to succeed, and others help us process emotion. When in balance, they help us live in alignment with our values. When out of balance, they create internal conflict and self-doubt. Understanding the origins of these voices helps us realign with our authentic selves.

Examples of Internalized Voices

Internal voices often reflect early life experiences. For example, a child raised by a parent who emphasized achievement may internalize a message like: *"You're only valuable if you're the best."* As an adult, this may become a relentless pursuit of perfection, often at the cost of joy, rest, or self-worth.

Here are a few other common internal voices:

- **The Perfectionist Voice** – Echoes a critical parent: "If you don't do this perfectly, you'll fail."
- **The Fearful Voice** – Mirrors an anxious caregiver: "Don't try that—you might get hurt."
- **The Rebel Voice** – Responds to control or shame: "No one gets to tell me what to do."

These voices are not inherently bad. Many were formed to protect us in vulnerable moments. But left unexamined, they can undermine confidence, limit potential, and hinder personal growth.

The Science Behind Self-Talk

Self-talk—the ongoing inner dialogue we experience—is a core component of emotional and mental health. Far from being meaningless chatter, it directly impacts our performance, mood, and even physical well-being.

Research by Meichenbaum (1977) found that athletes who practice positive self-talk perform better under stress. Conversely, negative self-talk is closely linked to increased anxiety, depression, and avoidance behaviors.

Neurologically, this inner dialogue is processed through the *Default Mode Network* (DMN), a brain system active during self-referential thinking and daydreaming (Whitfield-Gabrieli & Ford, 2012). Overactivity in the DMN is associated with ruminative and negative thought loops, particularly in individuals with anxiety or depression.

The goal is not to silence these voices, but to engage with them intentionally—breaking unhelpful cycles and fostering healthier patterns of thought.

Understanding the Voices: Types and Functions

1. The Critic

This voice judges, corrects, and often shames. It typically stems from early criticism and is meant to keep us from making mistakes. When overactive, it fuels self-doubt and perfectionism.

Example: "You're not good enough. You'll never get this right."

2. The Protector

This voice seeks to prevent failure or harm. It often sounds cautious or anxious, warning us away from risk. While it's meant to keep us safe, it can hold us back from growth.

Example: "Don't try it. It's too risky."

3. The Pleaser

This voice prioritizes approval from others. Shaped by early rewards for being helpful or compliant, it can lead to self-neglect and a fear of conflict.

Example: *"If you don't please them, they won't like you."*

4. The Rebel

This voice resists authority and demands autonomy. Often born from control or shame, it can empower but also isolate if not managed.

Example: *"I'll do it my way—no one controls me."*

Real-Life Examples of Inner Scripts in Action

Carla's Inner Critic

Carla, a high-achieving marketing director, struggled with self-doubt despite consistent praise. A persistent voice told her, *"You're not smart enough to lead."*

Raised by a highly critical father, Carla internalized his unattainable standards. Over time, this voice grew louder, paralyzing her in moments of decision-making.

In therapy, Carla learned to recognize this voice as a reflection of her father's expectations, not her own truth. Naming and reframing it allowed her to reclaim her confidence.

James' Inner Debate

James, a successful entrepreneur, described his internal world as a mental boardroom: *"Half of them think I'm a fraud."*

His dominant inner voices included:

- The Critic: "You should've known better."
- The Protector: "Don't take risks—you'll fail."
- The Competitor: "Others are doing better than you."

These voices stemmed from early experiences with perfectionism and peer pressure. By identifying and dialoguing with these voices, James learned to separate his identity from them and step into his leadership with clarity.

Transforming the Voices: Practical Strategies

Changing your inner dialogue is not about shutting the voices down—it is about changing your relationship with them. Here is how:

1. Identify the Voice

Start by noticing repetitive thoughts. What do you hear most often? What is the tone or emotion behind it?

2. Personify the Voice

Give the voice a name or persona. This makes it easier to externalize and examine. (e.g., "Critical Carl," "Anxious Annie")

3. Question the Voice

Ask: *Is this voice still serving me? Is it rooted in truth—or old fears?*

4. Respond with Compassion

Rather than shutting it down, try responding kindly: "Thank you for trying to protect me, but I can handle this now."

5. Replace with a Healthier Voice

Build a new narrative based on your values and present reality. Let this voice be your inner coach—not your inner critic. *Example:* "I am enough as I am. Mistakes are part of learning, not a reflection of my worth."

Key Takeaways

1. **We All Have an Inner Narrative**

   Even when we are unaware, our minds are constantly speaking. These voices shape how we think, feel, and act.

2. **Not All Voices Are Our Own**

   Many internalized voices were inherited from caregivers, peers, or culture. Understanding their origin helps us choose which ones to keep and which ones to challenge.

3. **Self-Talk Is Malleable**

   The dialogue in your mind can be rewritten. With awareness and practice, you can transform your inner world into a source of support and strength.

4. **Your Voice Matters Most**

   As you cultivate a more compassionate and conscious internal dialogue, you become the author—not the echo—of your story.

By practicing these steps consistently, you can begin transforming your inner dialogue into a source of strength, clarity, and self-compassion.

Reflection Questions

1. What is the loudest voice in your head? What does it typically say to you?
2. Where did that voice originate from? Is it a reflection of someone else's belief?
3. How can you challenge this voice and replace it with a kinder, more empowering one?
4. How does this voice affect your behavior in everyday situations?
5. What would a wise, compassionate version of yourself say to you in moments of doubt or fear?

✦ Chapter Summary

Chapter 2 explores a powerful yet often overlooked force in our lives: our inner dialogue. This constant internal conversation shapes how we think, feel, and act—often without our awareness. While some inner voices offer guidance and support, others, like the inner critic, can be harsh and limiting. These voices are frequently rooted in early life scripts and can profoundly influence our self-perception and choices. This chapter offers tools such as reframing and challenging negative self-talk to help shift the inner narrative. The aim isn't to silence these voices, but to integrate them in ways that foster resilience, compassion, and personal growth.

Chapter 3

The Language of Identity: *Rewriting Who You Believe You Are*

"Words are not just labels—they are the mirrors that reflect who we believe ourselves to be." – Iyanla Vanzant

If our internal voices are the raw material of our mind scripts, then language is the instrument that writes, defines, and rewrites them. Language wields immense power—not only in how we communicate with others, but also in how we understand ourselves. The words we choose to describe our experiences, our relationships, and especially ourselves, shape our perception of reality and influence the direction of our lives. Most importantly, language is fluid—changeable and responsive. By intentionally changing the way we speak and think, we can shift the trajectory of our identity.

This chapter explores the deep connection between language and identity: how the words we absorb and internalize from childhood—labels, expectations, and cultural scripts—form the foundation of how we see ourselves. Whether we were called "the smart one," "the troublemaker," or "not enough," these early labels often become embedded narratives that define how we show up in the world.

You will discover that identity is not a fixed trait, but a dynamic, evolving story—one that we can consciously rewrite. By learning to challenge limiting language and embrace empowering alternatives, you can reshape your personal narrative to better reflect your truth, your growth, and your potential.

This chapter provides tools to help you move from inherited or imposed identities to consciously chosen ones—allowing you to reclaim authorship of your story and step into a more liberated, authentic version of yourself.

The Role of Language in Self-Identity

Our sense of self is never static. It continuously evolves through life experiences, relationships, and the internal dialogue we carry. At the center of this evolution is language—not just the words we say aloud, but also the silent, persistent narrative we repeat in our minds.

Language is more than descriptive; it is prescriptive. It tells us who we are and what is possible. The stories we tell ourselves do not just reflect reality—they *create* it. And central to these stories is the powerful phrase: "I am."

When we say, *"I am capable,"* we anchor ourselves in confidence. When we say, *"I am a failure,"* we confine ourselves to limitation. Such phrases shape not only our self-image but also our choices and behaviors.

Example: Language of Identity

Consider someone who has experienced a failed business venture. They may initially think, *"I am a failure because my business collapsed."* But this internal script can be rewritten: *"I am someone who is learning from this experience."* That small shift in language opens the door to growth, resilience, and a new narrative rooted in possibility.

As philosopher Ludwig Wittgenstein (1953) said, *"The limits of my language are the limits of my world."* When we change the words we use, we expand the possibilities of who we can become.

Example: From Victim to Survivor

Someone who has experienced trauma might say, *"I am a victim of my circumstances."* This language reinforces passivity and powerlessness. But if they reframe their identity as, *"I am a survivor who is healing,"* they step into an empowered story that emphasizes agency, strength, and recovery.

The Power of Reframing: Shifting the Narrative

Reframing is the practice of seeing a familiar experience through a different lens. It does not deny reality—it reinterprets it in a way that empowers rather than limits. This technique is central to breaking negative cycles of thought and behavior, offering a path from helplessness to hope.

Example: The Language of Failure

Imagine someone who did not meet a goal and says, *"I failed, which means I'm not good enough."* This story reinforces shame and discouragement. A reframe might be: *"I didn't succeed this time, but I learned something valuable that I can apply moving forward."* This revised narrative supports growth and self-compassion.

Example: From "Failure" to "Opportunity"

A person who was laid off might initially think, *"I'm a failure."* But through reframing, they could say, *"This is an opportunity to explore new paths and realign with what matters most to me."* This shift transforms a painful event into a catalyst for reinvention.

Reframing gives us the power to transform setbacks into opportunities for growth and enables us to tell more compassionate and courageous stories about ourselves.

Language and Neuroplasticity: Rewiring the Brain with Words

Neuroplasticity is the brain's remarkable ability to adapt, reorganize, and form new neural connections throughout life. It is a foundational concept in neuroscience that reveals how our thoughts, behaviors, and experiences can reshape the physical structure of the brain. But one of the most powerful and accessible tools for harnessing neuroplasticity is language. The words we use—both in our self-talk and our communication with others—are not merely symbolic; they are physiological triggers that can rewire the brain over time.

The Science Behind Language and Brain Change

Every time we use a word or phrase, we activate specific neural circuits. Repeated use of certain phrases can strengthen these pathways, making them more automatic. For example, if someone frequently thinks, *"I'm not good enough,"* this negative script becomes deeply ingrained as a dominant pathway in the brain. This is because neural pathways operate on a "use it or lose it" principle—those that are frequently activated become stronger, while those that are neglected weaken over time (Doidge, 2007).

41

However, the same principle applies to positive language. By intentionally using affirmations like *"I am capable," "I am worthy,"* or *"I am growing every day,"* we can create and strengthen new neural connections that support confidence, resilience, and self-acceptance. These positive scripts can gradually replace old, limiting beliefs.

Words as Tools for Cognitive Rewiring

Dr. Norman Doidge (2007), in *The Brain That Changes Itself,* provides compelling examples of how individuals have used language to reprogram their minds. His research highlights that language-based practices, including affirmations and mindfulness, can foster lasting cognitive and emotional transformation. Through consistent engagement with empowering language, individuals can effectively rewire their brains, replacing automatic negative thoughts with constructive, growth-focused ones.

But why is language so powerful in this process? The answer lies in the brain's connection between language and emotion. When we speak or think, we activate not only the language centers of the brain but also the limbic system—the area responsible for processing emotions. This means that words do not just convey information; they evoke feelings, trigger memories, and influence how we perceive ourselves and the world.

42

Breaking Free from Negative Language Loops

Negative self-talk, such as *"I always fail"* or *"I can't do anything right,"* creates a cycle of self-doubt and anxiety. These thoughts activate the brain's stress response, flooding the body with stress hormones like cortisol. Over time, these repetitive negative thoughts can lead to anxiety, depression, and low self-esteem.

But by intentionally choosing a more positive, constructive language, we can interrupt this cycle. For instance, instead of saying, *"I'm not good at this,"* we can say, *"I am learning, and I will improve with practice."* This subtle shift in language reduces emotional stress and helps the brain form new, empowering connections.

How to Harness the Power of Language for Brain Change

1. **Identify Limiting Beliefs:** Pay attention to negative scripts you frequently tell yourself. Write them down without judgment.
2. **Challenge Negative Language:** Replace limiting statements with more accurate, constructive ones. Instead of *"I'm always messing up,"* try *"I'm learning, and I'm making progress."*

3. **Use Daily Affirmations:** Create a list of positive affirmations that align with your goals and values. Repeat them daily with intention.

4. **Visualize Success:** Combine affirmations with mental imagery. Visualize yourself embodying the qualities you are affirming.

5. **Practice Mindful Language:** Be intentional with the words you use in your self-talk and conversations. Choose words that uplift and inspire.

The Physical Benefits of Positive Language

Research has shown that positive self-talk not only improves mood and mental health but also has physiological benefits. Studies in psychoneuroimmunology demonstrate that optimistic language can enhance immune function, reduce stress hormone levels, and promote faster recovery from illness (Segerstrom & Miller, 2004). In other words, the language we use does not just change our minds—it changes our bodies.

Ultimately, language is more than just a tool for communication; it is a tool for transformation. By becoming aware of the words we use and intentionally choosing those that empower, we can harness the power of neuroplasticity to reshape our thoughts, emotions, and lives. *More on this in a later chapter.*

The Importance of Positive Self-Talk

Positive self-talk is more than feel-good encouragement—it is a powerful psychological tool that influences mood, motivation, and resilience. Studies in positive psychology show that individuals who engage in affirming self-talk experience higher levels of well-being, better stress management, and healthier relationships (Seligman, 1998).

On the flip side, negative self-talk can fuel anxiety, depression, and self-doubt. The more we criticize ourselves, the more we reinforce the mental grooves of fear and failure.

Example: Shifting the Inner Critic

You might catch yourself thinking, *"I'll never get this right."* That inner critic thrives on certainty and finality. Instead, reframe it to: *"This is hard, but I've overcome challenges before—and I can learn this too."* The shift is subtle, but the impact is powerful.

Example: The Language of Resilience

A student who fails an exam might say, *"I'm just not smart enough."* This locks them into a fixed identity. But if they say, *"This is a learning opportunity—I'll come back stronger,"* they plant the seeds of perseverance, not defeat.

When we shift our internal dialogue, we shift our entire identity. Through conscious language, we do not just describe who we are—we decide who we become. Your story is still being written. Choose your words like they matter—because they do.

Creating New Narratives: Writing Your Own Story

Perhaps the most powerful way to reshape your identity is to become the conscious author of your story. Your story is not something that happens to you—it is something you *create* with intention. It is not about denying the past, but about giving it new meaning through your chosen lens.

Rewriting your story begins with awareness: What are the dominant scripts running in your mind? Are they serving your highest self—or limiting it?

Exercise: Rewriting Your Life Story

1. Write a short version of the story you've been telling yourself. Be honest and unfiltered.
2. Read it aloud and observe how it feels. Does it uplift or diminish you?
3. Now, take a breath—and rewrite it. Tell a new version that honors your resilience, values your growth, and leaves space for transformation.

Example:

- *Old Story:* "I've always struggled with confidence. I never get things right and I'm afraid of failing."
- *New Story:* "I am someone who has faced challenges and continues to grow stronger. Each step forward builds my courage and clarity."

This exercise is more than a journal prompt—it is a declaration. By choosing new words, you choose a new identity. One based not on fear or failure, but on truth, self-empowerment, and potential.

Key Takeaways

1. **Language Shapes Our Identity**

   The words we use to describe ourselves are not just labels; they actively shape how we see ourselves and how we interact with the world. Our internal narrative, made up of self-talk and external feedback, creates the lens through which we view our identity.

2. **Words Are Powerful Tools**

   The language we use, both internally and externally, influences our emotions, behaviors, and choices. Positive affirmations can boost confidence, while negative self-talk can perpetuate feelings of inadequacy or self-doubt.

3. **Early Language Forms Our Sense of Self**

   From childhood, we internalize the messages we hear. Words from parents, teachers, peers, and media contribute to the foundational beliefs about who we are, what we deserve, and how we fit into the world.

4. **Changing the Script Begins with Awareness**

   The first step in rewriting your story is recognizing the language you have inherited and how it is shaping your beliefs. Are you using language that empowers you, or are you reinforcing limiting beliefs with every word?

5. **The Stories We Tell Ourselves Become Our Truth**

   The stories we tell about our past, our failures, and our potential often define our present. By changing the narrative, we can shift how we perceive ourselves and what we believe is possible for our future.

6. **Empowering Language vs. Limiting Language**

   Empowering language encourages growth and resilience (e.g., "I am capable of change"), while limiting language keeps us stuck in old patterns (e.g., "I'll never be good enough"). The language we choose determines whether we remain static or evolve.

7. **Rewriting Your Script Requires Practice**

   Reframing your language is not a one-time event—it is an ongoing practice. The more you practice using empowering language, the more natural it becomes, gradually shifting your internal and external narratives.

8. **Language Reflects Our Core Beliefs**

   The way we talk about ourselves often reflects deep-seated beliefs. For instance, phrases like "I always mess up" can signal an underlying belief of unworthiness or fear of failure. Rewriting these beliefs requires changing the language that reflects them.

9. **Language Can Break the Cycle of Negative Patterns**

   Negative language patterns, when left unchecked, perpetuate cycles of self-doubt, anxiety, and depression. Changing the script is a powerful way to break free from these cycles and take control of your narrative.

10. **You Have the Power to Reclaim Your Story**

    Ultimately, the power to rewrite your script lies within you. By consciously choosing the language that aligns with your authentic self, you create the foundation for a healthier, more empowered identity.

By practicing these exercises regularly, you will begin to notice how your language transforms not just your thoughts, but your identity and actions as well. This consistent effort will empower you to rewrite your story with intention and clarity.

Reflection Questions

1. What is one limiting story you have been telling yourself about your life? How can you begin to reframe this narrative?

2. In what areas of your life could you benefit from positive self-talk? Write a few affirmations that you can use in challenging situations.

3. How can you reframe a current challenge or failure in your life as an opportunity for growth?

4. What new narrative can you write for your life that empowers you to embrace your strengths, values, and future possibilities?

✦ Chapter Summary

Chapter 3 explores the profound impact that language has on shaping our identity and the way we perceive ourselves. Our words not only reflect our thoughts but actively construct and reinforce our self-image. The language we use, both internally and externally, directly influences our beliefs, our sense of worth, and how we relate to others. This chapter discusses the transformative potential of conscious language, emphasizing how we can rewrite the narrative of our lives by choosing words that empower rather than limit us. By recognizing the power of language to reshape our reality, we begin to take responsibility for the stories we tell about ourselves. The chapter offers practical tools to challenge negative self-talk, reframe limiting beliefs, and use affirmations and positive language to create a new, empowering identity. Through the power of words, we can begin to step into the life we want to create.

Chapter 4

Shifting Beliefs: *Transforming the Subconscious Mind with Language*

"The words we choose build bridges or walls between hearts." – Thich Nhat Hanh

The subconscious mind holds the blueprint of our life experiences, guiding how we perceive and interact with the world. What is truly fascinating is that our subconscious beliefs do not have to be permanent. They can be rewired. One of the most profound ways to do this is through the deliberate use of language.

In this chapter, we probe onto how language acts as a powerful key to accessing and transforming the subconscious mind. The beliefs we hold—often shaped in childhood or through repeated life experiences—form the lens through which we interpret the world. Many of these beliefs operate beneath the surface, deeply influencing our behaviors, emotions, and decisions without conscious awareness.

You will learn how habitual language patterns—both internal and spoken—reinforce subconscious beliefs, for better or worse. We will explore how phrases like *"I always mess things up"* or *"I'm just not that kind of person"* can keep us stuck in self-limiting loops, while intentional language can begin to rewire those patterns and open new pathways for growth and self-trust.

This chapter introduces techniques drawn from cognitive restructuring, affirmations, visualization, and mindfulness to help shift internal narratives. You will discover how to identify outdated scripts, speak new truths into your life, and gradually reshape the subconscious landscape with empowering, aligned language.

Understanding the Subconscious Mind

The subconscious mind is responsible for about 95% of our mental activity, yet it operates below the level of conscious awareness. Unlike the conscious mind, which is deliberate and analytical, the subconscious functions automatically and continuously. It stores everything we've ever learned—our memories, beliefs, habits, emotions, and even trauma—and heavily influences our worldview, often without us realizing it (Bargh & Chartrand, 1999; Kahneman, 2011; Lipton, 2005). This vast internal system shapes our reactions, decisions, and behaviors long before our conscious mind catches up.

Think of the subconscious as a vast internal archive—a powerful file cabinet storing every belief, habit, and emotional response we have picked up along the way. These mental "programs" quietly shape how we react to stress, pursue success, navigate relationships, and interpret the world around us. Most of these programs were written in early childhood, a time when our minds were especially open and impressionable. During those formative years, we absorbed messages from our environment—words, tones, behaviors—without question or conscious filtering. Over time, these early imprints solidified into core beliefs, reinforced by repeated experiences and the language consistently used around (and within) us. For example, a child who is repeatedly told, *"You're not good enough,"* internalizes this message. The subconscious mind takes this as truth, and the individual may carry this belief into adulthood. This subconscious programming then manifests as behaviors and actions that reflect low self-worth, such as avoiding new opportunities or sabotaging relationships.

Metaphor: The Subconscious as a Silent Operating System

Think of your subconscious mind as the silent operating system running in the background of your life. Like the software beneath a computer's interface, it stores and executes all the default settings, shortcuts, and automatic responses you rely on each day. From the way you handle stress to how you form relationships, these hidden programs quietly influence every thought, feeling, and decision.

Most of this "code" was written when you were young—before you had the tools to question, filter, or understand the input. Instead, you absorbed everything: the tone of a parent's voice, the rules of your household, the unspoken lessons about love, success, or worth. Over time, these inputs became default settings, reinforced by repetition and woven into the language you heard—and eventually, the language you used with yourself.

But just like outdated software, these programs can be revised. With awareness and intention, you can rewrite the code.

Example: Repeating Patterns

Sarah, a 30-year-old woman, always felt like she was not capable of achieving her goals. She grew up in a family where success was always out of reach, and phrases like, *"People like us don't get ahead,"* were frequently heard. As she entered adulthood, Sarah's subconscious mind was programmed to expect failure, which led her to avoid pursuing her career goals. She internalized this belief so deeply that she subconsciously sabotaged opportunities for success through procrastination or withdrawal.

Example: The Hidden Power of Subconscious Beliefs

Imagine someone who has always struggled with self-worth, believing deep down that they are not good enough. This belief might have been formed early on through criticism, neglect, or societal messages. As an adult, this belief influences how they approach relationships, career opportunities, and self-care. They may shy away from challenging opportunities or stay in unhealthy situations because their subconscious mind believes they do not deserve anything better. By addressing and shifting these beliefs, they can begin to take more empowering actions that align with their true potential.

This is the result of subconscious programming: behaviors are shaped by beliefs that we often do not even recognize.

The Role of Language in Shaping Subconscious Beliefs

Language is not just a tool for communication; it is a tool for shaping our inner world. The words we use, both in thought and speech, carry significant power. Every thought we have, whether conscious or subconscious, is expressed through some form of internal language. When we repeat thoughts and words over time, they become embedded in our subconscious mind.

Language can serve as the bridge between our conscious desires and our subconscious programming. Words influence our mental states, guide our emotions, and determine how we view the world. When we speak words of limitation, we reinforce beliefs that hold us back.

Conversely, when we speak words of possibility, we create space for new beliefs and behaviors.

Example: The Influence of Positive Language

For example, when someone says, *"I can't do this,"* the subconscious mind registers this limitation. However, if the same person changes their language to *"I can handle challenges, and I am capable of learning new things,"* they create a new pathway in the subconscious. This shift in language begins to reprogram the belief system, reinforcing an image of competence and resilience.

Example: The Language of Empowerment

If you have a deep-seated belief that you are incapable of succeeding, changing your internal language to something more empowering can begin to shift this belief. For instance, instead of saying, *"I'm just not good enough,"* you could start saying, *"I am worthy of success and capable of achieving my goals."* The repetition of this new language gradually rewires the subconscious mind to accept this empowering belief.

This is the power of language: it can shape our thoughts, change our emotions, and guide the subconscious mind toward more empowering beliefs.

Affirmations and Visualization: Tools for Transformation

One of the most powerful ways to shift subconscious beliefs is through the intentional use of affirmations paired with visualization. Affirmations are positive, present-tense statements that affirm a truth about who you are or what you're becoming. They help rewire the subconscious mind by gently replacing negative self-talk and limiting beliefs with empowering thoughts rooted in possibility.

When combined with visualization, affirmations become even more potent. Visualization involves vividly imagining yourself living the life you desire—seeing, feeling, and experiencing your goals as if they are already real. The subconscious mind responds powerfully to this practice because it does not distinguish between reality and imagination. What you consistently picture in your mind, especially when paired with strong emotion and repetition, becomes a blueprint your subconscious begins working toward.

Personal Story:

I remember when I was just starting out in life. I would sit in quiet moments of prayer and visualize the kind of home I wanted to live in. I imagined tall trees and beautiful dogwoods swaying gently in the breeze, land with a peaceful pond, and a house with a specific number of bedrooms and bathrooms— fully furnished, warm, and affordable. I could feel myself walking through that space, surrounded by serenity and gratitude. Six months later, it manifested. Every detail I had visualized became reality. It was not just a wish—it was a blessing, made real through faith, focus, and unwavering belief. And unbeknownst to me, that was just the beginning.

This is the power of aligning your inner script with your vision. When your thoughts, emotions, and language align with what you truly desire, transformation follows.

Putting Affirmations and Visualization in Practice

Let us consider how affirmations and visualization can work together to transform a limiting belief into an empowering one—particularly in the context of career growth.

Imagine someone who struggles with feeling inadequate in their professional life. To shift this belief, they begin using the following affirmation:

- *"I am worthy of professional success, and I have the skills and resources to achieve my goals."*

Each day, they pair this affirmation with visualization—seeing themselves confidently walking into meetings, speaking with clarity, collaborating effectively with colleagues, and completing high-level projects with success. The more they visualize these scenarios while repeating the affirmation, the more their subconscious begins to internalize this new belief.

As this belief becomes more deeply rooted, their actions naturally begin to reflect it. They speak with more confidence, take on new challenges, and approach their work with a sense of purpose. Eventually, their external reality begins to mirror their internal shift—success follows belief.

Now let us apply this same principle to a different kind of internal transformation:

Visualization and Affirmations in Daily Life

Suppose someone wants to move from the belief *"I can't handle stress"* to *"I am calm, capable, and resourceful in the face of stress."* To anchor this shift, they might use the following tools:

- **Affirmation:** "I am calm, capable, and resourceful when faced with challenges."

- **Visualization:** With eyes closed, they imagine themselves in a previously stressful situation—this time responding with clarity and composure. They see themselves breathing deeply, thinking clearly, and taking thoughtful, effective actions.

By practicing this daily, the subconscious begins to accept the new narrative as truth. Over time, when real-life stress arises, the individual responds with greater calm and control—mirroring the inner transformation they have cultivated. Transforming the subconscious mind is not an overnight process—it's a daily commitment to speaking, thinking, and living in alignment with your true self. As you continue to choose empowering words and visualize the life you desire, you will begin to witness the quiet but consistent transformation that language can create.

Reprogramming Limiting Beliefs: The Power of Repetition

Repetition is a foundational tool in transforming beliefs. Just as negative thoughts—when repeated over time—can solidify into deeply rooted limitations, the same process can be used to instill empowering and affirming beliefs. The subconscious mind learns through consistency, and what we tell ourselves regularly eventually becomes our internal truth.

When we consciously repeat affirmations, empowering language, and visualizations, we begin to create new neural pathways in the brain. These new pathways gradually override the old ones that were built on fear, doubt, or past conditioning. With time, the subconscious starts to accept these new, positive beliefs as reality

Example: Repetition as a Tool for Change

Take John, for instance. For years, he carried the belief, *"I'm not good enough."* It echoed in his mind through self-doubt and hesitation. But John decided to rewrite this narrative. Every morning, he began reciting affirmations such as:

- "I am good enough."
- "I am capable of success."
- "I deserve happiness and abundance."

He wrote them in his journal, spoke them aloud in the mirror, and repeated them silently throughout the day. At first, they felt foreign—like trying on clothes that did not quite fit. But over time, something shifted. His confidence began to rise. He spoke up more in meetings, took risks he used to avoid, and pursued goals he once believed were out of reach.

Through repetition, John did not just change his words—he rewired his sense of self-worth.

Example: Rewriting the Story

If you have spent years believing things like *"I'm not smart enough," "I don't have the resources,"* or *"It's too late for me to change,"* those beliefs have likely shaped your reality. But they are not permanent. Start by identifying the old narratives, then intentionally replace them with affirmations that reflect your potential.

- "I am capable and intelligent enough to achieve my dreams."
- "I have everything I need—and I am attracting more every day."
- "It's never too late to start living the life I truly desire."

Repeat them. Say them out loud. Write them down. Visualize them as already true. The more often you do, the more your subconscious mind will begin to align with these new truths. And as your internal script changes, so will your external world—through your actions, your choices, and your renewed belief in what is possible.

The Impact of Language on Emotional Responses

The connection between language and emotion is both powerful and deeply rooted in the subconscious mind. Our beliefs—especially the limiting ones—are not just abstract thoughts; they are emotionally charged scripts that influence how we feel, respond, and show up in the world. These internalized narratives often trigger emotional states like fear, anxiety, shame, or frustration. What is important to understand is that much of this emotional response is shaped by the language we use—internally and externally.

Language acts as the bridge between thought and feeling. The words we choose to describe our experiences have the power to intensify or diffuse our emotional responses. When we consistently speak or think in disempowering ways, we reinforce the negative emotions connected to those thoughts. Conversely, when we consciously shift our language, we can also shift our emotional state.

For instance, consider the difference between these two statements:

- "I'm angry because of what they did to me."
- "I'm feeling frustrated by this situation, but I have the tools to respond with clarity."

The first sentence places blame and positions the speaker as a passive recipient of harm, fueling feelings of powerlessness and reactivity. The second acknowledges the emotion but reclaims control—it reframes the experience and opens the door for a calmer, more empowered emotional state.

Another common example is the phrase, *"I can't handle this."* That statement signals helplessness to the brain, activating stress responses and emotional shutdown. Now consider reframing it as, *"This is difficult, but I've handled hard things before, and I'll get through this too."* This simple shift in language tells the brain a different story—one of resilience and capability.

Language does not just describe our emotional experiences—it shapes them. It gives form and structure to feelings that might otherwise remain raw or overwhelming. By labeling emotions in healthier ways and using language that reflects hope, growth, and strength, we can regulate our emotions more effectively and foster emotional resilience.

This is why practices like mindfulness and cognitive reframing are so transformative. They teach us to slow down and become aware of the words we use—internally and externally—especially when we're in emotional distress. The moment we change our language, we begin to change our brain's response to a situation.

Practical Application: Reframing Emotional Triggers

When you notice yourself using emotionally charged language, pause and ask:

1. What am I really feeling right now?
2. Is there a more empowering way I can describe this experience?
3. How can I speak to myself with compassion instead of criticism?

Over time, this intentional use of language becomes a habit. It not only shifts how we feel in the moment but also begins to rewire the subconscious beliefs that keep us stuck in negative emotional cycles.

Language is not just how we express emotion—it is how we experience and transform it. When we choose our words with care, we can move from feeling overwhelmed and reactive to grounded and empowered.

Example: Language Shifting Emotional Responses

Sarah, a woman struggling with stress, typically uses language like *"I'm so overwhelmed, I can't cope,"* which amplifies her anxiety. Instead, she begins to shift her language to *"I am feeling stressed right now, but I am calm, and I know I can find a way to manage this."* Over time, this shift in language helps Sarah feel more in control of her emotions. She begins to recognize that stress is not something that controls her, but rather something she can manage through perspective and action.

Key Takeaways

1. **The Power of Subconscious Beliefs**

   Our subconscious mind holds deep-rooted beliefs that often dictate how we perceive ourselves, others, and the world around us. These beliefs are formed over time through our experiences, especially those from childhood, and can be positive or limiting.

2. **Language Shapes the Subconscious**

   Language is a powerful tool in shaping our beliefs and perceptions. The words we use, both consciously and unconsciously, influence our thoughts, emotions, and behaviors. Repetitive language patterns—whether self-talk or external dialogue—can reinforce or challenge our deep-seated beliefs.

3. **Beliefs Drive Behavior**

   Our beliefs, especially those held in the subconscious, play a crucial role in determining how we act and respond to life's challenges. Limiting beliefs can result in self-sabotage, while empowering beliefs open up possibilities and guide us toward success and fulfillment.

4. **The Subconscious Mind Does Not Distinguish Between Reality and Belief**

   The subconscious mind accepts everything as true, whether it is based on actual reality or perceived truths. This means that the beliefs we hold in our subconscious can shape our reality, even if they are not based on objective facts.

5. **Reprogramming the Subconscious**

   Shifting beliefs involves reprogramming the subconscious mind by actively changing the language we use. This can be achieved through affirmations, visualization, and intentional self-talk that challenge limiting beliefs and promote more empowering perspectives.

6. **Repetition is Key**

   The subconscious mind responds to repetition. Repeating positive affirmations, mantras, and empowering language helps to overwrite limiting beliefs with more constructive ones. Over time, these new beliefs begin to influence our actions, feelings, and thought patterns.

7. **The Role of Consistency and Patience**

   Shifting deeply ingrained beliefs takes time and consistent effort. It is not a one-time fix, but an ongoing process of practicing new language patterns and consciously engaging with your internal dialogue. Patience is crucial, as change does not happen overnight.

8. **Visualizing the Desired Outcome**

   Visualization is a powerful tool for shifting beliefs. By vividly imagining the person you want to become or the life you wish to create, you can communicate these new possibilities to your subconscious mind. The more detailed and emotionally engaged the visualization is, the more effective it will be in creating lasting change.

9. **Challenging Old Beliefs with New Language**

   To shift your beliefs, you need to challenge the old, limiting beliefs by asking critical questions like:

   • Is this belief true?

   • Where did it come from?

   • Does this belief serve me?

   This questioning, paired with new, more empowering

language, allows you to break free from limiting beliefs and replace them with more constructive narratives.

10. **Empowerment Through Choice of Language**

We have the power to choose the language we use, both with ourselves and others. By intentionally choosing a language that reflects empowerment, self-love, and growth, we can create new belief systems that align with our authentic desires and goals.

These takeaways illustrate the importance of language in reshaping our subconscious beliefs. By understanding how language affects our internal dialogue and taking proactive steps to reframe and challenge old beliefs, we can create lasting transformation in our lives.

Reflection Questions:

1. What are some of the most limiting beliefs you have held about yourself? How have they influenced your decisions and actions?

2. How can you reframe these beliefs using more empowering language?

3. What would your life look like if you consistently used positive affirmations and visualization to reprogram your subconscious mind?

4. How has the language you use affected your emotional responses in difficult situations? What changes can you make in your language to transform your emotional experiences?

These reflective questions will help you use language consciously to shift your beliefs, reprogram your subconscious, and ultimately change your experience of the world. With practice, you will begin to replace limiting beliefs with empowering ones that align with your authentic self and desires.

✦ Chapter Summary

Chapter 4 dives deep into the subconscious mind and its role in shaping our beliefs, behaviors, and realities. It reveals how early experiences and repeated messages from our environment become ingrained as subconscious scripts that influence the way we interact with the world. These beliefs often operate silently, outside of our conscious awareness, dictating our choices, responses, and interactions. Language is a key tool in transforming these subconscious scripts. By using intentional language—such as affirmations, visualization, and reframing— we can reprogram limiting beliefs that have been formed over time. This chapter introduces the concept of "mind reprogramming," showing how repetition and positive language can create lasting change. It empowers readers to shift from a fixed mindset to a growth mindset, offering them the tools to transform the very foundation of their thoughts and beliefs. With this transformation, we unlock the potential to rewrite our story, aligning our subconscious mind with the reality we want to create.

Chapter 5

The Ripple Effect: *How Your Words Shape Your Relationships*

"You are not the story you were handed—you are the author of what comes next." – Oprah Winfrey

Words are powerful. They hold the potential to build or break relationships, to strengthen or weaken bonds. Our language serves as a mirror to our thoughts and attitudes, shaping how we relate to others. Whether we realize it or not, the words we use with friends, family members, partners, and colleagues create a ripple effect that impacts not only the present conversation but also the future trajectory of the relationship.

In this chapter, we explore the profound impact of language on our relationships—with partners, family, friends, and even strangers. The words we choose do not just express how we feel—they shape how others experience us, how conflict unfolds or resolves, and how trust is built or broken. Language is both a mirror and a bridge: it reflects our inner world and connects us to the hearts of others.

We will examine the difference between reactive and mindful communication, the importance of emotional ownership through "I" statements, and how empathy-driven language fosters deeper emotional intimacy. You will also learn how negative language—such as criticism, sarcasm, or passive-aggression—can corrode relationships over time, while compassionate and intentional communication has the power to heal and strengthen bonds.

This chapter offers practical tools for transforming how you speak and listen in your relationships, revealing how even small shifts in language can create a ripple effect of connection, understanding, and mutual respect.

Language as a Mirror and a Bridge

At the core of every relationship is communication. How we speak to others, how we listen, and how we respond shapes the dynamic of that relationship. Words are much more than expressions; they are the carriers of emotion, meaning, and intention. Whether we realize it or not, our words can either build bridges or create walls between us and those we care about.

Language is not just a tool for conveying information—it is also a tool for shaping our reality. It reflects our beliefs and carries emotional weight. For instance, the words we use can reveal whether we see relationships as a struggle or a source of joy.

For example, if we believe that relationships require constant effort, we might say things like, "*We need to work on this all the time.*" If we believe relationships can be harmonious and growth-oriented, we might instead say, "*We communicate well and continue to grow together.*"

Our language shapes how others feel about themselves and the relationship. Words of encouragement, appreciation, and empathy strengthen bonds. In contrast, criticism, blame, and judgment often lead to tension and disconnection.

Example: Building a Positive Dynamic

Imagine a workplace where one colleague regularly praises another's contributions with comments like, "*You did an amazing job with that presentation—your skills are impressive!*" These words uplift confidence and create a cycle of trust. Now consider if the same colleague often said, "*This is okay, but it could have been better.*" Over time, this pattern can create resentment and erode morale.

The Impact of Positive Language in Relationships

Positive language is one of the most powerful tools for nurturing healthy, thriving relationships. Affirming, empathetic, and supportive words create a sense of safety, appreciation, and trust.

In romantic relationships, words play a central role in maintaining emotional intimacy. Phrases like *"I love you," "I appreciate you,"* or *"Thank you for being here for me,"* foster deeper emotional bonds.

In conflict, positive language helps de-escalate tension. Saying, *"I understand your point of view,"* or *"Let's find a solution together,"* expresses empathy and collaboration—key components of emotional safety.

Example: Language in Healthy Relationships

Consider a couple where one partner feels overwhelmed with work. The other might say, *"I see you're stressed, and I'm here for you. How can I support you?"* This compassionate language communicates love and partnership. Contrast this with, *"You're always stressed—just deal with it,"* which increases disconnection and stress.

Example: Language in Conflict

When disagreements arise, how we speak matters. If one partner says, *"You never listen to me,"* the other may feel attacked. Reframing this to *"I feel unheard right now—can we try to listen to each other more intentionally?"* shifts the tone from blame to understanding.

The Destructive Impact of Negative Language

While positive language can uplift, negative language can cause lasting harm. Words that criticize, belittle, blame, or dismiss can chip away at trust and connection.

Criticism is especially damaging when it targets a person's character rather than their behavior. For example, saying *"You're so lazy"* attacks identity, whereas saying *"I noticed you didn't follow through today—can we talk about what happened?"* focuses on behavior.

"You" statements like *"You never listen!"* often feel accusatory and trigger defensiveness. In contrast, "I" statements shift the focus to the speaker's experience: *"I feel hurt when I don't feel heard"* encourages openness rather than conflict.

Example: Shifting from Criticism to Understanding

A frustrated parent might say, *"You never listen to me!"* Instead, they could say, *"I'm feeling unheard and frustrated. Can we talk about this together?"* This shift prevents the child from feeling attacked and invites conversation.

Sarcasm, judgment, and blame also erode communication. Remarks like, "Why do you always make such stupid decisions?" foster shame and resentment, while constructive alternatives invite growth.

Example: Criticism vs. Constructive Communication

A parent who says, *"You never do anything right. I'm disappointed in you,"* may leave a child feeling worthless. A better approach is: *"I believe you can do better next time. Let's work on it together."* This reframing communicates belief in the child's potential, promoting resilience and a growth mindset.

Language and Emotional Regulation

Words do not just affect others—they influence how we regulate our own emotions. In emotionally charged situations, our choice of words can either escalate or calm the storm.

When we are angry or upset, pausing before responding allows us to choose words that reflect intentionality rather than reactivity. Mindfulness practices—like taking a deep breath before speaking—can help us respond with clarity and compassion.

Rather than saying, *"I'm so mad I can't think straight!"* we can reframe to, *"I'm feeling frustrated, but I want to respond thoughtfully."* This not only manages our emotional state, it also models emotional maturity.

Example: Emotional Regulation in Difficult Conversations

Imagine someone receives harsh feedback at work and feels angry. Instead of lashing out, they might say, *"I'm feeling upset about what was said. Can we have a calm conversation about it?"* This invites resolution instead of confrontation.

Why Listening Is Vital for Vulnerability

Vulnerability is often understood as emotional openness—
sharing our innermost thoughts, feelings, and fears with others.
It involves letting our guard down and allowing ourselves to be
fully seen. However, vulnerability cannot exist in a vacuum. It
requires a receptive, empathetic listener to truly flourish.

When we are vulnerable, we share parts of our emotional selves
that may feel raw or exposed. For this to be a healing and
constructive experience, the listener's response must be one of
acceptance, understanding, and compassion. Without this,
vulnerability can quickly lead to feelings of shame or rejection,
which may further distance us from those we seek to connect
with.

In intimate relationships, whether with a romantic partner,
family member, or friend—vulnerability deepens connection
and fosters trust. While vulnerability involves risk, it also opens
the door to deep emotional connection and intimacy.

The Role of Non-Judgmental Listening in Vulnerability

To create a space where vulnerability can thrive, the listener must be non-judgmental. Listening without criticizing, interrupting, or offering unsolicited advice gives the speaker freedom to express their emotions without fear of rejection. Non-judgmental listening means holding space for someone's feelings without feeling the need to fix or change them.

For example, imagine a partner confides their fear of failing in their career. Instead of responding, *"You're being dramatic, it's not that big of a deal,"* a more empathetic response would be, *"I can see why you're feeling anxious. It must be tough to carry that fear."* The listener's ability to sit with the speaker's vulnerability and hold space for those emotions is what makes the connection meaningful and transformative.

Vulnerability as a Bridge to Deeper Emotional Connection

Vulnerability plays a crucial role in deepening emotional connections by creating an opportunity for individuals to share their authentic selves. When we share our fears, desires, and insecurities, we invite others into our emotional world in a way that fosters closeness. Vulnerability is not weakness—it is courage and emotional honesty.

In relationships, the willingness to be vulnerable demonstrates trust and encourages reciprocity. When one person opens up, it creates a safe environment for the other to do the same. This mutual sharing strengthens bonds and fosters a deeper understanding of each other's emotional experiences.

Example: Vulnerability in Family Dynamics

Consider a parent-child relationship. When a parent admits, "*I don't have all the answers, and I'm doing the best I can,*" it allows the child to see them as a human being rather than an authority figure with all the answers. This moment of vulnerability can lead to greater empathy and understanding on both sides, helping the child feel more comfortable expressing their own struggles and emotions.

Vulnerability in relationships also opens the door to healing old wounds. For example, a person who was hurt in the past might find it difficult to open up again. But by allowing themselves to be vulnerable and sharing their hurt with a trusted partner, they express their emotions and move toward healing. In return, the listener's supportive response fosters trust and emotional recovery.

Practices for Cultivating Vulnerability Through Language

1. **Share Your Fears:**

   Begin by openly expressing your fears, even if they seem trivial or embarrassing. For example,

   "I'm feeling really anxious about this situation, and I'm afraid it might not go well."

   Putting vulnerability into words invites others to understand you more deeply.

2. **Express Your Needs:**

   Often, we expect others to understand our needs without expressing them. Sharing your emotional needs allows others to respond with care. For example,

   "I'm feeling really overwhelmed, and I just need some quiet time to recharge."

   This clarity invites meaningful support.

3. **Use Vulnerable Language:**

   In conversations where you might usually hold back, try using phrases like

   "I'm struggling with this," "This is really hard for me," or *"I'm not sure how to handle this, but I'm doing my best."*

   Such language opens space for deeper emotional connection.

4. **Encourage Vulnerability in Others:**

   When you listen empathetically and validate someone's emotions, you create an environment that encourages vulnerability. Respond with words like,

   "I'm so glad you felt comfortable sharing that with me. I'm here for you."

   This affirms their vulnerability and strengthens your relationship.

Listening and Vulnerability in Conflict Resolution

Conflict is inevitable in any relationship, but how we handle it makes all the difference. Listening and vulnerability are especially important during disagreements because they create the foundation for resolution and healing.

During conflict, it is easy to focus on our own emotions and defensiveness, but active listening and vulnerability shift the focus from "winning" to understanding each other's perspectives. Instead of using language that attacks or blames, vulnerability allows us to express feelings without causing further harm.

Example: Vulnerability in Conflict

Instead of saying, *"You always ignore my needs!"* (a blaming statement), try saying,

"I'm feeling really hurt because I don't feel heard. I need to feel understood and supported right now."

This acknowledges your emotions without accusing the other person, creating space for empathy.

By listening deeply and being vulnerable, we can transform conflict into an opportunity for growth and understanding, rather than disconnection.

Key Takeaways

1. **Words Have Power**

   Every word influences others, positively or negatively. Our language can build connections or create division, shaping relationship dynamics.

2. **Words Create Perceptions**

   The words we choose shape how others perceive us and themselves. Positive, affirming language boosts confidence; negative language creates distance.

3. **Emotional Impact**

   Words have a profound emotional effect, intended or not. Encouragement uplifts, criticism harms. Mindfulness of this impact fosters healthier relationships.

4. **Active Listening and Empathy**

   True connection requires thoughtful speaking and active listening. Combined with empathy, words create stronger bonds and deeper communication.

5. **Language Reflects Beliefs and Values**

   How we communicate reveals our underlying beliefs and values, which can align or clash with those of others.

6. **Conflict Resolution Through Language**

   Words are key to resolving conflicts. Compassionate, respectful, and clear communication de-escalates situations and fosters understanding.

7. **The Role of Vulnerability**

   Honest and vulnerable communication makes others feel safe and seen, promoting trust and intimacy.

8. **Building Connection Through Shared Language**

   Shared language creates belonging and identity. Inside jokes, common values, and understanding help us bond deeply.

9. **The Impact of Nonverbal Language**

   Communication is more than words—body language, tone, and facial expressions affect how messages are received.

10. **The Long-Term Effects of Words**

    Language spoken today ripple into the future. Positive language creates lasting trust; negative words can cause enduring emotional scars.

These points highlight how language shapes our relationships. By choosing words consciously, we create positive ripples that foster empathy, understanding, and healthier connections.

Reflection Questions

1. When was the last time you felt truly heard in a conversation? How did that affect your relationship with the listener?

2. How often do you allow yourself to be vulnerable in relationships? What holds you back?

3. How can you practice active listening to deepen emotional connections?

4. How can you use vulnerability to strengthen relationships, especially when feeling afraid or insecure?

5. How does your language impact how others perceive and respond to you?

6. In what ways has language helped or hindered your ability to communicate openly and honestly?

7. How can you use language to build trust and deepen emotional connections?

8. What changes can you make to foster more empathy, understanding, and support through your words?

✦ Chapter Summary

Chapter 5 investigates the profound impact of our words on the relationships we nurture. Language is more than communication; it is the foundation for trust, intimacy, and understanding. The words we choose, whether in casual conversation or deep conflict, can strengthen or erode connections with family, friends, colleagues, and strangers. This chapter highlights mindful communication and the power of intentional language to foster empathy, compassion, and respect. It discusses language's role in both healing and harming relationships and encourages readers to recognize the power of spoken and unspoken words. Practical strategies are offered to transform destructive communication patterns into nurturing dialogues, helping readers build healthier, more fulfilling relationships.

Chapter 6

Rewriting Your Script: *Shifting the Narrative to Create Lasting Change*

"Feelings are much like waves; we can't stop them from coming, but we can choose which ones to surf." – Jonatan Mårtensson

One of the most powerful tools we have in shaping our lives is the ability to change the stories we tell ourselves. The narratives we internalize—about our worth, our capabilities, and our potential—hold incredible influence over the decisions we make and the outcomes we experience. However, for many, these stories are based on past experiences, societal expectations, or limiting beliefs that no longer serve them.

In this chapter, we will explore how to intentionally shift the inner narrative that guides your thoughts, emotions, and behaviors. Many of us operate from unconscious scripts—deeply rooted patterns of thinking shaped by past experiences, cultural conditioning, and limiting beliefs. These internalized stories can hold us back from growth, connection, and purpose.

You will learn how to identify the thought patterns and language that reinforce self-doubt, fear, and emotional pain, and how to replace them with conscious, empowering narratives rooted in self-compassion and resilience. We will discuss the power of mindful awareness, emotional regulation, and intentional language as tools for rewriting your script.

This chapter will guide you through practical exercises to challenge outdated beliefs, reframe your internal dialogue, and begin creating a new narrative aligned with your values, goals, and true identity—one that fosters lasting transformation and inner freedom.

The Power of Self-Talk and the Inner Script

Self-talk refers to the ongoing internal dialogue we have with ourselves. It is the voice inside our heads that narrates our thoughts, reactions, and interpretations of the world around us. This voice can either empower us or limit us. It is the lens through which we view our experiences, and it shapes how we perceive our abilities, relationships, and our potential for success (Beck, 1976).

The inner script is the collection of stories and beliefs we have internalized about who we are and how the world works. These scripts can be positive, full of self-love and optimism, or negative, filled with self-doubt and fear. Over time, we may begin to act in alignment with these scripts, even if they are outdated or limiting (Seligman, 2011).

Example: The "Not Good Enough" Script

One common negative script many people carry is the belief that they are not good enough. This script might develop from past experiences of criticism, failure, or rejection, and it can influence future decisions. For example, if you have experienced repeated failures in your career, you may start to internalize the story that you are incapable of succeeding. This narrative can result in self-sabotage or avoidance of new opportunities because you have convinced yourself that you will fail again.

However, this script is just one interpretation of your experiences. It can be rewritten. A person who recognizes this limiting narrative might choose to challenge it by actively focusing on their successes, learning from failures, and practicing self-compassion. With time, their script might evolve into one that affirms their ability to learn, grow, and overcome challenges (Gilbert, 2006).

The Role of Awareness in Rewriting Your Script

The first step in changing your inner narrative is to become aware of it. Often, we operate on autopilot, unaware of the negative scripts that drive our behavior. We may not even realize the extent to which we limit ourselves by constantly telling ourselves that we are not good enough or capable of achieving our dreams (Beck, 1976).

Awareness begins by paying attention to your thoughts. Notice what you say to yourself when you face challenges or when you think about your goals. Are your thoughts empowering or disempowering? Do you focus on your strengths and achievements, or do you highlight your shortcomings and failures?

Mindfulness as a Tool for Awareness

Mindfulness—the practice of paying attention to the present moment without judgment—can be an invaluable tool in this process. By becoming more mindful of your thoughts, you create space for conscious reflection and choice. Instead of reacting automatically to negative thoughts, mindfulness allows you to pause, observe, and choose a more constructive response (Kabat-Zinn, 1990).

For example, let us say you are facing a tough project at work and immediately think, *"I'm terrible at this. I'm going to fail."* If you pause and become mindful of that thought, you may realize that it is not based on facts, but on a fear of failure. You can then challenge that thought with a more empowering one: *"I've overcome challenges before, and I have the skills to succeed."*

Techniques for Rewriting Your Inner Script

Once you are aware of the negative stories you have been telling yourself, the next step is to rewrite them. This is not about ignoring the past or pretending everything is perfect, but rather about shifting your perspective to see your experiences from a place of strength and growth (Seligman, 2011).

Here are some techniques to help you rewrite your inner script:

1. **Challenge Limiting Beliefs**: When you notice a limiting belief (e.g., *"I'm not good enough"*), ask yourself, *"Is this really true? What evidence do I have to support this belief?"* More often than not, limiting beliefs are based on old experiences or assumptions that no longer apply to your current life. By questioning these beliefs, you can begin to loosen their grip on your life (Beck, 1976).

94

2. **Reframe Negative Thoughts**: Reframing is the process of taking negative thoughts and viewing them from a different angle. For example, instead of thinking, *"I failed at this project,"* reframe it as, *"I learned valuable lessons from this project that will help me do better next time."* Reframing helps you see challenges as opportunities for growth rather than as personal failures (Gilbert, 2006).

3. **Affirmations and Positive Self-Talk**: Affirmations are positive statements that you repeat to yourself to reprogram your subconscious mind. For example, if you have a fear of public speaking, you might repeat to yourself, *"I am confident and capable of speaking in front of others."* By consistently repeating positive affirmations, you begin to shift your internal narrative toward one that supports your growth and success (Seligman, 2011).

4. **Visualize Your Desired Future**: Visualization is a powerful tool for creating change. Take time each day to visualize yourself living the life you desire, experiencing success, peace, and fulfillment. The more vividly you can imagine your ideal future, the more likely you are to start taking actions that align with that vision (Beck, 1976).

Creating New Narratives in Relationships

The stories we tell ourselves also influence how we interact with others. The way we perceive and communicate with our friends, family, and partners is often shaped by our internal scripts. If we believe that people will let us down or that we are unworthy of love, we may unintentionally sabotage our relationships or keep ourselves at a distance.

To rewrite your relationship scripts, start by examining your beliefs about love, trust, and connection. Are they based on past disappointments or fears? Are they serving you, or are they holding you back?

For example, if you have a narrative of *"I'm always the one who gives, and no one ever gives back,"* it may be time to reassess that belief. Is it true that people are not giving to you, or have you been so focused on giving that you have missed opportunities for others to show up for you? By rewriting this narrative to one of mutual reciprocity, you open the door to healthier, more fulfilling relationships (Gilbert, 2006).

The Power of Language in Shaping Your Script

As we have discussed, the language we use plays a crucial role in shaping our beliefs and behaviors. The words you choose, both in self-talk and in your interactions with others, influence how you perceive yourself and the world around you (Seligman, 2011).

For example, the way you speak about challenges can affect how you approach them. If you say, *"This is impossible, I'll never be able to do this,"* you are reinforcing the belief that failure is inevitable. But if you say, *"This is difficult, but I can figure it out,"* you shift your mindset to one of possibility and resilience (Beck, 1976).

The Impact of "I Am" Statements

One of the most profound ways to shift your inner narrative is through the use of "I am" statements. These declarations are not just words—they are affirmations of identity. When you say, *"I am strong," "I am capable,"* or *"I am worthy,"* you are not merely describing a trait—you are claiming it as a core part of who you are. This linguistic structure has a powerful psychological impact, influencing both your self-perception and your behavior.

"I am" statements are particularly powerful because they speak directly to your sense of self. For example, saying, *"I am a confident speaker,"* reinforces the belief that you already possess the qualities of a confident speaker. Over time, this kind of identity-based affirmation shapes your actions and choices, making it more likely that you will behave in ways that align with that self-perception (Seligman, 2011).

Why "I Am" Is So Powerful

In cognitive psychology, the concept of self-schema refers to the mental framework we hold about ourselves—essentially, the lens through which we view our identity (Markus, 1977). These self-schemas are formed through experiences and internalized messages and guide how we interpret our behaviors, choices, and interactions with the world. When we use "I am" statements, we directly speak to these schemas. Over time, repeated these statements—especially when emotionally charged—can help rewire these self-concepts (Beck, 1976).

"I am" statements also tap into what is known as the self-fulfilling prophecy, where beliefs and expectations—especially those that begin with 'I am'—shape our behaviors in ways that make those beliefs more likely to become true (Rosenthal & Jacobson, 1968). According to this theory, the beliefs we hold about ourselves can lead to behaviors that confirm those beliefs

(Merton, 1948). For instance, if you continually say, *"I am a failure,"* you are more likely to approach challenges with defeatism, subconsciously making choices that reinforce that narrative. On the other hand, saying, *"I am a learner,"* even in the face of failure, can help you persist and grow.

Rewiring the Subconscious

From a neurological perspective, repeated positive "I am" statements can help recondition the brain. The brain responds to repeated thoughts as if they are truths—this is the essence of neuroplasticity, the brain's ability to reorganize itself by forming new neural connections in response to learning and experience (Doidge, 2007). When we consistently use empowering "I am" statements, we strengthen the neural pathways associated with confidence, hope, and resilience.

Over time, affirming statements such as:

- "I am resilient."
- "I am enough."
- "I am deserving of love and success."

…can become ingrained in the subconscious, replacing older, more negative beliefs that no longer serve our well-being.

Using "I Am" Statements Intentionally

To maximize the power of "I am" statements:

1. **Be consistent**: Repetition is key. Speak your affirmations daily—out loud, in writing, or silently in your mind.

2. **Tie them to values**: Choose affirmations that reflect your core values and desired identity. For instance, if authenticity is a value, you might say, "I am free to be my true self."

3. **Say them with emotion**: Emotion reinforces belief. The more you feel the truth of your statement, the more likely it is to take root.

4. **Visualize yourself by embodying the statement**: Visualization helps align your mental, emotional, and physical energy with the affirmation (Gilbert, 2006).

"I Am" and Spiritual or Faith-Based Identity

For many people, "I am" statements also carry spiritual significance. In many sacred texts, "I Am" is used as a divine declaration—representing power, authority, and creation. In this context, "I am" becomes a spiritual affirmation of one's alignment with divine purpose and truth. Statements such as *"I am fearfully and wonderfully made"* (Psalm 139:14) or *"I am made in the image of God*" (Genesis 1:27) can deeply reinforce identity, self-worth, and spiritual grounding.

Whether used in a psychological or spiritual framework—or both—"I am" statements serve as tools of empowerment, helping you reclaim your narrative and author your own sense of self.

Rewriting your life's script is not a one-time event—it is a lifelong journey of growth, discovery, and transformation. Much like editing a manuscript, the process involves revisiting old chapters, refining your language, and aligning your inner dialogue with the person you are becoming. As life unfolds, new experiences, relationships, and challenges will inevitably bring old patterns and limiting beliefs to the surface. However, with self-awareness, intentional language, and a growth-oriented mindset, you can continue to shape a narrative that reflects your values, strengths, and vision for the future.

Psychologist Martin Seligman (2011), a pioneer in positive psychology, highlights that the narratives we create about ourselves play a vital role in our well-being and sense of empowerment. When we consciously replace language rooted in fear, self-doubt, or inadequacy with words of compassion, strength, and possibility, we not only rewrite our internal narrative—we reshape our entire lived experience. This act of narrative transformation becomes a practice of reclaiming authorship over our lives.

Your story is not set in stone. It is dynamic, fluid, and open to revision. Every thought you entertain, every word you speak, and every belief you challenge is an opportunity to realign with your truest self. The more consciously you engage with your internal script, the more empowered you become to redirect the plot of your life—toward healing, authenticity, and purpose.

In moments of doubt, return to your narrative. Ask yourself: *Is this belief helping or hindering my growth? Is this the story I want to continue telling?* With intention and practice, you can revise the narratives that no longer serve you and write new ones rooted in clarity, confidence, and courage.

Key Takeaways

1. **The Power of Personal Narratives**

   Our personal narrative is the story we tell ourselves about who we are, where we have been, and where we are going. This script is powerful because it influences our thoughts, emotions, behaviors, and life choices. Shifting the narrative can lead to profound transformation.

2. **We Are Not Defined by Our Past**

   Our past experiences, especially negative ones, do not define us. We have the power to reinterpret our past and create new meanings, allowing us to let go of limiting beliefs and rewrite our story in a way that serves our future.

3. **Awareness is the First Step**

   The process of rewriting our script begins with awareness. We must recognize the stories we have been telling ourselves and identify which ones are unhelpful or limiting. This awareness helps us challenge the validity of these narratives and decide if they align with our true potential.

4. **Language Shapes Our Reality**

   The language we use to describe our lives is instrumental in shaping our reality. By changing how we talk about ourselves, our challenges, and our future, we can shift our perceptions and open up new possibilities for growth.

5. **Identifying Core Beliefs**

   Our core beliefs form the foundation of our personal script. These deep-seated beliefs, often formed in childhood, influence how we see ourselves and the world. Rewriting our script involves uncovering and questioning these beliefs to see if they still serve us or need to be updated.

6. **Empowering Self-Talk**

   Rewriting your script involves transforming self-talk from a source of negativity and self-criticism into an empowering narrative that promotes growth, resilience, and self-compassion. Positive self-talk can help us overcome obstacles and stay focused on our goals.

7. **Visualization as a Tool for Change**

   Visualization is a powerful tool for rewriting your script. By imagining the life you want to create and seeing yourself living that story, you begin to program your mind for success. This mental imagery helps solidify the new narrative and primes you for action.

8. **Affirmations Reinforce New Beliefs**

   Using affirmations is a practical way to reinforce a new, positive narrative. Repeating affirmations aloud or in writing can reprogram the subconscious mind and support lasting change by replacing old, limiting beliefs with empowering ones.

9. **Small Shifts Lead to Big Change**

   Rewriting your script does not require an overnight transformation. Small, consistent shifts in how you think, speak, and act can lead to significant changes over time. Each step toward a new narrative is progress.

10. **Resilience Through Rewriting**

Shifting your narrative increases resilience by teaching you to frame challenges as opportunities for growth. When faced with setbacks, a positive, growth-oriented script helps you navigate adversity with a mindset of learning and improvement.

11. **You Are the Author of Your Life**

Ultimately, rewriting your script means taking ownership of your life story. You have the power to write the next chapter, regardless of where you have been or what has happened to you. You are not a passive participant in your life; you are the author.

This chapter emphasizes that we have the ability to change the stories we tell ourselves and, in doing so, transform our lives. By shifting our personal narrative to one that is empowering and aligned with our values, we can create lasting change and step into a life of purpose and fulfillment.

These exercises are designed to help you actively engage in the process of rewriting your personal narrative, using language, awareness, and intentional action to transform your beliefs and life experience. By integrating these practices into your daily routine, you can make lasting changes and shift towards a more empowered and fulfilling life.

Reflection Questions

1. What limiting beliefs or negative scripts do you hold about yourself, and how can you begin to challenge or reframe them?

2. In which areas of your life do you feel stuck, and how can rewriting your narrative empower you to move forward?

3. What positive *"I am"* statements can you start using to shift your inner dialogue and reinforce your self-worth?

4. How can you incorporate visualization or affirmations into your daily routine to create the future you desire?

5. What part of your current life script are you ready to rewrite, and what new beliefs or language will support your growth and transformation?

6. Are your current beliefs empowering or limiting? How do they affect your confidence, motivation, and relationships?

7. What new *"I am"* statements would support your growth and healing?

8. How can you incorporate these affirmations into your daily routine?

✦ Chapter Summary

Chapter 6 explains the transformative power of rewriting the stories we tell ourselves. Our personal narratives, often rooted in past experiences and beliefs, shape how we perceive ourselves and the world around us. However, these stories are not fixed—they can be rewritten to create lasting change. This chapter dives into the process of recognizing and challenging the limiting narratives that keep us stuck in patterns of self-doubt, fear, or unfulfilled potential. Through the practice of reframing and reshaping our inner dialogue, we learn to empower ourselves to create a new story—one that aligns with our values, goals, and aspirations. The chapter provides practical tools such as mindfulness, affirmations, and visualization to help readers reprogram their mindset and rewrite their personal scripts. By doing so, they can cultivate a more authentic, resilient, and purpose-driven life. This chapter serves as a reminder that the power to change our lives lies within our ability to change the narrative we live by.

Chapter 7

The Influence of External Narratives: *How Society and Others Shape Our Stories*

"Talk to yourself like someone you love." – Kristin Neff

In this chapter, we will explore how the stories we live by are not created in isolation but are deeply shaped by the voices of others—our families, cultures, media, and society at large. From early childhood, we begin to internalize messages about who we should be, what success looks like, how we are expected to behave, and what makes us worthy of love or belonging. These external narratives can uplift and inspire, but they can also limit, distort, or suppress our authentic selves.

We will examine the powerful role of family expectations, cultural norms, and societal standards in shaping identity, self-worth, and life direction. You will learn how unconscious scripts passed down through generations—often rooted in survival, tradition, or social roles—can either support personal growth or perpetuate cycles of shame, comparison, and fear.

Through self-reflection and practical tools, this chapter will help you begin to separate your true voice from the voices around you, empowering you to question inherited beliefs and reclaim authorship of your own story.

The Role of Society in Shaping Our Narratives

Our personal scripts are shaped not only by the inner voice that narrates our thoughts but also by the external narratives we encounter throughout life. These stories—transmitted through family, peers, society, culture, and media—profoundly influence how we see ourselves and the roles we play. While some of these narratives uplift and empower, others confine and distort our sense of self. In this chapter, we examine how external influences shape our identities and explore how we can reclaim authorship of our stories to align more closely with our authentic selves.

From childhood, we are immersed in a cultural landscape filled with expectations about who we should be and what we should strive for. These societal messages—often subtle but pervasive—begin to define our beliefs about success, relationships, morality, and personal worth.

Societal Expectations and the Pull of Conformity

From a young age, we are immersed in a cultural landscape filled with messages about what is acceptable, desirable, and valuable. These messages—often subtle and unspoken—form a set of societal scripts that influence how we define success, beauty, intelligence, gender roles, and even happiness. The pressure to conform to these expectations can be powerful, especially when they conflict with our internal values and authentic sense of self.

Classic social psychology research by Asch (1951) revealed just how strong the drive to conform can be. In his famous conformity experiments, participants were willing to give clearly incorrect answers to simple visual tasks simply because the majority group did so. This phenomenon demonstrates a fundamental human need: the desire for social belonging, even at the expense of one's own perception of truth.

In the context of life choices, this pressure to conform may manifest in more subtle but equally profound ways. Many people follow predetermined life paths not out of passion or purpose, but because society has deemed those paths "successful" or "normal." For instance, someone may pursue a high-paying career in law or finance, not because it aligns with their values or interests, but because cultural narratives equate professional status and financial gain with personal worth and achievement (Seligman, 2011). When the external script dominates, individuals may find themselves living lives that look successful on the outside but feel empty or unfulfilling on the inside.

This dissonance between societal expectations and personal values can lead to internal conflict and identity confusion. The more we internalize cultural messages about who we should be, the more difficult it becomes to hear our inner voice. We may begin to question our desires, suppress our uniqueness, or minimize our dreams in order to fit in or avoid rejection (Brown, 2010). Over time, this disconnection from our true selves can result in feelings of anxiety, depression, or low self-worth.

Moreover, societal expectations are not one-size-fits-all—they are often shaped by intersecting factors like gender, race, age, and socioeconomic status. For example, women may face conflicting expectations to be both ambitious and nurturing, while men may feel pressure to suppress vulnerability in the name of strength. These conflicting messages can further complicate one's ability to form an authentic identity.

The journey toward rewriting our script involves recognizing where we have conformed out of fear, habit, or social pressure—and choosing instead to align with our own values and truth. This process requires courage and self-awareness, but it also opens the door to a life that feels more authentic, fulfilling, and personally meaningful.

Scripted from the Start: How Family Shapes Our Inner Narratives

The family is the first place we encounter stories about who we are, what we are worth, and what is expected of us. Long before we have the words to describe ourselves, we absorb messages—spoken and unspoken—about our identity, place in the world, and how we are to relate to others. These early experiences are powerful. They serve as the initial drafts of our personal script, laying the groundwork for the inner narratives we carry into adolescence and adulthood.

Whether through direct communication or subtle cues, caregivers and close relatives impart values, beliefs, and expectations that become internalized over time. A child praised for being "the responsible one" may grow up clinging to the role of caretaker, even when it comes at the expense of their own needs. Similarly, a child labeled as "difficult" or "emotional" may internalize shame around expressing their feelings, resulting in self-censorship and emotional withdrawal later in life.

These family-formed narratives are often not questioned until we find ourselves stuck—repeating the same patterns in relationships, struggling with self-worth, or feeling disconnected from who we truly are. It is in these moments that we begin to realize that the stories we have inherited may not align with the person we wish to become. And that realization marks the beginning of narrative transformation.

Understanding the origins of our internal dialogue gives us the power to reflect, reframe, and rewrite. By identifying the specific family messages that have shaped our beliefs—both empowering and limiting—we open the door to conscious change. We are not bound by the narratives passed down to us. With intention and self-awareness, we can become the authors of new stories that reflect our truth rather than just our past.

The "Family Script"

Every family tells a story—and within that story lies an unwritten script. This "family script" consists of implicit rules, expectations, and emotional roles that guide behavior, communication, and identity within the family system (Minuchin, 1974). These scripts are rarely stated outright, yet they are deeply understood and internalized by each member of the family, often without conscious awareness. They influence how children view themselves, how they relate to others, and what they believe is required to receive love, acceptance, and safety (Bowen, 1978).

For example, a child raised in a household where academic excellence is highly praised may come to equate their worth with performance. The underlying message—whether ever explicitly spoken or not—is that success earns love and approval. If that same child later experiences failure, the pain is not merely about a grade or missed opportunity. It touches a deeper wound: the fear of being unworthy or unlovable unless they meet certain expectations (Beck, 1976). This narrative can persist into adulthood, manifesting as perfectionism, imposter syndrome, or chronic anxiety around failure (Gilbert, 2009).

Family scripts do not only center around achievement. They also shape how emotions are expressed or suppressed, how conflict is managed, and how identity is formed. In some families, emotions are openly discussed, and compassion is modeled; in others, emotional expression is viewed as weakness or is actively discouraged. A child in a household where anger or sadness is silenced may learn to deny or invalidate their own emotions, creating disconnection from their inner world (Neff, 2011).

These scripts can be both empowering and limiting. A family that emphasizes kindness, resilience, and open communication may instill values that nurture healthy self-esteem and emotional intelligence. Conversely, a family that rewards independence but discourages vulnerability may produce individuals who struggle to ask for help or trust others with their feelings (Siegel, 2012).

Recognizing the family script is a powerful first step in rewriting it. While we cannot choose the environment we were raised in, we can choose how much power those early narratives continue to have over us. By identifying and challenging the limiting beliefs inherited from our family systems, we begin to loosen their grip and reclaim authorship of our own stories (Brown, 2012).

The Formation of Early Narratives and Attachment

From our earliest moments of life, we are actively forming internal narratives about who we are and how the world responds to us. These foundational stories begin to take shape through our relationships with primary caregivers—parents, guardians, or other close adults—who serve as the first mirrors through which we begin to understand ourselves and our place in the world.

The tone of a caregiver's voice, the consistency of their presence, and the way they respond to our needs all contribute to the messages we internalize. When a caregiver is attuned, nurturing, and emotionally available, the child receives a message that says, *"I am valued. I am safe. I am worthy of love."* These early interactions form what psychologists refer to as an attachment style—a blueprint for how we expect to be treated in relationships and how we relate to others throughout life (Bowlby, 1969).

Conversely, if a caregiver is inconsistent, dismissive, or emotionally unavailable, a child may begin to internalize beliefs like *"I must earn love,"* or *"My needs are too much."* These narratives, though often unconscious, can become core beliefs that shape our adult relationships, self-esteem, and coping mechanisms. The child's understanding of the world becomes rooted in the idea that connection is conditional, or that expressing emotions leads to rejection or punishment.

These early attachment-based narratives are not formed through isolated events but through repetitive patterns of interaction. Over time, they become woven into the subconscious and serve as scripts that guide our thoughts, emotions, and behaviors. A securely attached individual may approach relationships with trust and openness, while someone with an anxious or avoidant attachment may struggle with fear of abandonment or emotional intimacy (Ainsworth et al., 1978).

Language also plays a vital role in shaping these early stories. The way caregivers talk to and about the child—labeling behaviors, offering praise or criticism, validating or invalidating emotions—begins to shape the child's self-concept. Statements like *"You're so sensitive"* or *"Be strong, don't cry"* may seem harmless on the surface but can contribute to lifelong patterns of emotional suppression or self-doubt. On the other hand, affirming language like *"Your feelings matter"* or *"I'm here for you"* can plant seeds of resilience and emotional security.

Understanding how these narratives are formed allows us to recognize that many of our current patterns—how we relate to ourselves, how we seek validation, how we express emotions—are not random. They are rooted in early relational experiences. The good news is that these narratives are not fixed. Through self-awareness, therapeutic work, and nurturing relationships, we can begin to revise the stories we inherited and form healthier, more empowering ones.

Attachment and Self-Worth

Attachment theory, first introduced by Bowlby (1969) and later expanded upon by Ainsworth (1978), posits that the quality of the emotional bond formed between a child and their primary caregiver lays the foundation for psychological development and interpersonal functioning. These early interactions serve as a blueprint for how individuals come to see themselves and others.

Children who experience secure attachment, typically with caregivers who are emotionally available, consistent, and attuned to their needs, tend to develop a positive internal working model of self. They are more likely to view themselves as worthy of love, capable of handling life's challenges, and able to form healthy relationships (Bretherton, 1992; Mikulincer & Shaver, 2007). This secure foundation contributes significantly to self-worth and emotional regulation throughout life.

Conversely, children raised in environments marked by inconsistent, neglectful, or rejecting caregiving may form insecure attachment styles—including anxious, avoidant, or disorganized attachments. These children often internalize beliefs that they are unlovable, unimportant, or a burden to others (Cassidy & Shaver, 2016). Over time, these beliefs can become ingrained narratives of unworthiness, affecting everything from self-esteem to how individuals perceive their value in romantic, familial, and professional relationships (Bartholomew & Horowitz, 1991).

Insecure attachment does not only impair the way individuals relate to others—it also deeply influences their self-talk and the language of their inner world. Adults with unresolved attachment wounds may engage in harsh self-criticism, sabotage their achievements, or struggle to assert needs and boundaries, all stemming from the original narrative: *"I'm not enough."*

Example: Maria's Story

Maria, a 32-year-old nurse, has always been described as competent and reliable by her coworkers. Yet despite her outward success, she struggles with deep feelings of inadequacy. Every time she receives praise, her instinct is to dismiss it or attribute it to luck. In relationships, she often feels anxious and fears abandonment, even when there is no real threat.

During therapy, Maria began to explore her childhood. Her father was emotionally distant, often criticizing her efforts and rarely expressing affection. Her mother, while loving, was overwhelmed and inconsistent—sometimes nurturing, sometimes unavailable. As a child, Maria learned that love had to be earned through perfection and emotional self-reliance. She developed a strong inner critic that constantly told her she was not enough.

Through this lens, Maria's adult struggles made more sense. Her attachment style, anxious-preoccupied—had led her to seek approval from others while constantly doubting her own worth. Her internal narrative, shaped by early attachment experiences, sounded like: *"I'm only lovable if I do everything right."*

With time and guided support, Maria began challenging these beliefs. She practiced positive self-talk, acknowledged her feelings without judgment, and started to rewrite her internal story. Through secure relationships and emotional processing, she gradually moved toward a more secure attachment style. Her new inner narrative became: *"I am worthy of love, even when I'm not perfect."*

Fortunately, research in attachment theory and therapeutic modalities such as emotionally focused therapy (EFT) and internal family systems (IFS) highlights that attachment styles are not fixed. Through conscious self-awareness, corrective emotional experiences, and nurturing relationships, individuals can begin to rewrite these early stories and rebuild a more empowered, secure sense of self (Johnson, 2019; Siegel, 2012).

Key Takeaways

1. **External Narratives Shape Our Identity**

   Our personal narratives are not created in a vacuum; they are influenced by societal expectations, cultural norms, and the people around us. Family, friends, media, and larger cultural messages play a significant role in shaping how we see ourselves.

2. **Social and Cultural Norms**

   Society imposes stories about success, beauty, gender roles, race, and what is considered "normal." These cultural scripts can be limiting, pushing individuals to conform to external definitions of who they should be, often at the expense of their true selves.

3. **The Power of Family Narratives**

   Our family dynamics often contribute to the foundation of our identity. The way our family communicates, values, and treats us can leave a lasting impact, either empowering or limiting our personal growth.

4. **Media and Pop Culture**

   Media plays a huge role in shaping external narratives, with its portrayal of beauty, success, relationships, and values. These images and messages can influence how we view our own lives and aspirations.

5. **Social Comparison**

   Constant exposure to the curated lives of others, especially through social media, can lead to unhealthy comparisons. It often results in feelings of inadequacy or the desire to live up to unattainable standards set by others.

6. **The Impact of Negative Feedback**

   The opinions and criticisms of others can become internalized over time, contributing to feelings of shame, doubt, or self-criticism. These external voices can shape our self-worth if we allow them to dominate our inner narrative.

7. **Breaking Free from External Influence**

   Becoming aware of the external narratives that influence our lives is the first step in reclaiming control. By questioning societal norms and evaluating the feedback we receive from others, we can rewrite our own stories and live in alignment with our authentic selves.

8. **Redefining Our Narrative**

   While external narratives are powerful, they are not permanent. We have the ability to challenge societal expectations and external pressures to create a narrative that truly reflects who we are and what we value.

9. **The Role of Empowerment in Narrative Change**

Empowering ourselves to recognize and resist the influence of others allows us to rewrite our scripts in a way that aligns with our personal truth. This involves embracing self-love, authenticity, and the courage to be different from what society expects.

9. **Creating a New Story**

To create lasting change, we must learn to actively create a story that reflects our values, strengths, and dreams—not one that is dictated by others. This requires intentionality and self-awareness, but it is key to personal transformation.

These exercises can help you step back from the external narratives that influence your story, allowing you to create a more empowering and authentic self-narrative.

Reflection Questions

Take a few quiet moments to reflect on the messages you received in your earliest relationships. Find a journal or a blank sheet of paper and write freely in response to the following prompts. Try not to censor yourself—let your thoughts flow with curiosity and compassion.

1. What do you remember feeling most often as a child in your home environment?

    (Safe? Anxious? Invisible? Loved? Responsible? Confused?)

2. How did the adults in your life respond to your emotions? Were your feelings validated or dismissed? Did you feel like it was okay to cry, ask for help, or express anger?

3. What unspoken rules or expectations existed in your family? Was achievement prioritized? Were there beliefs about strength, gender roles, success, or failure that shaped how you viewed yourself?

4. What were you praised for, and what were you criticized for? How did this shape your sense of worth?

5. Complete this sentence several times, as honestly as possible:

   "As a child, I learned that I am _____ if I _____."

6. Looking at your responses, what patterns do you notice? Do these early messages still influence how you speak to yourself today?

Your early story is not your final story. Awareness is the first step in change. As you uncover the roots of your self-narrative, know that you now have the power to rewrite the beliefs that no longer serve you—and create new ones that reflect your truth, your worth, and your capacity for growth.

✦ Chapter Summary

Chapter 7 explores the profound impact that external influences—such as family, culture, societal expectations, and media—have on the stories we internalize and the identities we form. From an early age, we are exposed to narratives that are handed down by those around us, shaping our worldview and our sense of self-worth. These external narratives can be powerful, often dictating what is deemed acceptable, successful, or valuable in society. However, many of these stories may not align with our true essence or personal values. The chapter examines how these external forces can either empower or limit us, as well as how we can consciously challenge and rewrite them. By recognizing the external narratives that influence us, we can begin to discern which ones resonate with our authentic selves and which ones need to be rewritten. This chapter offers insights into how to reclaim your voice, resist societal pressures, and create a personal narrative that reflects your true identity, values, and aspirations.

Chapter 8

Parenting Styles and the Stories We Inherit: *How Early Family Dynamics Shape Our Inner Narratives and Beliefs*

"Parenting is not about perfecting our children, but about reexamining and transforming the stories we've inherited, so that we can give our children the freedom to become who they truly are." – Shefali Tsabary

From the moment we take our first breath, we are immersed in a world shaped by the beliefs, behaviors, and expectations of those who raise us. According to attachment theory, our earliest bonds with caregivers play a critical role in shaping our emotional development and internal working models of self and others (Bowlby, 1969; Ainsworth, 1979). Secure attachments foster a sense of safety and self-worth, while insecure bonds can contribute to anxiety, avoidance, or confusion in relationships and self-concept. Our earliest caregivers—whether nurturing, critical, absent, or overprotective—become the authors of our first stories. Their words, reactions, and silent messages carve pathways in our minds, teaching us what it means to be loved, valued, and understood. These initial scripts form the foundation of our identity, influencing how we perceive ourselves, others, and the world around us. But the stories we inherit are not always written with clarity or kindness. A parent's anxiety can become a child's self-doubt. An overly critical voice can transform into an internal critic that echoes for decades. Even well-intentioned parents can pass down limiting beliefs, creating narratives that hinder rather than help. Whether we were guided with warmth and wisdom or struggled in the shadow of neglect, the stories we received were written long before we had a say.

This chapter navigates through the various parenting styles— authoritative, authoritarian, permissive, and neglectful—shape the stories we tell ourselves. You will gain insight into how the beliefs, emotional reactions, and communication patterns of your caregivers were passed down and woven into the scripts you carry today. By recognizing these influences, you will be better equipped to identify which stories serve you and which may need rewriting.

Most importantly, this chapter is not about assigning blame but about cultivating awareness. Understanding the origins of your internal narratives allows you to step out of unconscious patterns and consciously choose a new path. Regardless of the parenting style you experienced, you have the power to rewrite your story.

Let this chapter be a journey of discovery—one that invites you to reflect on the past, understand its impact, and begin crafting a narrative rooted in self-awareness, compassion, and authenticity.

Authoritative Parenting: Nurturing Self-Worth

Authoritative parenting, characterized by warmth, structure, and responsiveness, tends to foster a healthy sense of self-worth. Parents who balance high expectations with emotional support help children develop a positive self-concept and a strong sense of autonomy (Baumrind, 1991). These children are encouraged to express their emotions and opinions, which strengthens their self-confidence and resilience.

The narrative they develop is one where they believe in their own abilities and feel supported by others, creating a story of competence and value. For example, a child raised by authoritative parents might internalize the belief: *"I am capable of overcoming challenges because I have the support I need and the skills to succeed."*

For Example:

Emma's parents are warm and loving, but they also set clear boundaries and expectations. They encourage open communication and respect her opinions. When Emma struggles with schoolwork, her parents sit down with her, provide emotional support, and help her create a plan to improve. They praise her effort and encourage her to keep trying, even if she does not get perfect grades. Emma feels valued and capable because her parents balance support with appropriate expectations.

Effect on Self-Narrative:

As a result, Emma develops a narrative where she believes in her own abilities and feels empowered to face challenges. She internalizes the message that her worth is not based on perfection but on her efforts and the support she receives from others.

Example of Self-Narrative:

"I am capable of learning from my mistakes, and I have the support I need to grow."

Authoritarian Parenting: Restrictive and Perfectionistic Narratives

In contrast, authoritarian parenting emphasizes strict obedience and control, often at the expense of warmth or understanding (Baumrind, 1991). Parents with this style typically set rigid rules and enforce them without much room for discussion or emotional validation. Children raised in this environment may internalize messages of inadequacy or fear of failure, believing that their worth is contingent upon meeting external standards.

This can result in an internal narrative like: *"I am only valued when I follow the rules or achieve perfection."* Such children often struggle with self-esteem and may become overly dependent on external validation, fearing rejection or criticism.

For Example:

Kyle's parents enforce strict rules and demand obedience without explanation. If Kyle does not clean his room or get top grades, he faces harsh punishment, such as grounding or loss of privileges. His parents rarely praise his efforts but instead focus on the mistakes. Kyle learns to suppress his emotions, avoids asking for help, and feels that his value is tied to meeting high expectations. He feels anxious about making mistakes because he fears disappointing his parents.

Effect on Self-Narrative:

Kyle internalizes a narrative of inadequacy and fear of failure. He believes that his worth is contingent upon meeting high standards and that he must avoid failure at all costs, even if it means suppressing his own needs or desires.

Example of Self-Narrative:

"I am only valuable when I meet others' expectations. If I fail, I am not enough."

Permissive Parenting: Warmth Without Boundaries

Permissive parenting is characterized by high levels of warmth and emotional availability but minimal enforcement of rules, expectations, or consequences (Baumrind, 1991). These parents are nurturing and accepting, often striving to be more of a friend than an authority figure. While this approach fosters emotional closeness and a sense of being loved, it often lacks the structure children need to develop discipline, self-regulation, and accountability.

Instead of learning limits and responsibility, children raised in permissive households may be indulged, shielded from consequences, or allowed to make significant decisions without appropriate guidance. As a result, their developing self-narrative may revolve around entitlement, dependency, or a skewed sense of how the world works. They may internalize beliefs such as, *"I deserve to have my needs met without effort,"* or *"Someone else will fix things for me when they go wrong."*

For Example:

Sarah's parents are loving and supportive, but they avoid setting clear expectations or following through with discipline. When Sarah skips her chores or neglects her schoolwork, her parents excuse the behavior, reasoning that she's still young and should enjoy her freedom. They often buy her gifts to lift her mood or avoid conflict. As she grows older, Sarah becomes accustomed to getting what she wants with minimal effort and begins to expect others to accommodate her needs without question. She struggles with time management, responsibility, and emotional resilience when things do not go her way.

Effect on Self-Narrative:

Children raised with permissive parenting may construct internal stories that center around entitlement and a lack of accountability. They may develop unrealistic expectations about effort and reward, believing they are inherently deserving without needing to contribute or persevere. This can hinder emotional maturity and lead to difficulties in relationships, school, or work settings—especially when faced with limits, rejection, or consequences. Over time, this mindset can diminish self-efficacy and the ability to take ownership of one's life.

Example of Self-Narrative:

"I deserve to get what I want, and if things go wrong, it's not really my fault. I shouldn't have to try so hard—life should just work out for me."

Permissive parenting, though often well-intentioned, can unintentionally deprive children of the essential lessons that structure and accountability provide. While these children may feel emotionally safe, they often miss out on the internal development of perseverance, self-control, and responsibility. However, like all narratives, these beliefs can be re-examined and rewritten through intentional practice, self-awareness, and experiences that promote growth and accountability.

Neglectful Parenting: Absence That Shapes Identity

Neglectful parenting, sometimes referred to as uninvolved parenting, is marked by low responsiveness and a lack of both emotional warmth and structure. These parents may be physically present but emotionally distant, often overwhelmed, distracted, or disengaged from their child's daily needs and emotional life. While neglect can vary in degree—from emotional unavailability to complete withdrawal—it communicates a powerful message: *"You are on your own."*

Children raised in neglectful environments often internalize a sense of invisibility. They may come to believe that their needs, feelings, or achievements do not matter. Without the guidance, validation, or security that comes from consistent caregiving, children are left to fill in the gaps, often crafting internal narratives of unworthiness, self-doubt, or hyper-independence. As Bowlby (1980) noted, emotional unavailability from primary caregivers can disrupt a child's ability to form secure attachments, leading to long-term difficulties in trust, emotional regulation, and relational intimacy. These children may internalize beliefs such as, *"If I don't take care of myself, no one else will,"* or *"I must not be important enough to be noticed."*

For Example:

Marcus's parents are rarely home, and when they are, his parents are preoccupied with work or personal stress. They rarely check in on his school progress, emotional well-being, or friendships.

Marcus often eats alone, handles his own schedule, and finds comfort through screen time or peers. Over time, he stops seeking approval or emotional connection because he has learned not to expect it. Although independent on the surface, Marcus feels disconnected, unworthy of attention, and unsure of his value.

Effect on Self-Narrative:

Children raised in neglectful homes often develop stories centered around emotional isolation or a diminished sense of self-worth. They may internalize the idea that their presence—or absence—has little impact on others. This can manifest as difficulty forming trusting relationships, low self-esteem, or an intense need for control in adulthood as a way to compensate for early instability.

Example of Self-Narrative:

"My needs don't matter. I can't rely on anyone but myself. If I disappear, no one will notice."

These examples show how each parenting style can create different self-narratives, influencing how children perceive their abilities, worth, and place in the world.

Impact on Self-Worth

The parenting styles we experience as children play a significant role in shaping our self-worth and the stories we construct about ourselves. These early influences form the foundation for how we view our competence, value, and place in the world. The narratives we internalize about who we are often stem from how we were treated, nurtured, and guided during our formative years. Here is how each parenting style contributes to different perceptions of self-worth and identity:

1. Authoritative Parenting: Fostering Balanced Self-Worth

Impact:

Authoritative parenting is characterized by a healthy balance of warmth, responsiveness, and clear boundaries. Children raised with this style tend to develop a strong sense of self-worth rooted in the belief that they are valued and capable. They internalize the message that they are worthy of love and respect not only when they succeed but also when they face challenges. This creates a positive self-concept where children believe that their efforts matter and that they can be successful as long as they are willing to work for it (Baumrind, 1991).

Narrative Development:

Children raised by authoritative parents often develop narratives that emphasize effort, resilience, and self-efficacy. These children are taught that their worth is not based on perfection but on their intrinsic value as individuals. They see themselves as competent, responsible, and capable of growth. (Seligman, 2011).

Example of Self-Narrative:

"I am worthy of love and success, not because I am perfect, but because I am committed to trying my best and growing from my experiences."

2. Authoritarian Parenting: Restrictive and Perfectionistic Narratives

Impact:

In contrast, authoritarian parenting, which emphasizes obedience, control, and strict adherence to rules, often leads to children internalizing a narrative that ties their self-worth to their ability to meet external expectations. Children raised in authoritarian households often feel that their value is conditional, contingent upon their ability to achieve and perform at a high level. This can lead to feelings of inadequacy or shame when they fail to meet these standards (Baumrind, 1991).

Narrative Development:

These children may internalize beliefs that they are only worthy when they meet perfectionistic standards, often at the expense of their emotional well-being. The message they internalize is one of "*I am only valuable if I succeed*" or "*I am not enough if I fail.*" This can foster a fixed mindset, where failure is seen as an inherent flaw rather than an opportunity for growth (Dweck, 2006).

Example of Self-Narrative:

"I am not enough if I don't succeed. My value is only recognized when I meet the expectations of others, and failure means I am inadequate."

3. Permissive Parenting: Entitlement and Lack of Accountability

Impact:

Permissive parenting is marked by warmth and affection but often lacks the structure and discipline necessary for children to develop a sense of responsibility and accountability. While these children may feel loved and cherished, they may also develop a sense of entitlement, believing that they deserve things without the need to earn them. The absence of boundaries and consequences can lead to difficulties with self-regulation, and children may struggle to understand the importance of effort, responsibility, and self-discipline (Baumrind, 1991).

Narrative Development:

Children raised in permissive households may internalize narratives that focus on entitlement or a lack of accountability. They may come to believe that their needs and desires should be met without having to work for them, which can later lead to challenges in personal growth and healthy relationships. These children may have difficulty accepting the reality of setbacks, and instead of developing resilience, they may expect things to always go their way (Seligman, 2011).

Example of Self-Narrative:

"I deserve to get what I want, and it's not my fault if things don't go as planned. I shouldn't have to work hard for things; they should come easily."

4. Neglectful Parenting: Invisible and Unworthy Narratives

Impact:

Neglectful parenting is marked by emotional unavailability, lack of supervision, and minimal involvement in the child's life.

Children in these environments often internalize a deep sense of unimportance or invisibility, believing their needs and feelings do not matter.

Narrative Development:

These children may form core beliefs like *"I am not worth caring for"* or *"I must do everything myself."* This can lead to challenges with emotional regulation, hyper-independence, or a fear of vulnerability in relationships (Bowlby, 1980).

Example of Self-Narrative:

"I can't rely on anyone. If I don't take care of myself, no one will."

Recognizing and Rewriting the Stories

Understanding how these early experiences shape our inner narratives is the first step in reshaping our self-concept for better mental and emotional well-being. The stories we inherit from our families and caregivers have a profound impact on how we view ourselves and our potential. However, recognizing the origin of these narratives empowers us to take control of our inner dialogue. We can begin the process of rewriting our stories to reflect healthier, more empowering beliefs about our worth, capabilities, and place in the world (Beck, 1976).

By acknowledging how the parenting styles we experienced shaped our sense of self, we can challenge limiting beliefs and create new, more supportive narratives. This process of rewriting allows us to develop a more authentic, positive self-concept and fosters emotional resilience. We can learn to embrace our strengths and accept our imperfections, knowing that our worth is not contingent on meeting external standards but on our inherent value as individuals (Seligman, 2011).

Rewriting Your Story for Healthy Self-Worth

Rewriting the story of who we are involves developing a more balanced view of ourselves, recognizing that we are deserving of love, respect, and success not because we are perfect, but because we are worthy as we are. Whether we were raised in an authoritative, authoritarian, or permissive household, it is possible to break free from limiting narratives and create new ones that empower us to lead more fulfilling lives. This process demands self-awareness, compassion, and a commitment to change.

Ultimately, the stories we tell ourselves about our worth and identity are not set in stone. By examining the messages we received from our families, challenging the limiting beliefs we have internalized, and replacing them with healthier, more supportive narratives, we can rewrite our self-concept and build the life we truly deserve (Dweck, 2006).

Each style contributes differently to the stories children tell themselves about their value, competence, and role in the world.

Key Takeaways

The following takeaways summarize how parenting styles influence our identity formation and self-worth, offering insights into how we can begin to transform inherited narratives.

1. **Parenting Styles Shape Our Early Narratives**

   The way we are raised significantly impacts the stories we tell about ourselves. Whether through authoritative, authoritarian, permissive, or neglectful parenting styles, the messages we receive from our parents influence how we view the world, our relationships, and our self-worth.

2. **The Impact of Parenting on Self-Esteem**

   Parenting that is emotionally supportive and encouraging helps build self-confidence, while parenting that is critical or neglectful may contribute to lower self-esteem. Our parents' behavior becomes internalized as part of our self-narrative, shaping our belief in our own value and potential.

3. **Inherited Family Stories**

   We often inherit not only our parents' values and expectations but also their emotional patterns, communication styles, and coping mechanisms. These "family scripts" become the foundation for how we interpret our own lives and how we interact with others.

4. **Positive Parenting Styles Foster Resilience**

   Positive parenting—characterized by warmth, communication, and appropriate boundaries—helps children develop resilience and healthy coping mechanisms. These children are more likely to create positive, empowering personal narratives as they grow older.

5. **The Influence of Unresolved Parental Stories**

   Unresolved trauma, neglect, or emotional unavailability in childhood can create negative beliefs that continue to affect an individual into adulthood. These unresolved issues often play out in the form of limiting beliefs, self-doubt, or anxiety, shaping the way we see ourselves and the world.

6. **Parenting Styles and Attachment Theory**

The type of attachment we form with our caregivers (secure, anxious, avoidant, or disorganized) influences how we relate to others in our adult relationships. Attachment patterns can manifest as part of our internal dialogue and contribute to the ways we tell our life story in terms of love, trust, and security.

7. **Parenting Styles Evolve Over Time**

   Parenting is not static. The way we parent ourselves and our children can change over time. Awareness of the stories we inherit from our parents allows us to rewrite these narratives, either by healing past wounds or by adopting healthier patterns for future generations.

8. **Breaking Negative Cycles**

   One of the most powerful ways to shift our own stories is to recognize negative parenting patterns and consciously work to break them. By becoming aware of how past family dynamics influence our current beliefs and actions, we can actively choose to rewrite the story for ourselves and future generations.

9. ## Rewriting Our Own Parental Narrative

   Just as we can rewrite our personal narratives, we can also revisit and reframe our stories about our parents. This may involve letting go of resentment or recognizing that our parents did the best they could with the tools they had. Rewriting this story allows for healing and growth.

10. ## Conscious Parenting and Storytelling

    As parents, it is essential to be mindful of the stories we tell our children. Our words, actions, and emotional support shape how they view themselves and the world around them. Consciously telling empowering stories will help them create healthy, resilient narratives of their own.

These takeaways emphasize the strong link between parenting styles and the formation of personal and family narratives. Understanding and reflecting on these influences can be key to transforming limiting beliefs and fostering healthier, more empowering stories for ourselves and our children.

Reflection Questions: Parenting Styles on Self-Worth

1. How did your parents or caregivers show love and affection when you were growing up? How did that shape your sense of self-worth?

2. Reflecting on your childhood, how would you describe your parents' parenting style (authoritative, authoritarian, permissive, or neglectful)? How did their approach affect your self-esteem and beliefs about your abilities?

3. How did your parents' expectations (whether academic, behavioral, or emotional) influence your perception of success and failure? Did you internalize these expectations as part of your identity?

4. In what ways did your parents' feedback (positive or negative) influence your self-image? Did you feel encouraged to be yourself, or did you feel pressure to conform to their standards?

5. How did your parents handle mistakes or failures? What messages about failure did you internalize, and how does that affect your current self-worth?

6. Did your parents model healthy self-esteem and self-respect? How did their behavior shape your own self-worth and self-concept?

7. Reflecting on your upbringing, how did your parents' level of emotional support impact your sense of being valued? Did you feel emotionally secure in your family environment?

8. How did your parents' communication style (whether open and supportive or critical and restrictive) affect how you communicate your needs and express yourself in relationships today?

Reflection Questions: Self-Worth and Parenting Influence in Adulthood

1. In adulthood, how do you notice your childhood experiences influencing your self-worth? Are there any particular stories or beliefs that you still carry from your upbringing?

2. How do you find yourself reacting to praise or criticism? Does it align with the parenting style you experienced, or have you learned to develop your own responses over time?

3. Reflect on a time when you felt "not good enough"—how did your early experiences with your parents contribute to this belief?

4. When facing challenges in your personal or professional life, do you find yourself seeking approval from others? How does this relate to your early experiences with parental expectations?

5. What messages about your worth were communicated to you as a child that you would like to change? How can you rewrite these messages in your current life?

6. How do you navigate relationships now? Do you find yourself mirroring the parenting style you experienced (for example, being overly controlling, permissive, or emotionally distant)?

7. How do you respond when you feel "unloved" or unappreciated? Do these responses reflect early patterns of behavior you learned from your parents?

Reflection Questions: Parenting and Self-Worth in Your Own Parenting (if applicable)

1. If you are a parent, how do you try to balance warmth, discipline, and responsiveness with your children? How do you ensure you are fostering healthy self-worth in your child?

2. When you discipline your child, how do you communicate their value or worth? Are you mindful of how your parenting style might impact their self-esteem?

3. In what ways do you try to create a supportive environment where your child feels safe to express their emotions without judgment?

4. How do you ensure that your child feels empowered to make mistakes and learn from them without internalizing negative messages about their worth?

5. How can you consciously break any negative patterns from your own upbringing to ensure your child develops a healthy self-concept and emotional security?

These questions aim to help you reflect on how parenting styles—whether experienced or practiced—shape self-worth, and how those influences may carry over into adulthood or your own parenting practices.

✦ Chapter Summary

Chapter 8 focuses on the pivotal role that parenting styles play in shaping the narratives we inherit and how these early experiences influence our sense of self-worth and inner dialogue. From the moment we are born, the way our parents or caregivers interact with us forms the foundation of our internal story. Parenting styles—whether authoritative, authoritarian, permissive, or uninvolved—have lasting effects on how we perceive ourselves, how we respond to challenges, and how we relate to others. This chapter examines how these early interactions contribute to the development of both empowering and limiting beliefs about ourselves. For example, parents who provide consistent love, validation, and encouragement help to create an internal narrative of worthiness and confidence, while those who are neglectful or overly critical may foster feelings of inadequacy or fear. Through reflection and mindfulness, the chapter encourages readers to identify the parenting styles that shaped their early lives and explore the impact these stories have on their current self-perception. By understanding these inherited narratives, readers can begin the process of rewriting them, freeing themselves from old patterns and embracing a more authentic, empowered narrative.

Chapter 9

Sibling Dynamics and Culture: *How Our Roles Shape Us*

"Your siblings are the only people in the world who know what it's like to have been raised the way you were." – Betsy Chassney

Our siblings—whether they are our closest confidants, our rivals, or absent altogether—play a significant role in shaping the stories we carry throughout life. From the moment we share a home, our interactions with siblings help shape how we perceive ourselves, navigate relationships, and interpret our roles within the family.

Beyond just birth order, cultural norms and family traditions further shape these sibling stories. Whether raised in a culture that values independence or one that emphasizes collective harmony, the dynamics we experience with our siblings influence our beliefs about competition, love, loyalty, and fairness. These experiences often extend beyond childhood, subtly influencing how we relate to others, assert ourselves, and navigate conflict as adults.

In this chapter, we will investigate how sibling dynamics and cultural influences intertwine to create lasting internal narratives. By examining these interactions and the beliefs they formed, we can better understand how to break free from limiting patterns, heal unresolved tensions, and embrace healthier ways of relating to ourselves and others.

Siblings influence identity formation not only through direct interactions but also through implicit comparisons within the family system. From how affection was distributed to which child was praised or disciplined, these subtle cues help shape how children view themselves and their value. Among the most studied aspects of sibling dynamics is birth order, which has long been linked to personality development and self-perception (Adler, 1930).

The Hierarchy Within the Family System

According to Adler's (1930) birth order theory, a child's position in the family—firstborn, middle, youngest, or only child—can significantly impact the narratives they construct about who they are and what is expected of them.

Firstborns, for example, often take on responsibility early and may be viewed as leaders within the family, which can foster traits such as conscientiousness and perfectionism.

These children may internalize the belief that they must lead by example and meet high expectations (Sulloway, 1996).

In contrast, middle children may feel overlooked or caught in between, struggling to define their unique identity. Lacking the authority of the eldest or the attention often given to the youngest, they might seek validation outside the family or adopt independent, competitive traits (Leman, 2009). Youngest children are frequently seen as the "babies" of the family and may receive more leniency and less responsibility. This dynamic can nurture a sense of playfulness and dependence but also foster a desire to break away from expectations and assert individuality, sometimes through rebellion or humor (Dunkel & Langenbucher, 2004).

Only children, lacking sibling comparisons, often experience a different dynamic altogether. Without the influence of sibling rivalry, they may develop a strong sense of self and responsibility, yet they may also struggle with peer relationships or perfectionism due to heightened parental focus (Falbo, 1991).

These birth order positions often come with unspoken family roles that become woven into one's internal narrative. A firstborn might take on the role of the "caretaker" or "enforcer," a middle child might act as the "peacemaker" or "mediator," and the youngest might become the "entertainer" or "troublemaker" in order to stand out. Only children may adopt the role of the "mini-adult," taking on more mature traits early in life due to increased interaction with adults (Leman, 2009; Sulloway, 1996).

These roles and the stories they create do not just influence family life—they shape how we relate to others well into adulthood. Sibling rivalry, favoritism, and birth order comparisons can leave lasting impressions on self-esteem and contribute to limiting beliefs about our place in the world. Though the specific dynamics may evolve as we grow, the scripts written in childhood often continue to inform our adult relationships, behaviors, and self-worth.

Firstborns: The Responsible Leaders

Firstborn children are often cast into roles of leadership, responsibility, and achievement. They may internalize the narrative that they are expected to set an example for younger siblings, leading to a strong sense of duty and, sometimes, perfectionism. This pressure can manifest in high-achieving behaviors, a fear of failure, or difficulty delegating tasks (Sulloway, 1996; Paulhus, Trapnell, & Chen, 1999). Firstborns are also more likely to identify with parental authority and align with traditional values, especially in families that emphasize hierarchy and discipline (Ernst & Angst, 1983).

For example, a firstborn might carry an unspoken family script such as, *"I must always hold it together so others don't fall apart,"* which can result in self-neglect or burnout in adulthood.

Middle Children: The Diplomats and Peacemakers

Middle children often find themselves navigating a complex emotional space between older and younger siblings. With less undivided parental attention, they may develop stories of invisibility or of being the "forgotten" child (Salmon & Daly, 1998). However, this same position can foster adaptability, strong negotiation skills, and a tendency to avoid conflict—hallmarks of the classic peacemaker.

A common internalized message for middle children might be, *"I need to stay neutral to keep the peace,"* which can hinder the development of a strong personal voice or assertiveness later in life. Studies suggest that middle-born individuals may be more sociable and less conforming than their firstborn counterparts, possibly because they must find creative ways to stand out (Sulloway, 1996).

Youngest Children: The Charmers or Dependent Ones

Youngest siblings are often viewed as the "baby" of the family, receiving more leniency and emotional support. This can foster confidence, sociability, and creativity, as they often use charm or humor to gain attention (Stewart & Campbell, 1998). However, this role can also come with challenges—youngest children may internalize messages of dependency, believing they always need help or that they are less capable than their older siblings.

For example, a youngest child may grow up with the belief, *"Someone will always be there to rescue me,"* which can translate into difficulty with independence, decision-making, or self-efficacy as adults.

Only Children: The Independent Perfectionists

Only children, often receiving the full attention of parents, may develop strong self-esteem and maturity but also face intense pressure to meet expectations. Without siblings to share responsibilities or roles, they may internalize both the achiever and caretaker scripts. This can foster a sense of independence and high achievement, but also a fear of failure and social comparison (Falbo & Polit, 1986).

Only children may adopt beliefs such as, *"If I don't succeed, I'll disappoint everyone,"* reflecting the weight of concentrated parental hopes and projections.

These roles, while shaped in childhood, often carry into adulthood unless consciously rewritten.

The Power of Family Stories and Cultural Narratives

Beyond our daily interactions with the world, we carry within us inherited multigenerational narratives—stories of perseverance, trauma, identity, and deeply held values. These narratives, often absorbed unconsciously, serve as a kind of psychological inheritance that reflects both family identity and the broader cultural norms we grow up within (McAdams, 2006). They influence how we see ourselves, how we respond to life challenges, and what we believe is possible for our future.

Family stories are more than nostalgic anecdotes or cautionary tales; they function as internalized scripts that guide our behavior and worldview (Fivush, 2011). For example, a family with a long history of overcoming adversity may pass down a strong narrative of resilience. While this can instill a sense of strength and pride, it may also carry implicit messages that discourage vulnerability or emotional openness—traits deemed less compatible with "survival." Similarly, families that emphasize achievement may implicitly communicate that one's worth is tied to productivity or accolades, leaving little room for rest or creative exploration (Grych, 2015).

Cultural Scripts and Identity Development

Family narratives do not develop in isolation—they are profoundly shaped by the cultural contexts in which families exist. These cultural scripts serve as socially constructed guidelines for how individuals are expected to think, feel, behave, and relate to others within a given society (Schank & Abelson, 1977). Cultural scripts act as invisible blueprints, passed down through generations, subtly guiding individuals toward certain ideals, roles, and values.

For instance, in collectivist cultures, such as those found in many parts of Asia, Africa, and Latin America, identity is often shaped around interdependence, family honor, and duty. Children may be raised with narratives that emphasize obedience, respect for elders, and the subordination of personal desires to group needs. In these environments, being a "good daughter" or "honorable son" might involve prioritizing family expectations over personal goals, even when it leads to inner conflict (Markus & Kitayama, 1991). Such scripts can promote a strong sense of belonging and identity within the group but may also discourage individuality and emotional authenticity.

Conversely, in individualistic cultures, such as those predominant in the United States and Western Europe, the cultural narrative often prizes autonomy, personal achievement, and self-expression. Families in these societies may foster stories around "being true to oneself," striving for personal success, or "making it on your own." While such messages can empower individuals to pursue their dreams and embrace uniqueness, they can also create pressure to perform, compete, and isolate—especially when emotional vulnerability or interdependence is undervalued (Triandis, 1995).

Cultural scripts also interact with gender roles, race, religion, and class—layering expectations that shape identity development in nuanced ways. For example, in some cultures, masculinity is associated with stoicism and dominance, while femininity is linked to nurturance and sacrifice. Children growing up under these influences may internalize rigid gender narratives that limit emotional expression and career choices (Bem, 1981). Similarly, cultural messages about race and social class can profoundly affect how individuals perceive their self-worth and opportunities (Helms, 1995).

Example: Amira's Story:

Amira grew up in a Middle Eastern family where women were expected to marry young and prioritize family life. While she respected her culture's emphasis on loyalty and connection, Amira dreamed of becoming an international human rights lawyer. This choice was met with disapproval and warnings that she would "miss her chance" at a fulfilling personal life. Through therapy and support from mentors, Amira learned to honor her heritage while choosing a different path—one that aligned with her passion for justice and service.

Example: Dylan's Story:

Dylan, a second-generation immigrant in the U.S., was raised with the belief that academic success equals worth. When he decided to leave medical school to pursue music, he wrestled with feelings of failure and shame. Over time, he realized these feelings came from a script that equated self-sacrifice with honor. By rewriting that narrative, Dylan embraced a new story—one where following his truth was also a form of courage and success.

It is important to recognize that cultural scripts are neither inherently good nor bad—they can both empower and constrain. They provide coherence and belonging, but when they conflict with personal values or limit potential, they may lead to internal tension or identity confusion (Phinney, 1990).

For individuals striving to rewrite their personal narratives, becoming aware of these broader cultural influences is crucial. Reflecting on which messages serve one's growth and which may be challenged or reframed is a key part of developing an authentic and empowered identity.

The Double-Edged Sword of Inherited Narratives

Whether inherited from family or culture, these narratives have a dual nature—they can empower, or they can confine. A family history marked by struggle, for example, might instill a strong work ethic and appreciation for perseverance. However, it may also pass down the belief that joy is fleeting or that safety is always fragile. Children growing up in such environments may unconsciously internalize the idea that happiness must be earned through hardship or that stability is an illusion (Yehuda et al., 2001).

Consider a child raised in a family where hardship and struggle were constant themes. Perhaps their parents lived through economic instability, experiencing periods of financial stress, or they grew up in an environment where emotional support was scarce. The child learns early on that life is tough, and success requires immense effort. As an adult, this person may internalize the narrative that "hard work is the only path to success" and that "joy is something to be earned." They may develop a strong work ethic, becoming highly motivated and driven to achieve their goals. This mindset can lead to professional success, the ability to overcome obstacles, and a sense of accomplishment.

However, this inherited narrative has a double edge. The belief that happiness must be earned through struggle may also create emotional barriers. The individual may find it difficult to relax, take breaks, or feel worthy of joy without having "earned" it through labor. For example, after completing a significant achievement, they may feel a brief sense of satisfaction, but it quickly fades because they feel they must immediately start working toward the next challenge, never truly allowing themselves to enjoy the fruits of their labor. This belief could lead to chronic stress, burnout, or feelings of inadequacy because happiness or peace feels always out of reach, requiring more effort to attain.

This internalized belief may be deeply ingrained, so much so that it operates in the background, affecting every area of life. In relationships, for example, they might feel like they have to "earn" love or approval from others through constant effort or sacrifice, leading to issues with self-esteem or boundary-setting. They may struggle to accept praise or affection without feeling guilty, perpetuating a cycle of emotional suppression and difficulty accepting joy without earning it through hardship.

These inherited beliefs—shaped by family history and cultural context—become part of their implicit schemas. As Beck (1976) explains, these schemas guide an individual's thoughts and behaviors unconsciously, reinforcing certain patterns. In this case, the schema might dictate that stability is precarious and that vulnerability or relaxation can lead to disaster. The individual may unknowingly recreate these patterns of behavior throughout their life, repeating cycles of overwork, emotional distance, or difficulty in enjoying life, because they have never paused to question or reframe the inherited narrative.

Thus, while the narrative of perseverance and resilience can serve as a strength, it also can limit the person's capacity for self-compassion, emotional rest, and joy, highlighting the double-edged sword of inherited narratives.

The Transformative Power of Reflection and Rewriting

While these narratives may feel deeply embedded, they are not unchangeable. In fact, one of the most empowering realizations we can come to is that we are not bound by the stories we inherit—we have the capacity to reflect, revise, and re-author our personal narratives. Research has shown that engaging with family stories—especially when they include both positive and negative experiences—can foster resilience, identity development, and emotional well-being. In a landmark study,

Duke, Lazarus, and Fivush (2008) found that children who knew a balanced, coherent narrative about their family's history—its triumphs, struggles, and how it overcame adversity—were more likely to exhibit strong self-esteem, a clearer sense of identity, and better coping skills during difficult times.

This reflective process begins with awareness. By taking the time to question where our beliefs, values, and self-concepts originated, we begin to discern which parts of our narrative are truly ours and which ones were absorbed from family, culture, or society. This kind of introspection can be both illuminating and liberating. For example, someone raised in a family that valued emotional restraint may discover they have inherited a narrative that equates vulnerability with weakness. Through reflection, they may realize that expressing emotion can be a strength—and begin to rewrite that inner script accordingly.

Rewriting does not mean erasing the past. Rather, it is about reframing it—choosing to see inherited challenges not as defining limits, but as invitations to grow. It involves asking critical questions: *What values have I inherited that serve me well? Which beliefs hold me back? Where do I need to give myself permission to change, grow, or let go?* In doing so, we do not discard our family or cultural stories—we integrate them more consciously, choosing how they will influence us moving forward (McAdams, 2001).

Moreover, reflecting on the broader context of these inherited narratives helps us develop compassion—for ourselves and for those who came before us. Understanding the struggles that shaped our caregivers' behaviors and beliefs allows us to move beyond blame and into understanding. This process not only supports healing but also opens the door for more intentional living—choosing how we want to relate to ourselves, others, and the world.

By rewriting our stories, we reclaim authorship over our lives. We begin to live less by default and more by design, creating new narratives that reflect our true values, strengths, and vision for the future.

Rewriting Childhood Narratives: A Path to Healing

The good news? Our early stories are not our final ones. While childhood experiences often lay the groundwork for our internal narratives, those scripts can be examined, challenged, and rewritten. Healing begins with self-awareness—the capacity to notice the stories we inherited and how they continue to shape our thoughts, behaviors, and self-worth (Siegel, 2010).

Two well-established therapeutic approaches that support this process are those focused on recognizing and reshaping distorted or harmful beliefs formed from past experiences, as well as Narrative Therapy, which centers on the stories we tell about ourselves (Beck, 1976). For example, a child who internalized the belief *"I'm only lovable when I succeed"* may learn to challenge and replace that belief with more compassionate and accurate affirmations.

Narrative Therapy, developed by White and Epston (1990), invites individuals to separate themselves from their problems by recognizing that "the person is not the problem—the problem is the problem." It encourages people to externalize unhelpful narratives and re-author their lives in ways that align with their values, hopes, and strengths. This therapeutic lens empowers individuals to take on the role of the author rather than passenger in their life stories.

Another vital practice in rewriting internal narratives is reparenting—the act of giving ourselves now what we may have lacked in childhood, such as emotional validation, consistent support, and healthy boundaries. Through self-compassion (Neff, 2003), mindfulness (Kabat-Zinn, 1990), and intentional inner dialogue, we can become the nurturing presence we needed. This process enables us to move from a narrative of inadequacy to one grounded in resilience, empowerment, and authenticity. Ultimately, rewriting childhood narratives is not about erasing the past—it is about understanding it with more context and compassion so we can grow beyond it. With time and intentional effort, old wounds can become a source of wisdom, empathy, and strength.

The Media and Cultural Narratives

In the digital age, media has become one of the most pervasive forces in shaping identity. From advertisements and films to music videos, news outlets, and social media platforms, we are constantly bombarded with messages about who we should be, what we should value, and how we should live. These media portrayals act as cultural scripts, subtly (or overtly) influencing our beliefs about beauty, success, gender roles, wealth, relationships, and even mental health.

Media does not just reflect culture—it actively constructs it. According to cultivation theory, prolonged exposure to media content can shape an individual's perception of reality (Gerbner, Gross, Morgan, & Signorielli, 1986). For instance, if someone constantly sees portrayals of thin, flawless bodies as the standard of beauty, they may internalize the belief that they must look a certain way to be loved or accepted.

Social media adds another layer, offering curated, idealized versions of life that are often filtered and staged. Users may compare their real, messy lives with others' highlight reels, resulting in feelings of inadequacy, anxiety, and low self-worth (Fardouly et al., 2015; Chou & Edge, 2012). The more we compare ourselves to these unrealistic portrayals, the more likely we are to adopt self-critical narratives and chase identities that are not truly our own.

Examples:

Case 1: The Instagram Illusion

Janelle, a 19-year-old college student, spends hours each day on Instagram. She follows influencers with luxury lifestyles and "perfect" bodies. Over time, she begins to feel as though she is falling behind in life, despite being successful in school and maintaining healthy friendships. Janelle starts to believe she needs to look a certain way or travel constantly to be considered valuable. It takes a digital detox and a shift in the accounts she follows to begin dismantling these harmful narratives.

Case 2: Media Stereotyping and Masculinity

Marcus, a 28-year-old teacher, grew up watching action movies where men were portrayed as tough, emotionless heroes. Crying or talking about feelings was seen as weak. As an adult, Marcus finds it difficult to express vulnerability in relationships.

Through therapy, he begins to unpack how media representations shaped his narrative around masculinity and discovers new, healthier ways to define strength.

The Influence of Media on Self-Image

Media consumption plays a powerful role in shaping how we view ourselves, particularly in terms of appearance, success, and worth. Constant exposure to idealized representations—whether through television, film, advertising, or social media—can distort our perceptions of what's normal, desirable, or attainable. These images often present unrealistic beauty standards, airbrushed physiques, and lifestyles that are selectively curated to show only the best moments.

Research supports this connection. Grabe, Ward, and Hyde (2008) conducted a meta-analysis of 77 studies and found a robust link between media exposure and body dissatisfaction among women. The more women consumed media that emphasized thin ideals, the more likely they were to report dissatisfaction with their own bodies. This dissatisfaction can contribute to the development of eating disorders, anxiety, and depression (Tiggemann, 2011).

Media influence isn't limited to appearance. Cultural scripts portrayed in media often equate success with wealth, fame, and power—standards that are unattainable for most people. When individuals compare their lives to the glamorized depictions of success, they may begin to question their own worth, even if they are personally and professionally fulfilled (Gilbert, 2006). This comparison trap can create internal narratives of "not being enough," undermining self-esteem and promoting chronic dissatisfaction.

Social media adds another layer of pressure. Platforms like Instagram and TikTok, which reward popularity and aesthetics, often encourage users to perform rather than express their authentic selves. The pressure to conform to viral trends or influencer lifestyles can result in individuals curating their identity to fit the dominant narrative, disconnecting from who they really are (Fardouly et al., 2015).

For Example:
Social Media and Body Image

Samantha, a 22-year-old college student, frequently scrolls through fitness influencer content on Instagram. Although she exercises regularly and eats well, she begins to feel insecure about her body because it does not match the toned, filtered images she sees online. She starts skipping meals and obsessively tracking her food—behaviors she never engaged in before social media exposure intensified her body dissatisfaction.

The Comparison Trap:

Luis, a 35-year-old graphic designer, enjoys his work and has a healthy family life. Yet, after seeing former classmates on LinkedIn celebrating promotions and luxury purchases, he begins to doubt his career path. Although he once felt successful, he now tells himself he has not achieved enough. This shift in self-perception stems not from actual dissatisfaction, but from a media-fueled script about what success should look like.

The Harmful Effects of Conformity and External Validation

Conformity to societal norms is often driven by one of the most fundamental human needs: the need to belong. According to Baumeister and Leary (1995), humans are biologically and psychologically wired for connection, which motivates us to align with social norms in order to be accepted and avoid rejection. This desire for inclusion is not inherently negative— shared norms can foster cooperation and harmony—but problems arise when belonging becomes conditional on suppressing one's authentic self.

Social comparison theory (Festinger, 1954) explains how individuals evaluate themselves by comparing their abilities, achievements, and appearance to others. While this can sometimes provide motivation for growth, it more often leads to chronic self-doubt, especially when comparisons are upward (i.e., comparing ourselves to those we perceive as "better"). In the age of social media, where carefully curated versions of others' lives dominate our screens, this effect is amplified (Fardouly et al., 2015). The result is a growing tendency to judge one's worth against artificial or superficial standards, leaving many people with a persistent sense of inadequacy.

When societal norms narrowly define success as wealth, beauty, productivity, or status, individuals internalize scripts that tell them they are only valuable if they meet these benchmarks. This external validation loop can lead to anxiety, burnout, depression, or imposter syndrome (Gilbert, 2006). People may pursue careers, relationships, or lifestyles that are socially approved but personally unfulfilling, leading to a sense of emptiness or existential dissatisfaction (Brown, 2012).

Moreover, this overreliance on external validation often suppresses emotional authenticity. We may silence our true feelings or preferences in order to be accepted or praised. Over time, this can erode self-trust and contribute to the development of a "false self"—a persona crafted for approval rather than a reflection of inner truth (Winnicott, 1965).

Example: Maya's Story – The High-Achiever Trap

Maya was raised in a family and culture where success was measured by external accomplishments—grades, awards, career prestige. From a young age, she learned that her worth was tied to achievement. Her parents praised her when she brought home straight A's and boasted about her to others. Although she felt loved, the love seemed conditional on performance.

Influenced by this narrative, Maya pursued a career in corporate law—not because she was passionate about it, but because it symbolized "success" in her community. She dressed the part, worked long hours, and climbed the ladder. Outwardly, she looked successful. But internally, she felt disconnected and drained. She rarely had time for creative pursuits or relationships that nourished her emotionally.

Despite her accolades, Maya struggled with anxiety and imposter syndrome. She constantly compared herself to colleagues on social media who seemed to have even more — a better title, a bigger home, a more luxurious lifestyle. Social comparison (Festinger, 1954) and her reliance on external validation made her feel like she was never enough.

It was not until she took a sabbatical and began journaling—
something she had not done since childhood—that she started
to reconnect with her inner voice. She realized her definition of
success had been inherited, not chosen. Slowly, she began
rewriting her script: she moved into a more flexible career,
returned to painting, and sought out relationships that honored
her authenticity rather than her resume.

Challenging these external scripts begins with awareness. By
questioning whose standards we are trying to live up to—and
why—we begin to loosen the grip of conformity and return to
a more authentic narrative. Recognizing that we are worthy not
because of how we compare to others, but because of who we
are, is the foundation of psychological freedom and well-being.

Reflection

Maya's story is a powerful reminder that living by inherited or
socially prescribed scripts can lead to emotional burnout and
identity confusion. Without examining these narratives, we risk
building lives that may impress others but do not fulfill us.

The Harmful Effects of Conformity on Self-Worth

While conformity can foster a sense of belonging and social unity, it can also come at a significant personal cost. When the desire to fit in outweighs the need to stay true to oneself, it can erode self-worth and negatively impact mental well-being. Let us explore how this happens:

1. Loss of Authenticity

When we conform to societal standards or group expectations that conflict with our true values and desires, we risk losing touch with our authentic selves. The more we shape our behaviors to align with external ideals, the more we drift from our internal compass. Over time, this disconnect can manifest as frustration, emptiness, or even identity confusion. It can feel like living someone else's life instead of our own.

For example, imagine someone who chooses a prestigious career path—such as law or medicine—not out of passion, but because of societal messages equating success with income or status. While they may achieve external validation, internally they may feel unfulfilled or out of alignment with their true interests, such as working in the arts or social justice (Seligman, 2011).

2. Increased Anxiety and Stress

Conforming often requires constant self-monitoring—carefully crafting your image, avoiding judgment, and striving to meet societal benchmarks. This vigilance can be mentally exhausting. When individuals feel pressure to maintain appearances in areas like career, beauty, or lifestyle, stress and anxiety tend to increase.

Studies show that people who feel compelled to conform to societal ideals are more likely to experience mental health issues such as anxiety and depression (Grabe, Ward, & Hyde, 2008). The fear of not measuring up fuels a cycle of self-doubt, leaving little space for growth, creativity, or self-compassion.

3. Negative Body Image and Low Self-Esteem

Few societal pressures are as pervasive—and damaging—as those surrounding physical appearance. Mainstream media often promotes narrow, unrealistic beauty ideals that exclude a wide range of body types, ages, and ethnicities. These portrayals foster widespread dissatisfaction and internalized shame.

For instance, the frequent depiction of idealized bodies—often thin, youthful, and Eurocentric—can lead individuals to feel inadequate or "less than" if they do not meet that mold. Research links these media-driven beauty ideals to lower self-esteem, increased body dissatisfaction, and higher rates of eating disorders (Grabe et al., 2008).

4. Imposter Syndrome

Societal standards of success can also contribute to the rise of imposter syndrome—a psychological experience in which individuals feel undeserving of their achievements and live in fear of being "found out." This is especially common among high achievers who internalize perfectionistic standards and tie their worth to external validation.

Even when they meet or exceed expectations, these individuals may feel like frauds, believing their accomplishments are the result of luck rather than ability (Clance & Imes, 1978). When success is defined by society in rigid terms—status, wealth, prestige—it can leave those on less conventional paths feeling unworthy, no matter how meaningful their contributions.

Example: Jordan's Story – The Pressure to Perform Masculinity:

Jordan grew up in a community where masculinity was defined by emotional stoicism, physical strength, and dominance. From a young age, he learned that showing vulnerability was a sign of weakness. When he cried as a child, he was told to "man up." When he wanted to pursue music instead of sports, he was mocked by peers and subtly discouraged by family.

Over time, Jordan internalized a script that said *"Real men don't feel deeply"* and *"Success means power, not passion."* He conformed by becoming highly competitive, emotionally distant, and obsessed with appearing "strong." On the outside, he was admired. On the inside, he felt lonely, disconnected, and anxious.

It was not until his late twenties—after a failed relationship and a bout of depression—that Jordan sought therapy. He realized his self-worth had been tethered to a version of masculinity that did not reflect his true self. Influenced by societal and cultural scripts (Connell, 1995; Mahalik et al., 2003), Jordan had been performing rather than living.

In therapy, Jordan began to rewrite the narrative. He embraced emotional vulnerability, reconnected with his love for music, and started building relationships based on authenticity rather than image. This shift helped him rebuild his self-worth on the foundation of *who* he was, not *what* he was expected to be.

Key Insight

Jordan's experience highlights how gendered societal expectations can shape identity and diminish self-worth when they conflict with a person's natural temperament or desires. His healing began when he challenged the inherited script and gave himself permission to redefine what it meant to be a man on his own terms.

Example: The Courage to Feel: A Teen's Journey Beyond the Mask of Masculinity

Jalen, a 16-year-old high school athlete, was known for being quiet, competitive, and "tough"—qualities praised by his coaches and peers. In his friend group, emotions were off-limits. Jokes about "acting like a girl" or being "soft" kept everyone in line. So when Jalen started struggling with anxiety after his parents' divorce, he hid it. He stopped sleeping well, lost interest in school, and even began lashing out at friends—all while trying to maintain the image of being strong and unaffected.

In health class, a lesson on mental health and masculinity hit home. For the first time, Jalen heard someone say that bottling up emotions isn't strength—it's a survival strategy, and not always a healthy one. Encouraged by the teacher's openness, he reached out to the school counselor. It was hard at first—words didn't come easily—but he began to unlearn the message that masculinity meant silence. Over time, Jalen found new ways to express himself and discovered that being vulnerable didn't make him less of a man—it made him more human.

Key Insight:

True strength isn't found in suppressing emotions, but in the willingness to face them. Jalen's journey reveals that challenging cultural expectations around masculinity can lead to deeper self-awareness, emotional healing, and more authentic connection with others.

Challenging Harmful Societal Norms

Societal norms may be powerful, but they are not immutable truths. They are constructed—shaped by culture, history, media, and power—and therefore, they can be questioned, redefined, and even dismantled. Reclaiming your narrative often begins with disrupting these imposed standards and creating space for a more authentic, values-based life.

1. Self-Reflection and Critical Thinking

The first step in breaking free from limiting societal expectations is self-inquiry. Ask yourself: *What beliefs or ideals have I accepted without question? Do they reflect who I truly am or who others expect me to be?*

By critically examining the messages absorbed from family, media, and culture, you begin to distinguish your authentic desires from imposed narratives. This awareness creates the foundation for meaningful change.

2. Redefining Success

True success is not one-size-fits-all. Rather than measuring achievement through society's lens—wealth, status, or accolades—consider how success feels on your terms. For some, it may mean creative freedom. For others, it might involve nurturing close relationships, maintaining mental health, or living in alignment with spiritual or ethical values.

When you redefine success around personal fulfillment rather than social comparison, you liberate yourself from the pressure to perform and begin to live with intention (Beck, 1976).

3. Building a Supportive Network

Surrounding yourself with people who value authenticity over conformity is a powerful buffer against societal pressure. When your community affirms your true self—rather than the version that fits a mold—it becomes easier to stay grounded and resist the urge to seek approval from outside sources.

Seek out mentors, friends, or groups that celebrate your unique path. Their presence can offer strength, validation, and encouragement as you rewrite your story.

4. Fostering Self-Compassion

To counter the damage inflicted by comparison and perfectionism, cultivate self-compassion. Speak to yourself with kindness, especially when you feel you are falling short.

Recognize that it is human to feel uncertain or imperfect—and that your worth is not determined by how well you fit societal ideals (Neff, 2011).

Practicing self-compassion does not mean settling for less. It means building resilience from a place of self-love, rather than fear or shame.

Key Takeaways

1. **Sibling Relationships Shape Identity**

   Our siblings play a significant role in shaping our identity and personal narrative. The dynamic between siblings, whether competitive, supportive, or indifferent, influences how we view ourselves and our relationships with others.

2. **Birth Order Influences Personality**

   Birth order can impact personality development. Firstborns, middle children, youngest children, and only children often develop distinct traits due to their position within the family structure. These traits can contribute to how we see ourselves and our role within the family and society.

3. **Firstborns Often Take on Leadership Roles**

   As the firstborn, individuals often take on leadership roles and feel a sense of responsibility for their younger siblings. They may develop traits like perfectionism, a strong sense of duty, or a drive for achievement, often because they feel the weight of setting an example.

4. **Middle Children May Strive for Attention**

   Middle children may feel overlooked and develop a desire to stand out or carve their own path. They might become peacemakers or, alternatively, rebellious, depending on how they navigate their relationships with older and younger siblings.

5. **Youngest Children Are Often Nurtured but May Lack Autonomy**

   Youngest children, often pampered or protected, may develop charm and playfulness but struggle with autonomy or asserting their voice. They may develop traits of being charming, playful, or spoiled, but they might also face challenges when trying to assert themselves.

6. **Only Children Carry the Weight of Parental Expectations**

   Only children are often the focus of their parents' attention and expectations, which can create a strong sense of responsibility but also pressure to succeed. They may struggle with feeling isolated or overprotected but often develop maturity beyond their years.

7. **Sibling Rivalry Can Influence Self-Perception**

   Rivalry between siblings can lead to comparisons and feelings of inadequacy. It can shape the narrative of who is "better" or "less than," which can impact self-esteem and personal identity well into adulthood.

8. **Family Narratives Are Often Shared Among Siblings**

   Siblings often share common family narratives, but each sibling might interpret these stories differently based on their unique perspective and role within the family. These varying interpretations can influence how each sibling perceives themselves and their place in the family dynamic.

9. **Sibling Roles Can Change Over Time**

   As siblings grow older, their roles within the family may shift. The dynamics that once defined their relationships can change due to life events such as marriage, parenthood, or other transitions, which may lead to evolving personal narratives.

10. **Awareness of Birth Order Narratives Can Promote Healing**

    Understanding how birth order and sibling dynamics have influenced your personal narrative can help you become more self-aware. It allows you to challenge yourself with limiting beliefs, heal old wounds, and create a more balanced and empowered self-identity. Whether shaped by family roles or societal scripts, our early identities are not fixed destinies.

With awareness, compassion, and courage, we can unlearn what no longer serves us—and write new narratives rooted in authenticity, not approval.

These takeaways highlight the powerful role that sibling relationships and birth order play in shaping personal identity. By recognizing these early dynamics, you can begin to understand yourself more deeply and cultivate healthier, more authentic connections with others.

The following exercises are designed to help you reflect on and rewrite the narratives shaped by your family role, fostering a more empowered and compassionate story about who you are and how you relate to those closest to you.

Reflection Questions

1. How have cultural expectations or family stories shaped your views on identity, success, or relationships? Are these narratives still serving you today?
2. What roles or values from your culture or heritage have positively influenced you, and which ones might need to be revisited to align more with your true self?
3. How has media or social media influenced your sense of self-worth or body image? What harmful messages have you unlearned or need to challenge?
4. In what ways can you redefine success to reflect your personal values rather than societal or cultural pressures?
5. What steps can you take to cultivate a community and media environment that supports authenticity and empowers you to be true to yourself?

✦ Chapter Summary

Chapter 9 explores how sibling dynamics, cultural scripts, and media influences collectively shape the stories we carry throughout our lives. Siblings often play a crucial role in the development of our identity, either by providing support and companionship or by introducing rivalry and competition. The unique positions we occupy in the family (oldest, youngest, middle child, only child) influence the scripts we inherit and the roles we adopt, which may carry into adulthood. In addition to family roles, cultural expectations and societal norms offer another layer of influence, often dictating how we are expected to behave and what values we should uphold. This chapter emphasizes the powerful impact of cultural scripts—such as gender roles, race, and community traditions—that shape the stories we tell ourselves about who we are and what we can achieve. Media also plays a significant part in shaping our narratives, presenting idealized images and messages that may or may not align with our true selves. The chapter encourages readers to reflect on the interplay between family, culture, and media in crafting their identity, urging them to question limiting beliefs and adopt more empowering perspectives. By unpacking these external influences, readers can break free from inherited scripts and embrace their authentic narratives, making conscious choices that align with their true values and desires.

Chapter 10

The Role of Language: *How It Shapes Our Life Story*

"Words are, of course, the most powerful drug used by mankind." – Rudyard Kipling

Language is more than just a tool for communication—it is the lens through which we perceive the world and define ourselves. From the stories we tell others to the silent dialogue within our minds, language has the power to shape thoughts, influence emotions, and create the framework of our personal identity. What we say to ourselves and how we interpret the words of others can become a powerful force—either reinforcing limiting beliefs or unlocking new possibilities.

We often think of language as external—something we use to express thoughts or share ideas. But in reality, it also operates internally, silently scripting the narratives that define our self-worth, relationships, and potential. For some, a childhood filled with affirmations can cultivate confidence, while others may carry the weight of critical or dismissive words, becoming their harshest critics.

But the beauty of language lies in its flexibility. Just as it can limit, it can also liberate. By becoming aware of the words we use—both out loud and in our thoughts—we gain the power to challenge negative scripts, reframe difficult experiences, and write a new story for ourselves.

In this chapter, we will explore the profound influence of language on our life narratives, beginning with the way self-talk shape's identity. You will discover how the words you use internally impact your beliefs, emotions, and behaviors. We will examine the power of reframing—transforming limiting thoughts into empowering ones through cognitive restructuring techniques. Our journey will also cover the impact of external language, revealing how cultural, familial, and societal messages can influence your self-concept and worldview. Through real-life examples, you will see how shifting language transformed the lives of others, offering a blueprint for your own change. Finally, this chapter will provide practical tools to help you become aware of your language patterns, replace negative scripts, and consciously choose words that align with your values and vision.

This chapter is an invitation to become the conscious author of your life story—one where your words become a source of strength, clarity, and possibility.

The Power of Words: How Language Shapes Our Perception of Reality

Language is not merely descriptive—it is generative. It does not just mirror our world; it creates and reshapes it. Philosopher Ludwig Wittgenstein famously said, *"The limits of my language mean the limits of my world"* (1953). This insight captures how the words we use shape the boundaries of what we believe is possible.

From early childhood, we assign meaning to our experiences through language. The words we choose—whether consciously or unconsciously—become the lens through which we interpret life events. When we describe a setback as a "failure," for example, we are more likely to internalize shame. But when we frame it as a "learning opportunity," we open ourselves to growth.

Language influences not just what we think, but how we think. Over time, repeated words and phrases form the blueprint of our inner world—defining our identity, shaping our relationships, and guiding our responses to challenges.

How Language Influences Self-Perception

Our self-talk—the internal dialogue that runs through our minds—plays a powerful role in shaping how we see ourselves. Whether we label ourselves as "capable," "broken," "resilient," or "not enough," those words influence our behavior, self-worth, and emotional health.

Psychologist Donald Meichenbaum (1977) highlighted the significant role self-talk plays in shaping our psychological patterns. Building on this understanding, harmful inner language—such as *"I'm a failure"* or *"I'll never be good enough"*—is recognized as a key contributor to anxiety, depression, and low self-esteem (Beck, 1976). These automatic thoughts often form the basis of negative self-narratives.

A fundamental technique involves identifying and replacing distorted thoughts with more balanced and empowering language. This process not only transforms our thinking but also reshapes how we feel and behave.

Example: Lisa's Story

Lisa, a 35-year-old teacher, frequently told herself: "I'm terrible at public speaking" and *"I'm going to mess this up."* These beliefs led her to avoid leadership roles and feel intense anxiety in the classroom. Lisa began to recognize these statements as distorted interpretations rather than facts. Gradually, she replaced them with affirmations such as, *"I care about my students, and I'm learning to speak with confidence."* This change helped her see her skills as adaptable rather than fixed, ultimately enabling her to present at a district-wide workshop—something she once believed was beyond her reach.

This transformation illustrates that self-talk is not trivial—it is central. When we change our internal language, we rewrite the story of who we believe we are and what we can become.

Personal Reflection

I experienced a similar transformation during my undergraduate studies. I dreaded public speaking, but I knew it was essential for both my academic performance and personal growth. To manage my anxiety, I relied on positive self-talk, repeating encouraging phrases like, *"You've got this," "It'll only be a few minutes, and you'll be done,"* and "Think of it as teaching them something they don't know." These simple affirmations helped me tremendously. In time, I went from avoiding presentations to being the first to volunteer to speak.

The Influence of External Language: Society, Media, and the Language of Judgment

While internal language shapes how we view ourselves, external language—the messages we receive from family, culture, media, and society—also profoundly influences our narratives.

Words and labels assigned to us, such as "lazy," "strong," "troubled," or "gifted," can become internalized over time, often affecting our self-perception more than we realize. For instance, someone repeatedly labeled as "dramatic" or "too emotional" may suppress their feelings or develop shame around emotional expression.

Media's Role in Shaping Self-Narratives

The media is a powerful force in shaping language around beauty, success, and self-worth. Advertisements, movies, and social platforms often promote narrow ideals, particularly around physical appearance. Research by Grabe, Ward, and Hyde (2008) found that media exposure to idealized images of thinness is strongly associated with body dissatisfaction, especially in women. Fouts and Burggraf (2000) further found that teen girls exposed to media messages emphasizing perfection were more likely to struggle with self-esteem and body image.

The language surrounding mental health also reflects and reinforces stigma. Phrases like "crazy," "unstable," or "weak" perpetuate shame and discourage people from seeking help. As Corrigan (2004) notes, internalized stigma—where individuals adopt society's negative language—can severely impact recovery and self-worth.

Redefining Success and Worth

Societal language around achievement often equates worth with productivity, external status, or material possessions. This dominant narrative can pressure individuals to strive for perfection, constantly feeling the need to prove their value to others (Brown, 2010). Such language fosters a mindset where self-worth is directly tied to achievements, leading to anxiety, burnout, and feelings of inadequacy.

However, research suggests that a shift in perspective can lead to more sustainable motivation and well-being. Carol Dweck (2006), in her groundbreaking work on growth mindset, emphasizes that when success is framed as effort-based rather than outcome-based, individuals are more resilient, open to learning, and willing to take on challenges. This approach encourages people to view setbacks as opportunities for growth rather than as reflections of their value.

Furthermore, language plays a critical role in shaping perceptions of beauty, success, and worth. Media and cultural norms often promote narrow standards of beauty and success, creating unrealistic expectations (Tiggemann & Slater, 2014). These narratives can negatively impact self-esteem, particularly among vulnerable populations. By consciously changing the way we speak about value—focusing on qualities such as kindness, perseverance, and authenticity—we empower ourselves to define our own standards and resist limiting labels.

This redefined approach to success allows for a more compassionate and authentic sense of self-worth. It encourages individuals to recognize that value is inherent, not earned, and that true success is found in personal growth, meaningful relationships, and self-acceptance (Neff, 2011).

The Power of Mindset: Effort Over Outcome

Carol Dweck (2006), in her groundbreaking work on growth mindset, emphasizes that when success is framed as effort-based rather than outcome-based, individuals are more resilient, open to learning, and willing to take on challenges. A growth mindset encourages individuals to view setbacks as opportunities for development rather than as reflections of their value. In contrast, a fixed mindset—where worth is seen as dependent on talent or inherent qualities—can cause individuals to avoid challenges for fear of failure.

By adopting a growth mindset, individuals begin to understand that their value is not defined by flawless performance but by their willingness to learn, adapt, and grow. This shift is not merely a change in thinking but a transformation in self-language. Statements like "*I failed*" can become "*I learned something new*," and "*I'm not good at this*" can become "*I haven't mastered this yet.*"

The Impact of Cultural Narratives

Beyond personal beliefs, cultural narratives also play a significant role in shaping perceptions of success and worth. Media and cultural norms often promote narrow standards of beauty and success, creating unrealistic expectations (Tiggemann & Slater, 2014). Social media, with its emphasis on curated images and achievements, can further amplify feelings of inadequacy (Fardouly et al., 2015).

Language in cultural narratives often categorizes individuals based on superficial traits—appearance, wealth, or status—leading to value judgments that are both limiting and harmful. By consciously challenging these narratives and adopting a broader, more inclusive language of worth, individuals can protect their self-esteem and develop a healthier sense of identity.

Redefining Success through Faith-Based Perspectives

From a faith-based perspective, worth is not determined by worldly achievements but by inherent dignity as a creation of God. As written in Psalm 139:14, "*I praise you because I am fearfully and wonderfully made; your works are wonderful, I know that full well*" (NIV). This scripture emphasizes that human value is intrinsic and divinely given, not earned through performance.

The teachings of Jesus also reinforce a different standard of success—one rooted in love, humility, and service. In Matthew 23:11, Jesus says, "*The greatest among you will be your servant*" (NIV), a reminder that true greatness is found in character, compassion, and selflessness, rather than in external status.

Practical Steps to Redefine Success and Worth

1. **Adopt a Growth Mindset**: Regularly reframe your self-talk using growth-oriented language. Instead of saying, "I can't do this," try saying, "I'm learning how to do this."
2. **Challenge Societal Narratives**: Reflect on where your standards of success come from. Are they based on your values, or are they influenced by external pressures?

3. **Embrace Your Inherent Worth**: Remind yourself that your value is not dependent on achievements. Use faith-based affirmations such as "I am wonderfully made" or "I am loved without condition."

4. **Surround Yourself with Positive Language**: Limit exposure to media that promotes superficial success. Instead, engage with content that emphasizes personal growth, kindness, and authenticity.

5. **Practice Gratitude**: Focus on what you have achieved in terms of personal growth, meaningful relationships, and acts of kindness, rather than on external accomplishments.

Redefining success and worth are an ongoing process that requires conscious effort. By transforming the language you use to define value—both for yourself and others—you can cultivate a mindset rooted in growth, authenticity, and self-compassion. You become free to define success on your own terms, finding fulfillment in who you are, not just in what you achieve.

The Role of Narrative Therapy in Rewriting Our Stories

Narrative therapy, developed by White and Epston (1990), is based on the idea that we are not our problems—we are the authors of our own stories. This approach helps individuals separate themselves from negative narratives and re-author their lives using language that supports empowerment and possibility.

A core practice in narrative therapy is externalization—the act of describing a problem as something one experiences, not something one *is*. For example, saying *"I am depressed"* reinforces identity fusion with the condition, whereas *"I'm experiencing depression"* recognizes that the condition is not the whole self.

Through re-authoring, individuals begin to construct new stories that highlight strength, power, and purpose. Therapists act as collaborators in helping clients identify "alternative plots"—those moments of strength, connection, or resilience that contradict the dominant, problem-saturated story.

The Language of Empowerment: Reclaiming Our Voice

Reclaiming the language of empowerment starts by changing how we speak about ourselves. Instead of internalizing fixed identities like *"I'm not good at this,"* try using growth-oriented statements such as, "I'm learning something new." This simple shift builds psychological flexibility and encourages self-compassion.

Dweck's (2006) concept of the *growth mindset* shows that when we frame challenges as learning opportunities, we are more likely to persevere. Similarly, affirmations—intentional, positive statements—can disrupt old scripts and build new neural pathways rooted in encouragement and possibility.

We also have the power to challenge and revise the external scripts imposed by culture. Redefining beauty to include authenticity, redefining success to include balance, and redefining strength to include vulnerability are all ways we reclaim our narrative.

Final Thoughts

Language is the foundation of every story we live. Whether it arises from within or is spoken over us by others, it has the power to define, confine, or liberate. When we become conscious of the words we use—especially in how we speak to and about ourselves—we gain access to profound personal transformation.

By the end of this chapter, you now have the tools to identify the limiting scripts shaped by language and begin rewriting your narrative using words that align with your truth. When you reclaim your language, you reclaim your life.

Key Takeaway

1. **Language Creates Reality**

    The language we use shapes the way we perceive and experience the world. Words not only describe our reality but also create and influence how we interpret events, ourselves, and others.

2. **Words are Powerful Tools**

    Our language can either limit or empower us. Negative self-talk or harmful language can reinforce limiting beliefs and hold us back, while positive, empowering language can help us create new possibilities and a more resilient mindset.

3. **Narratives Are Constructed**

    Life narratives are not fixed; they are constructed through the stories we tell ourselves and others. By changing the language we use, we can change the story we live.

4. **Internal and External Narratives**

    Both internal dialogue (self-talk) and external influences (family, culture, media) shape our personal narratives. Understanding and differentiating these influences helps us take control of our life stories.

5. **The Impact of Language on Identity**

    The way we speak about ourselves and others contributes to our sense of identity. Shifting language can help us rewrite who we believe we are and who we are becoming.

6. **Rewriting Your Narrative**

   Changing the language we use to describe ourselves and our experiences is a powerful tool in rewriting our life story. By reframing negative language, we can shift our focus toward growth, opportunity, and resilience.

7. **The Role of Mindfulness and Awareness**

   Becoming aware of the language we use, especially in moments of stress, challenge, or self-doubt, allows us to pause and choose more empowering words, contributing to emotional well-being and self-compassion.

8. **Conscious Language**

   To foster lasting change, we must practice conscious language, intentionally speaking in ways that support our growth, vision, and goals. This shifts our narrative from one of limitation to one of possibility.

By recognizing and shifting the language that shapes your thoughts and behaviors, you begin the powerful process of transforming your life narrative. Through intentional reflection and practice, you can harness the power of words to build resilience and create a more empowered, purposeful future.

Reflection Prompts

Think of a recent situation where you doubted yourself or felt overwhelmed.

1. What did your inner voice say in that moment?

2. How might your experience have shifted if you had responded with language rooted in self-compassion or encouragement instead?

Think about a recent conversation that left you feeling either deeply connected or emotionally distant.

3. What words were used?

4. How did the language either build a bridge or create a barrier between you and the other person?

Consider how using "I statements" or expressing vulnerability might have shifted the dynamic.

Reflection Questions

1. How has the language you use in self-talk influenced your self-worth and perception of your abilities?

2. What societal or cultural narratives have you internalized through the language used by others?

3. How can you begin to use language as a tool for empowerment, both in your internal dialogue and in your relationships?

✦ Chapter Summary

Chapter 10 explores the profound influence language has on shaping our life narratives. Words are not just tools for communication, they are the architects of our identity, the building blocks of our perceptions, and the drivers of our experiences. The language we use, both with ourselves and others, frames how we interpret the world around us and how we position ourselves within it. This chapter explores how the stories we tell through language can either empower or limit us, impacting our emotional well-being, our relationships, and our personal growth. The words we choose shape our sense of self-worth, our ability to navigate challenges, and our potential for transformation. By becoming more conscious of our language—whether in self-talk, interpersonal communication, or the narratives we internalize from society—we gain the ability to rewrite our personal stories. This chapter emphasizes the importance of using language to cultivate a mindset of possibility, resilience, and self-compassion. Through practical exercises and real-life examples, readers are encouraged to harness the power of words to reframe negative beliefs, shift perceptions, and create a narrative that aligns with their authentic self. Ultimately, the chapter invites readers to see language as a powerful tool for healing and transformation, capable of reshaping their identity and the course of their lives.

Chapter 11

The Transformative Power of Self-Talk

"Your self-talk is the script you're writing for your life. Choose your words wisely." – Unknown

Self-talk is an inherent part of our daily lives, comprising the inner dialogue that accompanies us—often unconsciously—throughout each day. It is the ongoing stream of thoughts that shapes the narrative through which we interpret and interact with the world. Research shows that self-talk plays a central role in influencing both our emotional experiences and behavioral responses. Beck (1976) explains that how we speak to ourselves—whether in an empowering or destructive way—plays a crucial role in our mental health and emotional well-being. Self-talk is not simply a mental event but a powerful psychological tool that, when harnessed correctly, can significantly influence our personal growth.

Psychological research also underscores the profound effect self-talk has on self-esteem, self-concept, and coping strategies. It's not only about the content of these thoughts but also about their emotional tone and the mental images they evoke. Whether we choose language that supports our growth or diminishes it, our confidence can significantly impact our

202

outcomes in life. Neff (2011) emphasizes that we can change our emotional landscape simply by adjusting the way we speak to ourselves.

In this chapter, the transformative power of self-talk is examined as a fundamental component of personal growth and emotional well-being. Self-talk, defined as the continuous internal dialogue that influences our perception of self and the world, plays a pivotal role in shaping our mental health, motivation, and behavior. Drawing on foundational cognitive-behavioral theories and contemporary psychological research, this chapter explores the mechanisms through which self-talk affects self-esteem, resilience, and coping strategies. Readers will gain insight into how negative self-talk can contribute to emotional distress and cognitive distortions, while positive self-talk fosters empowerment and psychological resilience. Furthermore, evidence-based techniques for cultivating constructive inner dialogue, including mindfulness and self-compassion practices, are presented to guide the reader in intentionally rewriting their internal narrative toward greater well-being and self-efficacy.

The Impact of Negative Self-Talk

Negative self-talk can be self-limiting, serving as an internal barrier that prevents us from realizing our full potential. According to Beck's cognitive model of depression (1976), negative self-talk stems from core beliefs that we hold about ourselves, which are shaped by early life experiences and reinforced over time. This negative self-talk is often automatic, repeating itself in the background of our minds. It can include harsh judgments and labels like *"I'm not good enough," "I always fail,"* or *"I'll never succeed."*

Studies have shown that people who engage in consistent negative self-talk are more likely to experience anxiety, depression, and feelings of hopelessness (Seligman, 1990). These distorted ways of thinking can create a vicious cycle: ruminating on past failures often leads to negative emotional states, which then trigger further negative self-talk. This cycle reinforces feelings of inadequacy, hindering people from attempting new challenges, and can ultimately contribute to learned helplessness—the belief that one has no control over their fate (Seligman, 1975).

Negative self-talk also increases self-critical perfectionism, a psychological state that leads to a constant fear of failure. According to Frost et al. (1990), perfectionists often engage in self-destructive self-talk that leads them to believe they can never meet their high standards. This perpetual self-criticism exacerbates stress and emotional distress, making it difficult to form healthy, adaptive ways of thinking and coping with setbacks.

Common forms of negative self-talk include:

- **Catastrophizing:** Believing the worst possible outcome will happen.
- **Overgeneralization:** Making broad statements based on a single event ("I always fail").
- **Personalization:** Blaming oneself for external events outside of one's control.
- **Filtering:** Focusing only on the negative aspects of a situation, ignoring the positive.

These patterns of thinking perpetuate emotional distress and hinder problem-solving, as they prevent individuals from seeing solutions and opportunities (Burns, 1980).

Example: Alex's Struggle with Negative Self-Talk

Alex, a 28-year-old graduate student, had always been an overachiever. From a young age, he internalized the message that his worth was tied to his performance. When he received a B on a major research paper, his inner dialogue immediately spiraled: *"I'm a failure," "I'll never be good enough," "Why even try?"*

These thoughts were automatic and relentless. What seemed like a small academic setback triggered deep-seated beliefs rooted in childhood—core beliefs formed when he was constantly praised for achievements but rarely affirmed simply for who he was. According to Beck's (1976) cognitive model, this automatic negative self-talk was a reflection of core beliefs that Alex held about himself: that he was only worthy if he was perfect.

Over time, this pattern of thinking began to erode his self-confidence. He started avoiding new challenges, withdrawing socially, and procrastinating on assignments—not because he was lazy, but because his fear of failure was paralyzing. His perfectionism, as described by Frost et al. (1990), made him set unrealistically high standards and then berate himself when he did not meet them.

Alex's thinking fell into multiple cognitive distortions:

- He **catastrophized** the B grade, telling himself it meant he'd never succeed.
- He **overgeneralized**, believing one poor performance defined his whole academic future.
- He **filtered** out praise and positive feedback from professors, focusing only on what went wrong.

This ongoing pattern contributed to depressive symptoms— low energy, hopelessness, and a sense of helplessness— mirroring what Seligman (1975) described as *learned helplessness*. The more Alex engaged in negative self-talk, the more convinced he became that no effort would change his trajectory.

Eventually, Alex sought support through therapy. He began learning how to identify and challenge his distorted thoughts, gradually replacing self-criticism with more balanced self-talk: *"I'm disappointed in this grade, but it doesn't mean I'm a failure. I can learn from it."* Over time, his emotional resilience strengthened, and his sense of self-worth became less tied to external outcomes.

Key Insight:

Alex's story illustrates how negative self-talk, rooted in early experiences and reinforced by perfectionism, can create barriers to emotional well-being and success. But it also highlights that these thought patterns are not permanent—they can be restructured with awareness, support, and intentional effort.

The Power of Positive Self-Talk

Conversely, positive self-talk involves the conscious choice to reframe negative thoughts and adopt a language that fosters self-compassion and empowerment. According to Seligman (1990), positive self-talk is a cornerstone of resilience and psychological well-being. It allows individuals to maintain a growth mindset, which is the belief that abilities and intelligence can be developed through effort and learning (Dweck, 2006). By speaking kindly to ourselves, we begin to counteract the automatic negativity that often dominates our thinking and pave the way for more hopeful and positive outcomes.

Research has consistently shown that engaging in positive self-talk leads to increased motivation, self-confidence, and overall well-being (Neff, 2011). For example, using affirmations such as *"I am capable of learning"* or *"I can handle challenges"* helps to promote an attitude of optimism and self-efficacy. Positive self-talk is also linked to reduced anxiety levels, as it reduces the impact of stressful events by reframing how we perceive them (Feldman et al., 2006).

Another example, someone preparing for a job interview may say to themselves, "*I am prepared and capable*," rather than focusing on fears or potential mistakes. This shift in language reduces stress and fosters a growth mindset—believing that abilities and intelligence can be developed over time (Dweck, 2006).

Another benefit of positive self-talk is its ability to combat imposter syndrome, which is the persistent feeling that one is undeserving of their achievements. Individuals who engage in positive self-talk can remind themselves of their strengths and past successes, helping to affirm their abilities and reduce feelings of self-doubt.

In the context of goal achievement, positive self-talk enables individuals to remain focused on their goals, reducing distractions caused by fear or self-doubt. By speaking to ourselves in a constructive way, we are better equipped to embrace setbacks as learning opportunities rather than failures. Bandura (1997) suggests that individuals with a strong sense of self-efficacy—often bolstered by positive self-talk—are more likely to engage in behaviors that lead to success, even in the face of adversity.

Techniques for Cultivating Positive Self-Talk

1. **Awareness of Thought Patterns**: As the first step in changing self-talk, it is crucial to become aware of automatic thoughts that arise throughout the day. Cognitive restructuring, helps individuals identify negative thoughts and challenge their validity (Beck, 1976). By journaling or engaging in daily mindfulness practices, people can notice when they fall into negative self-talk and consciously shift the narrative.

2. **Challenging Negative Beliefs**: Negative self-talk often arises from cognitive distortions—ways of thinking that are unbalanced or exaggerated (Burns, 1980). These distortions can be challenged by asking oneself questions like, "Is this thought really true?" or "What evidence do I have to support this belief?" Reframing negative thoughts into more balanced and realistic alternatives is an effective way of countering unhelpful thinking patterns.

3. **Affirmations and Visualization**: Positive affirmations, as proposed by Neff (2011), are an effective tool for shifting from negative to positive self-talk. Repeating affirmations such as "I am enough," "I have the skills to succeed," or "I am worthy of happiness" reprograms the brain to view challenges as manageable. Additionally, visualization—imagining oneself succeeding in future endeavors—can increase confidence and motivation.

4. **Mindfulness and Self-Compassion**: Self-compassion involves treating oneself with the same kindness and understanding that one would offer to a friend in times of difficulty. Kristin Neff (2011) highlights that self-compassion is a powerful antidote to self-criticism, enabling individuals to accept their flaws and mistakes without judgment. Mindfulness practices, which encourage non-judgmental awareness of thoughts, also help individuals detach from negative self-talk and view it from a place of acceptance rather than self-judgment (Kabat-Zinn, 1990).

5. **Reframing Challenges as Opportunities**: The language we use when confronted with challenges is critical. Instead of saying, "This is too hard for me," try reframing it as, "This is difficult, but I can handle it." According to Dweck (2006), adopting a growth mindset allows individuals to approach obstacles with a sense of curiosity and determination, rather than fear and avoidance.

Self-Talk and Mental Health

Self-talk can have a profound impact on mental health by influencing the way individuals perceive and respond to their emotions, thoughts, and external events. Negative self-talk, which often manifests in the form of self-criticism, perfectionism, and rumination, has been linked to psychological distress and the development of mood disorders such as anxiety and depression. According to Beck (1976), individuals with depression often experience distorted thinking patterns, including catastrophic thinking, black-and-white reasoning, and excessive self-blame. These cognitive distortions are reinforced through negative self-talk and lead to a downward spiral in emotional well-being.

For example, individuals with depression might constantly tell themselves, "*I'm a failure,*" or "*Nothing will ever get better,*" which reinforces feelings of hopelessness and helplessness. Over time, these repetitive negative thoughts contribute to learned helplessness (Seligman, 1975), where the individual believes they have no control over their circumstances. This state of mind can prevent them from seeking help, taking action to improve their situation, or engaging in activities that might boost their mood.

One of the most effective strategies for addressing depression and anxiety involves changing negative self-talk. Beck (1976) introduced the concept of cognitive restructuring, which helps individuals challenge and shift unhelpful thought patterns. Through this process, people learn to recognize automatic negative thoughts (ANTs) and replace them with more realistic, balanced perspectives. This shift supports improved emotional regulation and contributes to lasting gains in self-esteem and coping skills.

Personal Reflection

I remember a time when my self-talk was overwhelmingly negative. I constantly told myself, *"You'll never amount to anything,"* and *"You're not smart enough to compete with other people—they have it all together."* Those thoughts replayed so often that, eventually, they became part of how I saw myself. It wasn't until I began my healing journey that I realized just how much that inner voice had wounded me. I can still recall the way it made me feel—small, ashamed, and not enough. Every time I criticized myself, my body would tense, and I wanted nothing more than to disappear from the world.

But things started to shift when I began catching those thoughts and intentionally replacing them with kinder, more positive ones. I told myself things like, *"You've got this,"* and *"You're learning and growing every day."* Slowly, I noticed my self-esteem rising and my mood improving. It didn't happen overnight—it is an ongoing process. But I was determined to stop feeling like I was not good enough. Healing takes time. Just as physical wounds need care and patience, so do the emotional baggage we carry.

Research has demonstrated that individuals who engage in positive self-talk are more likely to experience improved mental health outcomes. According to Seligman (1990), individuals who practice learned optimism—which involves changing negative self-talk to more positive, optimistic language—report greater resilience in the face of adversity and are less likely to experience depressive symptoms. Positive self-talk allows individuals to challenge pessimistic thinking and reframe setbacks as opportunities for growth. It serves as an essential component of resilience, helping individuals manage stress and adversity with greater ease.

Mindfulness-based interventions also emphasize the importance of self-talk in mental health. Kabat-Zinn (1990) explains that mindfulness encourages individuals to observe their thoughts without judgment. This awareness allows them to recognize negative self-talk and step back from it, preventing these thoughts from dominating their emotional state. Research by Hayes et al. (2012) found that individuals who practiced mindfulness were able to reduce the impact of negative thoughts on their mental health by developing a more compassionate and non-judgmental attitude toward themselves.

In the process of rewriting our inner narratives, self-compassion plays a central and transformative role. Rather than meeting moments of failure or emotional difficulty with criticism or judgment, self-compassion invites us to respond with understanding, acceptance, and care. According to Neff (2011), individuals who practice self-compassion are significantly less likely to engage in harsh self-talk. Instead, they offer themselves the same kindness they might extend to a close friend, fostering resilience in the face of setbacks.

This shift from internal criticism to self-kindness has been shown to reduce the psychological impact of negative self-talk, easing symptoms of anxiety and depression while enhancing overall life satisfaction (Neff, 2011). It does not require us to ignore our struggles—it simply changes the tone of the conversation we have with ourselves. Where there was once blame or shame, there can now be empathy and encouragement.

At the same time, cultivating positive self-talk—the practice of intentionally challenging and replacing unhelpful thoughts—can further support mental and emotional health. Individuals struggling with depression or anxiety often engage in cognitive distortions, such as catastrophizing, overgeneralization, or all-or-nothing thinking, which amplify emotional suffering and diminish self-worth (Beck, 1976). When these distorted narratives are left unchecked, they become embedded patterns that shape how we interpret ourselves and the world around us.

For example, people with social anxiety may engage in self-talk that revolves around the fear of being judged or rejected. Replacing these thoughts with affirmations like, "*I am worthy of love and acceptance*" can reduce anxiety and enhance self-acceptance. Similarly, individuals dealing with depression can reframe negative beliefs such as "*I'll never get better*" into thoughts like *"I am working on improving my mental health, and progress is possible."*

Real Life Experience:

Beckie, a 28-year-old graphic designer, struggled with social anxiety, particularly in work settings. During team meetings, she often experienced racing thoughts like, *"Everyone's going to think I'm stupid if I say the wrong thing,"* or *"I shouldn't speak up because I might embarrass myself."* These thoughts led her to avoid speaking altogether, reinforcing her belief that she was not capable or confident.

Over time, this pattern not only limited her career growth but also impacted her self-worth. She began to internalize the idea that she did not belong or was not as competent as her peers.

Beckie learned to recognize these unhelpful thoughts and gradually replaced them with more balanced and affirming ones, allowing her to reshape the way she viewed herself and her potential. She practiced reframing her self-talk with phrases like:

- *"It's okay to be nervous—everyone feels this way sometimes."*
- *"I have good ideas, and my voice deserves to be heard."*
- *"Even if I make a mistake, it doesn't mean I don't belong."*

After several weeks of consistent practice, Beckie noticed a gradual shift. She still felt nervous in meetings, but her anxiety decreased, and she began participating more. That small shift in language changed the story she told herself—from one of inadequacy to one of self-compassion and resilience.

Similarly, during a period of mild depression following a breakup, Beckie's internal script turned harsh and absolute: *"I'm unlovable"* or *"I'll never feel happy again."* Using the same tools, she started gently challenging those thoughts:

- *"This pain is temporary."*
- *"I am learning and healing every day."*
- *"I am not defined by one relationship."*

Rewriting her internal narrative did not make the pain disappear overnight, but it empowered Beckie to move forward with more hope, emotional strength, and clarity about her self-worth.

Engaging in self-compassionate self-talk has also been shown to improve resilience following traumatic experiences. According to Tugade and Fredrickson (2004), individuals who practice self-compassion and use positive self-talk during times of stress exhibit better emotional regulation and quicker recovery from setbacks.

By learning to recognize and reframe these thoughts, individuals can disrupt the cycle of negativity. For example, replacing a thought like *"I always mess everything up"* with *"I made a mistake, but I'm learning and growing"* not only changes the emotional experience in the moment but also gradually reshapes one's self-concept. As the internal script becomes more supportive and balanced, the grip of anxiety and depression can begin to loosen.

Together, self-compassion and positive self-talk serve as powerful tools for healing. They allow us to take back control of our internal dialogue—not through denial or forced positivity, but through conscious, compassionate redirection. In doing so, we begin to live not from a place of fear or shame, but from a foundation of self-acceptance and hope.

The Role of Self-Talk in Overcoming Obstacles

Self-talk plays a pivotal role in how we approach challenges and obstacles in life. It can either serve as a barrier or an empowering force, depending on the nature of the language we use. When faced with a difficult situation, people with negative self-talk may immediately focus on failure and defeat, leading to feelings of helplessness and avoidance. On the other hand, individuals who engage in positive self-talk are more likely to view obstacles as challenges to be overcome, rather than insurmountable roadblocks.

The concept of self-efficacy, as proposed by Bandura (1997), is central to understanding how self-talk influences our ability to overcome challenges. Self-efficacy refers to an individual's belief in their ability to achieve a desired outcome through their actions. Those with high self-efficacy are more likely to approach challenges with confidence and perseverance, even in the face of setbacks. Positive self-talk reinforces this belief by encouraging individuals to maintain focus on their goals, rather than dwelling on doubts or perceived limitations.

For example, consider someone preparing for a public speaking engagement. If they engage in negative self-talk such as, "*I'll probably mess up,*" or "*I'm not good at speaking in front of people,*" they are likely to experience heightened anxiety, which may impact their performance. However, by practicing positive self-talk, such as "*I have the skills to succeed*" or "*I've prepared well for this, and I can handle it,*" the individual may reduce their anxiety and perform with greater confidence (Feldman et al., 2006).

Resilience is a key factor in overcoming obstacles, and research shows that self-talk has a direct impact on an individual's resilience. Tugade and Fredrickson (2004) found that people who engage in positive self-talk during times of stress demonstrate greater emotional regulation, optimism, and a greater capacity to bounce back from adversity. This is because positive self-talk helps individuals reframe challenges as learning opportunities, rather than threatening situations.

The power of reframing lies in the ability to transform obstacles into manageable problems. For instance, someone experiencing job loss might initially think, *"This is the end of my career,"* but with positive self-talk, they might reframe it as, *"This is an opportunity to explore new possibilities and grow."* This shift in perspective not only reduces feelings of helplessness but also opens up new avenues for problem-solving and growth.

Studies show that self-talk can help individuals engage in goal-setting and problem-solving behaviors. For instance, when individuals use empowering language like *"I can solve this"* or *"I will learn from this setback,"* they are more likely to take constructive steps toward resolution rather than giving up or becoming overwhelmed (Bandura, 1997). In fact, self-talk has been linked to enhanced goal achievement because it bolsters the mindset of persistence and determination. Those who use positive self-talk are more likely to approach challenges with a mindset that failure is not final but part of the learning process.

One of the most critical ways self-talk helps overcome obstacles is by influencing self-regulation. When we engage in positive self-talk, we become more likely to persist in the face of adversity and remain focused on long-term goals. For example, students preparing for exams may use positive self-talk such as *"I can handle this,"* or *"I've done the work, and I'm prepared."* This language promotes self-control and discipline, which are essential for achieving success.

Additionally, social support and the language of encouragement from others can amplify the effects of positive self-talk. For instance, when people hear affirming statements such as *"You're doing great"* or *"I believe in you,"* it can help them internalize these supportive messages and use them in their self-talk. Positive language from others serves as a reinforcement of the empowering messages we tell ourselves, helping to foster a cycle of confidence and perseverance (Feldman et al., 2006).

The Transformative Power of Self-Talk

Self-talk plays a profound and transformative role in shaping not only our mental health but also our capacity to overcome life's challenges. The language we use internally serves as the backdrop for our emotional and cognitive experiences—it can either reinforce cycles of anxiety, depression, and self-doubt, or it can empower us to approach life with confidence, clarity, and resilience.

When left unchecked, negative self-talk often becomes habitual, feeding limiting beliefs and distorting how we perceive ourselves and our abilities. Phrases like *"I'm not good enough"* or *"I always fail"* create mental roadblocks that erode motivation and self-worth. However, when we consciously shift our inner dialogue toward more supportive and constructive messages, we begin to dismantle these barriers. Reframing our internal narrative—choosing to say *"I am learning"* instead of *"I'll never get it right"*—opens up space for growth, curiosity, and hope.

The transformative power of self-talk lies in its ability to reshape our perceptions, influence our emotional states, and guide our behaviors. Positive self-talk does not mean denying reality or engaging in toxic positivity—for example, saying *"Just be happy, it could be worse"* to ourselves when we're struggling only suppresses real emotions. Instead, it means acknowledging challenges while affirming our capacity to grow through them. This internal shift enhances self-compassion, builds resilience, and fosters a deeper sense of mental and emotional well-being.

Whether we are striving to achieve goals, working through emotional pain, or simply trying to navigate the complexities of daily life, the words we choose to speak to ourselves matter deeply. They form the foundation of our mindset, influencing how we interpret setbacks and how we move forward. By choosing empowering language, we reinforce a cycle of self-belief, healing, and personal transformation.

Embracing positive self-talk as a tool for mental health and resilience is not just a therapeutic strategy—it is a lifelong practice that can lead to greater fulfillment, success, and personal growth.

Key Takeaways

1. **Self-Talk Shapes Our Reality**

   Self-talk is the inner dialogue we have with ourselves, and it profoundly influences our emotions, thoughts, and behavior. The way we talk to ourselves can either empower us or reinforce negative beliefs, affecting our mental health and overall well-being.

2. **Positive vs. Negative Self-Talk**

   Positive self-talk helps foster confidence, resilience, and growth, while negative self-talk can lead to feelings of inadequacy, fear, and anxiety. Recognizing the difference between these two types of self-talk is crucial to shifting our internal narrative.

3. **The Impact of Self-Talk on Mental Health**

   Negative self-talk is often linked to mental health challenges like depression, anxiety, and stress. By shifting to more positive and supportive self-talk, we can improve our emotional regulation, reduce self-criticism, and increase overall well-being.

4. **Awareness is Key**

   Becoming aware of your self-talk is the first step in transforming it. Many of us engage in automatic, negative self-talk without realizing how it impacts our lives. Mindfulness and self-reflection can help us catch these thoughts and interrupt harmful patterns.

5. **The Role of Self-Talk in Growth and Resilience**

   Self-talk influences how we respond to challenges. Encouraging, motivating self-talk can help us overcome obstacles and view setbacks as opportunities for growth, while negative self-talk may prevent us from trying new things or persevering in difficult situations.

6. **Rewriting Self-Talk with Compassion**

   Transforming self-talk involves practicing self-compassion. Rather than criticizing or punishing ourselves for mistakes, we can learn to speak to ourselves with love, kindness, respect, understanding, and patience, just as we would to a friend.

7. **Self-Talk and Beliefs**

   Our self-talk is often rooted in deeply held beliefs about ourselves, shaped by our past experiences, culture, and environment. To create lasting change, we need to identify and challenge these beliefs, replacing them with healthier, more empowering narratives.

8. **Intentionality in Self-Talk**

   By consciously choosing the language we use in our self-talk, we can rewire our thought patterns and reinforce positive, growth-oriented beliefs. Self-talk should align with our values and goals, serving as a tool for personal transformation.

9. **Self-Talk as a Reflection of Self-Worth**

   The way we talk to ourselves often reflects how we value ourselves. Positive self-talk supports a healthy sense of self-worth, while negative self-talk erodes it. Cultivating self-respect through affirmations and compassionate dialogue with ourselves enhances our overall self-esteem.

10. **Empowering Self-Talk for Success**

    Self-talk is a powerful tool in achieving personal success. By replacing limiting thoughts with affirmations and goal-oriented language, we can cultivate the mindset needed to overcome obstacles and achieve our desired outcomes.

When we recognize the influence of self-talk on our thoughts, emotions, and behaviors, we unlock the ability to reshape our internal dialogue and create a more positive, resilient, and empowering narrative. Through consistent practice of these exercises, you can transform your self-talk into a powerful tool for personal growth, emotional strength, and lasting change.

Reflection Questions

1. What does your inner voice sound like most of the time—kind or critical?

   Where do you think these messages come from?

2. How does your self-talk help or hinder you during moments of stress, disappointment, or fear?

   Can you recall a time when it helped you overcome a challenge?

3. How does your self-talk differ when talking about yourself vs. someone you care about?

   What would change if you showed yourself the same compassion?

4. What beliefs about yourself have been shaped by your internal dialogue?

   Are they empowering or limiting?

5. How could your life change if your self-talk became consistently affirming and hopeful?

   How would it impact your confidence, decisions, and relationships?

✦Chapter Summary

Chapter 11 explores the critical role of self-talk in shaping our mental health, resilience, and capacity for personal growth. Our internal dialogue is a constant companion, influencing how we perceive ourselves, interpret events, and respond to challenges. The voice within can either uplift us, fostering self-compassion, confidence, and resilience, or it can tear us down, reinforcing negative beliefs, fear, and self-doubt. This chapter emphasizes the power of consciously shifting our self-talk to promote positive transformation. By identifying harmful thought patterns and replacing them with affirming, constructive language, we can cultivate a mindset that supports healing, emotional regulation, and progress. The chapter highlights the connection between self-talk and mental health, showing how negative self-talk can contribute to anxiety, depression, and stress, while positive self-talk can enhance emotional well-being and coping skills. Practical tools and strategies are offered to help readers recognize their inner dialogue, challenge unhelpful thoughts, and foster a supportive internal voice. This chapter ultimately invites readers to embrace their inner dialogue as a powerful force for good, with the potential to shape their resilience, mental health, and overall life trajectory.

Chapter 12

Rewriting Your Story: *A Path to Empowerment*

"It's never too late to be what you might have been." – George Eliot

Our lives are shaped by the stories we tell ourselves—narratives constructed through a continuous interplay between our internal self-talk and the external voices that surround us. These stories influence not only how we perceive our identity but also the behaviors we adopt and the opportunities we recognize. Often, these narratives become deeply ingrained scripts that guide our actions unconsciously.

In this chapter, we will examine the powerful process of rewriting these internal and external narratives. By cultivating awareness of limiting beliefs and challenging outdated scripts, you can embark on a transformative journey toward greater empowerment, self-acceptance, and resilience. This process enables you to reclaim ownership of your personal story and intentionally shape a future defined by your own values and aspirations.

The Power of Narrative in Shaping Identity

The stories we tell ourselves about who we are profoundly influence how we perceive the world around us. Our self-identity is largely shaped by the narratives we internalize about our abilities, worth, and past experiences. According to McAdams (2001), personal narratives are the stories we construct about our lives to make sense of our experiences and provide a sense of coherence and purpose. These narratives often reflect the way we interpret events, challenges, and interactions.

For example, individuals who view themselves through the lens of failure may construct a narrative that reinforces a fixed mindset—believing they are incapable of change or success. Conversely, those who adopt a growth mindset—one that emphasizes learning, development, and resilience—tend to rewrite their stories to emphasize adaptability and progress. The ability to alter the way we interpret our experiences is essential in empowering ourselves to rewrite our personal narratives in a way that aligns with our values and aspirations.

Psychologist Carol Dweck (2006) argues that adopting a growth mindset allows individuals to view challenges as opportunities for development, which leads to more adaptive coping strategies and greater perseverance. Instead of seeing setbacks as a reflection of one's inherent limitations, they are viewed as stepping stones to future growth. This shift in perspective enables individuals to break free from the limitations of their previous self-concept, paving the way for greater empowerment.

Challenging the Past: Releasing Limiting Beliefs

Limiting beliefs are ingrained ideas that we hold about ourselves, others, and the world that restrict our growth and potential. These beliefs are typically developed in our early experiences—whether through familial messages, cultural norms, or personal struggles—and they tend to persist throughout our lives, shaping how we view the world and interact with it. These beliefs are often subconscious, meaning that we may not even be aware of their existence, but they subtly affect our thoughts, actions, and decision-making. Limiting beliefs can manifest as thoughts like, *"I'm not smart enough," "I don't deserve happiness,"* or *"I'll never succeed."*

The challenge is that we often see these limiting beliefs as truths, not recognizing that they are not inherent facts but interpretations of our experiences. The first step in rewriting our story is to identify and challenge these limiting beliefs. According to Beck (1976), individuals struggling with depression or anxiety often hold distorted beliefs about themselves and the world that exacerbate their mental health challenges. For example, someone might believe, "*I'm a failure,* or "*I can't do anything right*" even after experiencing a setback that is not truly indicative of their abilities or worth. This type of cognitive distortion reinforces negative self-concepts and hinders personal growth.

To begin the process of releasing limiting beliefs, it is essential to acknowledge their presence. Mindfulness practices can be particularly helpful in bringing awareness to these automatic thoughts that often operate beneath the surface. Journaling, another effective tool, allows individuals to externalize these internalized beliefs and examine them with more objectivity. For example, writing down thoughts like, "*I'll never be successful*" gives the individual an opportunity to challenge this belief: What evidence supports it? What past successes contradict it?

One of the most effective ways to challenge limiting beliefs is through cognitive reframing—the practice of shifting how we perceive and interpret situations, experiences, and events in order to see them from a more empowering perspective. For instance, if someone believes, "*I'm not good enough to get that promotion,*" cognitive reframing could involve asking themselves: "*What strengths do I possess that make me a strong candidate for this role?*" By identifying evidence-based truths (such as specific skills or achievements), they can start to rewrite their internal narrative, gradually replacing the limiting belief with a more empowering perspective.

Moreover, releasing limiting beliefs requires an active shift in mindset from victimhood to empowerment. This is the essence of growth mindset theory introduced by Carol Dweck (2006), which posits that individuals who believe their abilities and intelligence can grow through effort, learning, and persistence are more likely to overcome obstacles and achieve their goals. Embracing a growth mindset involves seeing challenges as opportunities for development, rather than insurmountable barriers. This shift in perspective helps individuals to confront their limiting beliefs head-on and to see failures not as personal shortcomings but as steppingstones toward greater achievement.

To fully release limiting beliefs, it is also important to practice self-compassion. According to Neff (2011), self-compassion involves treating yourself with the same kindness and understanding as you would offer a friend during times of struggle. When we are kind to ourselves during moments of doubt or failure, we can avoid internalizing shame or guilt and instead focus on learning and growth. This compassionate self-awareness can help us dismantle the negative inner dialogue that often reinforces limiting beliefs.

Example: Sarah's Belief About Success and Career Advancement

Sarah has always struggled with self-doubt and the belief that she is not smart enough to achieve her career goals. This belief has been deeply ingrained in her since childhood, when her parents often emphasized the importance of academic success. Growing up, Sarah faced challenges in school and was frequently compared to her more academically successful peers. As a result, she internalized the message that her intelligence was limited, which led her to believe that she would never be successful in her career.

This limiting belief—"*I'm not smart enough*"—has shaped Sarah's decisions throughout her adult life. When she was offered the chance to apply for a leadership position at work, her immediate reaction was to dismiss the opportunity. She thought to herself, "*I'm not qualified for this role. I'll never get the promotion. They'll probably hire someone more competent.*"

Step 1: Acknowledging the Limiting Belief

The first step for Sarah is to acknowledge and bring awareness to the limiting belief. She decides to take some time each morning for mindfulness practice and journaling to reflect on her thoughts. During these sessions, she identifies that she regularly tells herself, "I'm not smart enough" whenever she faces a new challenge or considers new opportunities.

Sarah realizes that this belief is not based on any recent evidence, but rather on her past experiences. As she writes down her thoughts in her journal, she begins to see the narrative more objectively: "What evidence do I have to support the idea that I'm not smart enough?" This awareness gives her the first step toward rewriting her story.

Step 2: Challenging the Belief

Next, Sarah engages in cognitive reframing to challenge her belief. She asks herself, "What strengths do I possess that make me qualified for this leadership role?" She writes down specific accomplishments:

- She successfully managed a team project last year, delivering results ahead of schedule.
- She regularly receives positive feedback from colleagues about her problem-solving abilities.

- She completed additional training in management and leadership skills to advance her career.

By listing these facts, Sarah can see that her belief about not being smart enough does not align with the reality of her capabilities. She reframes her thinking: "I am capable and skilled, and I have the potential to succeed in this role."

Step 3: Adopting a Growth Mindset

Sarah recognizes that her belief about being "not smart enough" is limiting her potential. She embraces Carol Dweck's growth mindset theory, which suggests that abilities and intelligence can develop over time through effort and perseverance (Dweck, 2006). Sarah begins to see challenges as opportunities for growth rather than barriers to her success.

She shifts her thinking about the promotion: "This is an opportunity for me to learn, grow, and develop my leadership skills. Even if I face difficulties, I can adapt and improve."

Step 4: Practicing Self-Compassion

During this process, Sarah practices self-compassion to ensure she is kind to herself when doubts arise. Instead of criticizing herself for not being perfect, she reminds herself that everyone faces challenges, and setbacks are part of the learning process. She tells herself, "It's okay to make mistakes and learn from them. I'm doing my best, and that's enough."

Whenever she faces moments of self-doubt, Sarah consciously replaces negative self-talk with self-affirming statements, such as, "I am capable, and I am deserving of this opportunity."

Step 5: Rewriting Her Story

Sarah begins to rewrite her internal narrative. Rather than seeing herself as someone who is "not smart enough" to succeed, she reframes her story to reflect her strengths, growth, and resilience. She now views herself as someone who is continuously learning and developing, capable of facing challenges with determination.

As Sarah approaches the leadership position once again, she feels empowered. She believes that her intelligence is not fixed, and that through effort and learning, she can excel in this new role. The limiting belief of "I'm not smart enough" no longer defines her. Instead, she embodies the narrative: "I am capable of growth, and I have the power to succeed in whatever I set my mind to."

This example illustrates how Sarah challenges her limiting belief about intelligence by applying mindfulness, cognitive reframing, embracing a growth mindset, and practicing self-compassion. Through these steps, she begins to rewrite her narrative, empowering herself to pursue new opportunities and embrace challenges with confidence.

Rewriting Your Story with Empowerment Language

The language we use in our self-talk plays a critical role in how we perceive ourselves and our future. Empowering language—which highlights possibilities, growth, and resilience—helps to strengthen a narrative of personal empowerment. Instead of saying, "*I can't,*" we might say, "*I can learn how,*" or "*I will figure this out.*" Language empowerment can be especially impactful when confronting obstacles. When faced with challenges, instead of adopting a victim mentality—for example, saying "*Nothing ever goes right for me, no matter what I do*"—individuals who rewrite their stories adopt a more active voice in their self-talk. They take ownership of their circumstances and use language that reflects their capacity for action and change.

The concept of empowerment in language is not just about positive affirmations; it is about making intentional choices about how we frame our experiences. According to Langer (1997), mindfulness in the present moment allows us to notice our language and the assumptions we make. When we become aware of limiting language, we can consciously replace it with more empowering language that reflects our sense of control and self-determination.

For instance, instead of saying, *"I'll never be able to change,"* one might say, *"Change takes time, and I am capable of learning and evolving."* This subtle shift in language can significantly alter the course of our lives by helping us cultivate the belief that we are empowered to make meaningful changes.

The Role of Forgiveness in Rewriting Your Story

Forgiveness is a powerful and transformative tool in rewriting our personal story. It serves as a means of liberation—freeing us from the emotional and psychological burdens that hold us hostage to the past. The act of forgiving—whether it involves forgiving others or ourselves—allows us to move forward in life without carrying the weight of unresolved resentment, anger, or guilt. Without forgiveness, we remain emotionally anchored to past events, and our ability to create a new and empowering narrative for our lives is severely hindered.

Forgiveness involves a shift in perspective—moving from a mindset of blame and victimhood to one of understanding and acceptance. This shift allows us to release the grip that past experiences have over us, enabling us to break free from the cycles of negativity that perpetuate limiting beliefs and self-sabotage. In the case of forgiving others, the focus is on letting go of the anger and resentment we hold toward those who have wronged us, recognizing that holding onto these emotions only serves to damage our mental and physical health. Research has consistently shown that forgiveness leads to better mental health, including reduced anxiety, depression, and stress (Toussaint & Cheadle, 2009). Forgiveness means choosing to love instead of holding on to resentment toward the person who has hurt you, while also discovering a deeper sense of love and compassion for yourself in the process. It is about freeing yourself from the emotional burden and reclaiming your peace.

However, forgiving others is often much easier than forgiving ourselves. Many people carry deep feelings of guilt, shame, and regret for past mistakes or failures. The emotional weight of self-blame can become a self-fulfilling prophecy, with individuals continuously punishing themselves for past actions or decisions, believing they are unworthy of change or redemption. This is where self-forgiveness comes into play.

Self-forgiveness is not about excusing harmful behaviors or denying responsibility for mistakes. Rather, it involves acknowledging our imperfections and accepting that being human means making mistakes. According to Enright (2001), self-forgiveness requires self-compassion and the recognition that our actions do not define our inherent worth. It involves releasing the self-judgment that keeps us stuck in cycles of guilt and shame, allowing us to see ourselves as worthy of growth, learning, and healing.

Self-forgiveness also requires emotional courage—the courage to face painful truths about ourselves and to accept that we can change. Often, individuals resist forgiving themselves because they feel they must remain accountable for their mistakes by continually punishing themselves. However, in order to truly heal and rewrite our personal story, we must release the emotional burdens of self-punishment and instead adopt an attitude of learning and growth. Forgiveness frees us from the past and allows us to step into a future where we can pursue our aspirations without being held back by the weight of past failures or regrets.

Forgiving ourselves also involves shifting our identity from one of a person defined by mistakes to someone who is capable of change and transformation. For example, someone who has struggled with addiction may have internalized a narrative of "*I will always be an addict*" or "*I am a failure.*" By practicing self-forgiveness, they can rewrite this story as one of resilience and empowerment, recognizing that they are not defined by their past behaviors but by their capacity to change, grow, and heal.

Importantly, forgiveness is not a one-time event; it is a continual practice that requires conscious effort. Just as we may have spent years cultivating limiting beliefs, we must spend time actively practicing forgiveness to dismantle these beliefs and rewrite our narratives. Every time we forgive ourselves or others, we take another step toward rewriting our story and reclaiming our personal power.

Reclaiming Your Narrative for a Bright Future

Rewriting your personal story is a dynamic process that requires courage, self-reflection, and intentionality. By challenging limiting beliefs, adopting empowering language, and practicing forgiveness, individuals can reclaim their narrative and transform their lives. The stories we tell ourselves shape our experiences and determine our future potential. By consciously choosing to rewrite our story, we create a life that reflects our highest aspirations, values, and dreams.

Through the process of narrative reconstruction, individuals gain the power to move beyond past limitations and construct a new, empowered version of themselves—one that is resilient, self-compassionate, and fully capable of embracing life's challenges with confidence and hope.

Rewriting your story involves the courageous act of challenging limiting beliefs and embracing the transformative power of forgiveness. These two elements—challenging the past and forgiving ourselves and others—are the foundation for creating an empowered, resilient, and hopeful future. Through this process, we release the psychological and emotional burdens that have held us back and embrace the possibility of growth, change, and self-empowerment. Ultimately, rewriting our story is about taking control of our narrative, stepping out of victimhood, and writing a new chapter that reflects our true potential and aspirations.

Key Takeaways

1. **The Power of Personal Narratives**:
   Our personal stories shape how we see ourselves, our past, and our future. Rewriting these stories gives us the power to redefine our identity and take control of our lives.

2. **Understanding the Past**:
   The stories we tell about our past can either limit or empower us. By examining these stories, we can identify patterns, beliefs, and experiences that no longer serve us.

3. **Recognizing the Impact of Language**:
   The language we use in our stories influences our thoughts, emotions, and actions. Shifting from negative, limiting language to positive, empowering language helps transform our mindset and approach to life.

4. **Challenging Negative Beliefs**:
   Many of the beliefs we hold about ourselves come from past experiences or external influences. Rewriting our story involves challenging these beliefs and replacing them with more positive, affirming ones.

5. **Empowerment Through Choice:**

   Rewriting our story is about taking ownership of our life's narrative. It is about recognizing that, while we cannot change the past, we can choose how we interpret it and how we move forward.

6. **The Role of Self-Compassion:**

   Self-compassion is essential in the process of rewriting our story. It allows us to let go of guilt, shame, and regret, and to approach our growth with understanding and kindness.

7. **Creating a Vision for the Future:**

   Rewriting your story is not just about the past. It is about shaping the future you want to create. By crafting a new narrative for the future, we can align our actions with our goals and values.

8. **Rewriting as a Continuous Process:**

   Rewriting our story is not a one-time event, but an ongoing practice. Each new chapter of our life presents an opportunity to update our narrative in ways that empower and align with our evolving self.

9. **The Impact on Relationships:**

   By changing the way we view ourselves, we can transform how we interact with others. A positive self-narrative leads to healthier relationships and better communication with those around us.

10. The Freedom of Choice:

Ultimately, rewriting your story means freeing yourself from the limitations imposed by old narratives. It is about stepping into a new version of yourself—one where you have the power to create and live out your own story.

These exercises are designed to help you actively engage in the process of rewriting your life story and empower yourself to create a new, more positive narrative moving forward.

Reflection Questions

1. What are the most prominent stories you tell yourself about your past?
   How have these stories shaped your identity and the way you approach challenges today?

2. How do the beliefs you've formed about yourself influence your decisions and actions?
   Are there any beliefs that you feel no longer serve your growth or well-being?

3. In what areas of your life do you feel empowered, and how can you build upon these stories to create more success and fulfillment in other areas?
   Reflect on your strengths and consider how to apply those narratives to other life domains.

4. How do you currently talk to yourself when faced with setbacks or obstacles?

   What can you do to shift from a critical or limiting voice to a more compassionate and empowering one?

5. What is one part of your life story that you are ready to rewrite?

   What new beliefs or narratives will you incorporate to support a healthier, more empowering future?

✦ Chapter Summary

Chapter 12 focuses on the transformative journey of rewriting your personal narrative by challenging limiting beliefs and embracing empowerment through language, forgiveness, and self-discovery. Our internal stories often trap us in a cycle of self-doubt, insecurity, and feelings of powerlessness. However, this chapter reveals that we have the ability to change those stories, freeing ourselves from the constraints of past experiences and societal expectations. By examining the language, we use to describe ourselves and our lives, we can identify the limiting beliefs that hold us back. Through the power of forgiveness, both for ourselves and others, we can release emotional baggage and unlock the path to personal liberation. The chapter digs into the concept of self-discovery, encouraging readers to reconnect with their authentic selves, rediscover their strengths, and rewrite their personal scripts in a way that aligns with their true potential. Practical exercises and guided reflections encourage readers to examine their current narrative, recognize opportunities for growth, and inspire them to create a new story grounded in resilience and strength. This chapter ultimately offers a blueprint for overcoming past obstacles and taking control of your future, one empowering word at a time.

Chapter 13

The Power of Rewriting Your Story: *Transforming Limiting Beliefs into Empowering Narratives*

"Your past does not define your future. The stories you tell yourself today shape the person you will become tomorrow." – Unknown

At the core of personal transformation is the realization that our narratives are not fixed. They are flexible, ever-evolving stories that we tell ourselves about who we are, where we have been, and where we are going. These narratives shape how we view the world, how we interact with others, and most importantly, how we view ourselves.

In this chapter, we will explore how the stories we tell can either empower and motivate us or limit our potential if they are shaped by negative experiences or limiting beliefs.

Limiting beliefs are mental patterns that we develop over time, often rooted in our upbringing, past failures, or societal conditioning. They are often framed in absolutes like, *"I'm not good enough,"* *"I don't deserve to be happy,"* or *"I'll never change."* These beliefs can form the lens through which we view ourselves and our abilities. And as we reinforce them with negative self-talk and language, they become ingrained in our identity, leading us to make choices that align with those beliefs.

However, the good news is that these beliefs are not fixed truths. We have the power to challenge and rewrite them. By identifying the stories that no longer serve us and reframing them, we can create empowering narratives that open the door to greater self-belief, growth, and transformation.

Understanding Limiting Beliefs: Where They Come From

Limiting beliefs are often formed during early childhood, when we are more susceptible to external influences like parents, teachers, peers, and societal expectations. For example, a child who is frequently told, *"You'll never be good at math,"* may internalize the belief that they are incapable of succeeding in mathematical subjects. Over time, this belief becomes part of their self-narrative, influencing their academic choices and their self-esteem.

Similarly, cultural narratives around success, beauty, and worth can deeply influence our sense of identity. In many cultures, external achievements like wealth, status, or appearance are heavily emphasized. Those who do not conform to these standards may feel as though they are lacking, unworthy, or "less than" others. The language we hear and internalize in society—whether it's through the media, family, or cultural expectations—shapes how we see ourselves and our potential for growth.

Research in social psychology shows that early experiences and societal messages significantly shape how we view our self-worth and capabilities (Bandura, 1997). These beliefs, though often unconscious, affect our choices, relationships, and overall happiness.

Common Limiting Beliefs That Inhibit Personal Growth

Although often unconscious, limiting beliefs can quietly shape our identity, decisions, and potential. The following categorized examples illustrate how these internal narratives commonly manifest in areas such as self-worth, achievement, change, relationships, purpose, and cultural identity.

Beliefs About Self-Worth

- *I am not good enough.*
- *I do not deserve happiness, love, or success.*
- *There is something inherently wrong with me.*
- *I must earn my value through performance or perfection.*
- *If others truly knew me, they would reject me.*

Beliefs About Success and Ability

- *I am not smart, talented, or capable enough.*
- *Success is reserved for others, not people like me.*
- *I'm too old, too young, or too inexperienced to begin.*
- *If I try, I will probably fail.*
- *I am not meant for greatness.*

Beliefs About Change and Growth

- *I can't change who I am.*
- *Personal growth is difficult, uncomfortable, and not worth the effort.*
- *Healing is for others—not for someone like me.*
- *I've already tried and failed; it's pointless to try again.*
- *If I change, I will lose people or become isolated.*

Beliefs About Relationships

- *Love always leads to pain or betrayal.*
- *I must meet others' expectations to be accepted or loved.*
- *I need to be perfect to be worthy of connection.*
- *Vulnerability leads to rejection or hurt.*
- *I am either too much or not enough for someone to truly love me.*

Beliefs About Work, Purpose, and Worth

- *I am not qualified enough to succeed.*
- *If I pursue my passion, I will struggle financially.*
- *I have to work harder than everyone else to prove myself.*
- *I must choose between purpose and security.*
- *Financial and personal peace cannot coexist.*

Beliefs Shaped by Culture and Society

- *My background limits what I can achieve.*
- *People like me don't get ahead.*
- *To be accepted, I must conform or stay silent.*
- *Expressing emotions is a weakness.*
- *I must meet cultural or family expectations, even if they contradict my truth.*

These beliefs are not fixed—they are learned, often early in life, and they can be unlearned. Awareness is the first step in dismantling these inner constraints. Once identified, these limiting narratives can be intentionally replaced with empowering beliefs that reflect self-compassion, potential, and authentic identity.

The Role of Language in Reinforcing Limiting Beliefs

One of the most subtle but powerful ways that limiting beliefs persist is through language. The words we use internally and externally reinforce the narratives we hold about ourselves. When we say things like, *"I'm not good enough,"* *"I can't do it,"* or *"I'll never succeed,"* we are reinforcing negative scripts that keep us trapped in a cycle of self-doubt.

This is where the practice of mindful language becomes important. Mindful language refers to being aware of the words we choose to describe ourselves, our experiences, and our capabilities. It is about becoming conscious of how we speak to ourselves and others, ensuring that our words support our growth rather than hinder it. For example, replacing *"I can't"* with *"I haven't yet"* creates room for growth, possibility, and action. By changing the way we speak to ourselves, we begin to shift our internal narrative from one of limitation to one of potential.

Another critical aspect of language is how we speak about our past. The language we use to describe past challenges can either trap us in a victim mentality or empower us to learn and grow. For instance, someone who has gone through a difficult breakup may view their past relationship as a "failure," reinforcing a belief of inadequacy or unworthiness. But reframing the language to say, "This relationship taught me valuable lessons about myself and what I want in the future" can shift the narrative toward personal growth and resilience.

Reframing: A Tool for Empowerment

Reframing is one of the most effective strategies for rewriting limiting beliefs and transforming the way we view ourselves. In essence, reframing involves looking at a situation, belief, or experience from a different perspective, allowing us to find new meaning and opportunities for growth.

For example, a person who has faced failure in their career might initially view it as a personal inadequacy, saying, "*I failed because I'm not good enough.*" However, through reframing, they can view the situation as a learning opportunity, saying, "This failure helped me gain valuable insights and skills that will make me more prepared for future opportunities."

Cognitive reframing (Beck, 2011) involves changing the way we interpret events, beliefs, and experiences. It requires us to challenge automatic negative thoughts and beliefs, replacing them with more balanced and constructive ones. Studies show that reframing not only helps us shift our mindset but can also improve emotional well-being, reduce anxiety, and enhance problem-solving skills (Kross & Ayduk, 2011).

To reframe effectively, ask yourself questions like:

- "What is the lesson I can learn from this experience?"
- "How might I view this situation as an opportunity for growth?"
- "How could this challenge contribute to my personal development?"
- "What would I tell a friend who is facing this same situation?"

These questions encourage a shift in perspective, helping you see challenges as steppingstones to greater resilience and success.

The Importance of Empowering Language in Rewriting Your Story

Empowering language is central to rewriting your story. When we replace limiting beliefs with empowering statements, we open ourselves up to new possibilities. Empowering language reflects self-acceptance, self-compassion, and self-efficacy—the belief in our ability to take action and influence our outcomes. Empowering language helps us step into a mindset of growth, where we see challenges as opportunities to learn and evolve rather than as obstacles to our success.

For example, instead of saying, *"I'm not good enough to succeed,"* an empowering reframe would be, *"I have the ability to learn and grow, and every setback is an opportunity for improvement."* This language is affirming, motivating, and action-oriented. It aligns with the belief that we have the power to influence our future, regardless of past experiences.

Empowering language also involves giving ourselves permission to be imperfect. Perfectionism often accompanies limiting beliefs, causing us to fear failure and avoid taking risks. By using language that emphasizes growth rather than perfection—such as, *"I am learning,"* or *"I am doing my best"*—we free ourselves from the paralyzing fear of not being enough and allow ourselves to progress without judgment.

Creating a New Narrative: Steps for Rewriting Your Story

1. **Identify Your Limiting Beliefs**: The first step in rewriting your story is to identify the beliefs and narratives that are holding you back. Reflect on areas of your life where you feel stuck or unfulfilled and notice the recurring thoughts or patterns that reinforce your limitations.

2. **Challenge and Reframe**: Once you have identified your limiting beliefs, challenge them. Ask yourself whether these beliefs are based on facts or assumptions. Reframe your beliefs to focus on what is possible, rather than what is impossible. Replace negative, self-defeating language with positive, empowering statements.

3. **Practice Affirmations and Visualization**: Use positive affirmations to reinforce your new narrative. Affirmations are short, positive statements that help shift your mindset. For example, "I am worthy of success," or "I am capable of overcoming obstacles." Additionally, visualize yourself living out your new narrative—imagine yourself succeeding and thriving in the areas where you once felt limited.

4. **Take Action**: Empowerment comes through action. Once you have shifted your internal narrative, take concrete steps toward your goals. Break down larger tasks into smaller, manageable actions, and celebrate each small victory along the way.

5. **Be Patient and Persistent**: Rewriting your story is a process that takes time. Be patient with yourself and acknowledge that it is normal to experience setbacks. The key is to stay consistent with your new narrative and language, even in moments of difficulty.

Key Takeaways

1. **The Impact of Beliefs on Our Story**:

   Our beliefs shape the narratives we tell ourselves, often guiding how we see ourselves and the world. Limiting beliefs can trap us in negative cycles, but rewriting these stories can help unlock new possibilities and self-empowerment.

2. **Identifying Limiting Beliefs**:

   To rewrite our stories, we must first identify the limiting beliefs that hold us back. These beliefs often stem from past experiences, societal influences, or inherited family narratives that no longer serve our growth.

3. **Challenging and Questioning Beliefs**:

   Rewriting our story begins with questioning the validity of limiting beliefs. Ask yourself if these beliefs are truly yours, if they are based on facts, and if they are helpful in achieving your goals.

4. **The Power of Language**:

   Language plays a key role in transforming limiting beliefs. By changing the way we speak to ourselves, we can begin to change our internal narrative, shifting from negative and self-defeating thoughts to positive, growth-oriented ones.

5. **Reframing the Past**:

   It is possible to look at past experiences from a new perspective. Reframing the past involves viewing old narratives through the lens of growth, resilience, and empowerment, rather than seeing them as setbacks or failures.

6. **Creating a New, Empowering Narrative**:

   Rewriting your story means consciously creating a new narrative that reflects your desired future. This narrative should align with your values, strengths, and goals, and it should inspire you to take positive action toward self-actualization.

7. **Consistency and Repetition**:

   Changing your narrative is a process that requires time and repetition. Consistently affirming the new beliefs and language will help solidify your new story and transform your mindset.

8. **Taking Action**:

   The shift in narrative is not just about changing thoughts; it is about aligning actions with the new story. Empowering narratives drive empowering actions, which will reinforce the new beliefs and continue the cycle of transformation.

9. **Self-Compassion in the Process**:

   During the process of rewriting your story, it's important to practice self-compassion. Understand that changing your narrative is a journey and that mistakes or setbacks are part of the learning process.

10. **The Ongoing Evolution of Your Story**:

    Your story is not fixed; it is constantly evolving. By embracing the process of rewriting, you give yourself the freedom to grow, change, and redefine who you are.

Through engaging in these exercises, you will actively reshape your inner dialogue and take control of your personal narrative, leading to greater empowerment and self-actualization.

Reflection Questions

1. What are some of the limiting beliefs you have held about yourself, and how have they influenced your decisions and actions?

   Reflect on how these beliefs have shaped your choices in relationships, career, or personal growth.

2. How does your current narrative affect the way you see yourself and your future?

   Consider how your beliefs about yourself and your potential might be shaping your confidence and vision for the future.

3. What new belief or narrative would you like to adopt about yourself, and how can you begin to live it out?

   Reflect on the positive changes you want to create and the beliefs that support that transformation.

4. In what areas of your life have you experienced a significant shift in your story, and how has this transformation impacted you?

   Think about times in your life when you've already begun rewriting your story, even in small ways, and what outcomes followed.

5. What challenges do you face when trying to rewrite your story, and what strategies can help you overcome them?

   Identify obstacles that arise when challenging old narratives and brainstorm ways to stay committed to your empowering story.

These questions can help guide deep reflection on how limiting beliefs shape your life and encourage you to envision and take steps toward rewriting a more empowering narrative.

✦ Chapter Summary

Chapter 13 highlights the transformative power of rewriting our personal narratives, emphasizing the journey from limiting beliefs to empowerment. Our inner stories shape the way we see ourselves, our potential, and the world around us. When we carry limiting beliefs—about our worth, abilities, or future—those stories can confine us, preventing growth and hindering our ability to achieve our fullest potential. In this chapter, we explore how identifying and challenging these beliefs is the first step toward rewriting our narrative. Through language, mindfulness, and self-awareness, we can replace disempowering thoughts with affirmations that reflect our strengths, resilience, and capacity for change. The chapter emphasizes the importance of recognizing the impact of past experiences but also offers a powerful perspective: our past does not define our future unless we allow it to. By shifting our mindset and transforming the way we speak to ourselves, we can reframe our life stories to reflect empowerment, courage, and a sense of possibility. Exercises and reflection prompts encourage readers to confront their limiting beliefs head-on, reframe negative self-talk, and replace outdated narratives with new stories that align with their true potential.

This chapter illustrates that rewriting your story is not just about changing words; it's about reclaiming your power, transforming your identity, and stepping into a future filled with possibility.

Chapter 14

The Impact of Collective Narratives:
Shaping Ourselves and Society

"The stories we share shape the reality we live. By rewriting our collective narratives, we transform the future for all." — Anonymous

As individuals, the stories we tell ourselves are powerful, but we are not the only ones creating narratives. We are also deeply influenced by the collective narratives of the society in which we live. Collective narratives, or the shared stories within a culture, community, or group, shape the values, beliefs, and behaviors that guide us. These societal stories influence how we perceive ourselves, how we relate to others, and how we make sense of the world.

In this chapter, we will explore how collective narratives shape our identities and behaviors, and how we can become conscious of these larger societal stories in order to reclaim our own narrative and live authentically.

Understanding Collective Narratives

Collective narratives are stories created by groups or societies that influence individuals within them. These stories are often deeply ingrained in cultural, political, and social systems. They are communicated through various channels such as family traditions, education, religion, media, and even politics. These narratives often address broad themes such as identity, success, failure, morality, and community values.

For example, many societies have collective narratives about what it means to be successful. In many Western cultures, success is often defined by individual achievement and material wealth. These cultural stories emphasize the importance of competition, self-sufficiency, and financial success. Those who do not align with these values may feel as though they are falling short or failing.

Similarly, in some cultures, collective narratives surrounding gender roles, racial identity, and social expectations can create limitations on what is considered acceptable or possible. For example, traditional gender roles may define success for women in terms of marriage and motherhood, while for men, it may be defined by career achievement and financial stability. These societal expectations, while often well-intentioned, can confine individuals to predefined paths, limiting their freedom to explore and express their true selves.

According to social identity theory (Tajfel & Turner, 1986), collective narratives are a key component of group identity. People's sense of self is influenced by the groups to which they belong, and these group affiliations help define the social roles and responsibilities they assume. When we internalize these collective narratives, they influence how we see ourselves and how we navigate the world.

The Power of Social Media and Mass Media

In modern society, mass media and social media play an enormous role in shaping collective narratives. Through television, movies, advertisements, and online platforms, we are constantly exposed to stories about beauty, success, relationships, and social norms. These stories influence not only how we see others but also how we see ourselves.

For example, social media platforms like Facebook, Instagram and TikTok have contributed to the creation of a "highlight reel" culture, where people only present the most curated, polished, and successful versions of their lives. This narrative can create unrealistic expectations for beauty, happiness, and success, leading to feelings of inadequacy and low self-worth among those who compare their lives to these idealized images.

Similarly, advertising is one of the most influential forms of media shaping collective narratives. Advertisements often reinforce societal expectations about beauty, wealth, and success, promoting the idea that happiness is attainable only through the purchase of certain products or services. These narratives, while designed to sell products, also shape how we perceive our own self-worth and value.

The Role of Religion in Collective Narratives

Religion is perhaps one of the oldest and most influential collective narratives in human history. It has provided communities with shared beliefs, moral frameworks, rituals, and explanations for existence, purpose, suffering, and the afterlife. These shared stories shape not only individual identities but also entire cultures, legal systems, traditions, and worldviews.

At the individual level, religious narratives can offer a profound sense of identity, belonging, and purpose. Phrases like *"You are made in God's image,"* or *"You are a sinner in need of grace,"* become internalized scripts that influence self-worth, behavior, and life choices. These statements can either empower individuals to live with dignity and compassion or, in some contexts, lead to guilt, fear, or a diminished sense of personal control—depending on the interpretation and delivery of these messages. At the societal level, religion has historically shaped laws, norms, and ethics—influencing everything from gender roles and family structures to political ideologies and human rights. For example:

- Judeo-Christian values have informed much of Western legal and moral systems.
- In many cultures, religious narratives dictate roles within families (e.g., patriarchy or matriarchy).
- Sacred texts are often interpreted as ultimate authority, influencing views on justice, sexuality, gender identity, and more.

Religious stories also serve as a mechanism for social cohesion and control. Shared rituals, holidays, and doctrines create a sense of unity, but they can also enforce conformity. When divergent beliefs are labeled as sinful, dangerous, or heretical, religion can become a source of division or oppression.

However, it is important to acknowledge the dynamic and evolving nature of religious narratives. Throughout generations, reinterpretation and reform have allowed many faiths to become more inclusive and aligned with contemporary understandings of human dignity, equality, and freedom.

Ultimately, religious narratives—like all collective scripts—are not inherently good or bad. Their impact depends on how they are interpreted, internalized, and enacted. As with any story we inherit from society, it's vital to examine which parts align with our values and contribute to our growth, and which may need to be questioned or reframed.

Conforming to Collective Narratives: The Pressure to Fit In

As individuals, we constantly navigate the tension between our personal narrative and the collective narrative. On one hand, we strive to honor our unique identity and pursue a life aligned with our values and desires. On the other, we are shaped— often subtly—by the stories society tells us about who we *should* be and what we *should* aspire to.

This societal pressure shows up in many forms—from expectations to reach certain career milestones, to the pressure to conform to specific beauty standards. The need for social acceptance and the desire to belong can push us to adopt societal norms, even when those norms do not reflect our true selves.

In some cases, conforming to these collective narratives can be harmful. Social comparison theory (Festinger, 1954) suggests that when we evaluate ourselves against others—especially those who represent societal ideals—we are more likely to experience negative emotions such as envy, shame, or inadequacy. These emotions can erode our mental health, damage self-esteem, and lead to disconnection from our authentic identity.

Sometimes, the effort to fit in comes at a greater cost than we realize—especially when it means conforming to the narrow and often unrealistic narratives that society paints for us. In our pursuit of belonging, we may silence our authentic selves, adopt roles that do not align with our values, or suppress parts of our identity just to be accepted. Over time, this can lead to internal conflict, emotional exhaustion, and a sense of disconnection from who we truly are. True belonging does not come from fitting into someone else's story—it comes from having the courage to write and live your own.

The Harmful Effects of Conformity on Self-Worth

The impact of collective narratives and societal pressure on self-worth can be profound. The more we internalize societal standards and ideals, the more likely we are to measure our worth against them. When we fail to meet these external expectations, we may experience feelings of inadequacy or unworthiness.

Cultural ideals—especially those perpetuated by media—often create narrow definitions of beauty that profoundly shape how individuals perceive themselves. Over time, these external standards can distort body image, foster insecurity, and erode a person's sense of self-worth, resulting in lasting emotional and psychological effects. Research shows that exposure to unrealistic beauty ideals is linked to dissatisfaction with one's appearance, depression, anxiety, and eating disorders (Grabe, Ward, & Hyde, 2008).

Additionally, the pressure to conform to career expectations—such as the idea that success is defined by financial wealth or job title—can lead to burnout, stress, and a diminished sense of self-worth for those who do not find fulfillment in these pursuits. Social expectations about relationship norms, such as the idea that happiness is achieved through marriage and children, can also create pressure for individuals who do not conform to these narratives.

The key issue is that when we rely too heavily on collective narratives to define our worth, we lose sight of our own values and desires. We end up living in a way that feels disconnected from our true selves and our unique potential.

Reclaiming Your Personal Narrative: Breaking Free from Societal Norms

To live authentically, we must learn to recognize the influence of collective narratives on our lives and question whether they are serving us. The process of reclaiming our personal narrative involves examining the societal stories that we have internalized and deciding which of these beliefs align with our true identity and which need to be discarded.

Here are some steps to reclaim your narrative:

1. **Become aware of societal expectations**: The first step in reclaiming your narrative is to become aware of the collective narratives that influence your thoughts, actions, and decisions. Reflect on the messages you have received about success, beauty, relationships, and worth. Are these messages in alignment with your values?

2. **Challenge the status quo**: Once you identify societal expectations, challenge them. Ask yourself whether these norms reflect who you truly are or whether they are simply external pressures that you have internalized. What are the consequences of conforming to these narratives? Are they helping you grow, or are they hindering your authenticity?

3. **Create your own definition of success**: Instead of relying on societal definitions of success—such as financial wealth, job titles, or relationship status—create your own definition of success that aligns with your values and desires. What does a fulfilling and meaningful life look like to you?

4. **Surround yourself with supportive communities**: Reclaiming your narrative often requires support from like-minded individuals who encourage you to embrace your true self. Seek out communities or mentors who share your values and will support you in challenging societal norms and creating a life that is authentic to you.

5. **Be patient with the process**: Rewriting your narrative and breaking free from societal norms is not a one-time event. It is an ongoing process of self-discovery, growth, and self-compassion. Be patient with yourself as you explore new paths and challenge old beliefs.

Key Takeaways

1. **Collective Narratives Shape Social Identity:**
    Collective stories, including cultural myths, historical accounts, and societal beliefs, significantly influence individual and group identities. These narratives guide how people perceive their roles in society, the values they uphold, and their sense of belonging.

2. **Power of Societal Influence:**
    From media to traditions, collective narratives can either empower or limit individuals. These shared stories have the power to reinforce stereotypes, perpetuate social norms, or challenge them. Understanding this influence allows for greater awareness and the ability to choose which narratives we embrace.

3. **Cultural and Societal Narratives are Fluid:**
    Collective narratives are not fixed. They evolve over time, often in response to social movements, changes in leadership, or shifts in public opinion. Participating in shaping these stories can lead to social change, as individuals and groups challenge outdated or harmful narratives.

4. **Influence on Personal Storytelling:**

   The narratives we inherit from society, such as those about gender, success, race, and family, play a crucial role in how we construct our own personal stories. These external influences can shape our self-worth, aspirations, and life choices, often in ways we are not fully aware of.

5. **Collective Narratives and Social Justice:**

   The stories we tell collectively can perpetuate inequality or drive social justice. By recognizing the power of narratives, individuals and communities can challenge harmful social norms and advocate for more inclusive and equitable stories.

6. **Individual Capacity in Shaping Collective Narratives**

   While collective narratives are powerful, individuals and groups have the ability to rewrite and influence these stories. By consciously engaging with and reshaping collective narratives, people can help create a more inclusive, empowered, and just society.

7. **Role of Storytelling in Social Movements:**

   Social movements often involve creating new collective narratives that challenge the status quo. These new stories can inspire collective action, build solidarity, and reframe societal values to address issues like inequality, injustice, and human rights.

Understanding the impact of collective narratives offers valuable insight into how societal stories shape individual lives and drive movements for change. Engaging with these exercises can deepen your awareness of the narratives that influence both your identity and your community—and empower you to take meaningful steps toward positive transformation.

Reflection Questions

1. What societal narratives have influenced your sense of identity?

   How have these narratives shaped your beliefs, behaviors, and decisions in life?

2. Which collective narratives have you internalized that you now recognize as limiting or harmful?

   How can you begin to challenge or rewrite these narratives to better align with your personal values?

3. In what ways do you see societal norms affecting how you perceive success, relationships, and identity?

   Are there any societal expectations that you feel pressure to conform to? How do these norms impact your well-being?

4. How can you use your personal story to challenge or shift the collective narrative around a specific societal issue (e.g., gender, race, success, family)?

   What actions or changes in perspective can you take to contribute to a positive shift in societal beliefs?

5. What are some stories, traditions, or cultural beliefs that
    you want to reclaim or rewrite for yourself and future
    generations?

    How can you reshape these collective narratives to be more
    inclusive, empowering, and reflective of your true self?

These questions encourage deep reflection on the impact of
societal narratives and prompt action towards creating more
empowering personal and collective stories.

✦ Chapter Summary

Chapter 14 explores the profound influence of collective
narratives—stories shared by groups, cultures, and societies—
and how they shape both individual identities and the broader
cultural landscape. Collective narratives are guided stories that
define social norms, values, and expectations, influencing how
we perceive ourselves and others. These narratives can be
rooted in history, culture, and societal beliefs, and they often
reflect the experiences and struggles of generations before us.
However, just as individual stories can limit or empower us, so
too can collective narratives. For example, societal narratives
around race, gender, success, and failure can either limit
opportunities and self-perception or foster a sense of belonging
and purpose. In this chapter, we examine the power of these
collective stories in shaping personal identity, social roles, and
the collective consciousness. We also explore the way societal

scripts can perpetuate harmful stereotypes and contribute to social inequality. But importantly, the chapter emphasizes that just as individuals can rewrite their own scripts, societies have the power to shift collective narratives. Through collective action, new perspectives, and an intentional focus on inclusivity, justice, and equity, we can reshape the stories that govern our shared experience. By doing so, we not only empower individuals but also influence the broader trajectory of societal change. Reflection prompts and exercises invite readers to consider the societal narratives they are a part of, challenge limiting collective beliefs, and actively participate in rewriting the stories that impact both themselves and the world at large.

Chapter 15

Rewriting the Narrative: *Creating a Conscious Story*

"Your story is not defined by the past, but by the choices you make today. Rewrite it with intention, and watch your future unfold." – Anonymous

In this chapter, we seek how to create a new narrative for your life by leveraging the power of neuroplasticity, the transformative potential of language, and the anchoring force of spirituality and faith. We live in the stories we tell ourselves, but those stories are not fixed. They are editable scripts shaped by our experiences, beliefs, and, most importantly, our interpretations. Rewriting your narrative is more than just changing words; it is about restructuring the neural architecture of your brain, challenging old paradigms, and integrating new ways of thinking that empower rather than limit.

Neuroplasticity: The Brain's Capacity to Rewrite the Script

For much of history, scientists believed the brain's structure was mostly fixed after early childhood. However, research in recent decades has radically shifted our understanding. Neuroplasticity refers to the brain's ability to reorganize itself by forming new neural connections throughout life (Doidge, 2007). This is the foundational scientific principle behind why and how we can rewrite our mental narratives.

Each time we engage in a thought or behavior, we strengthen the neural pathways associated with it—much like carving a groove into the brain. Repeated thoughts like *"I'm not good enough"* or *"I always fail"* become hardwired if practiced frequently. But, thanks to neuroplasticity, we can rewire those grooves by intentionally practicing new thoughts such as *"I am capable"* or *"I learn from challenges"* (Begley, 2007).

Functional MRI studies have shown that even individuals with deeply entrenched anxiety or depressive patterns can experience structural brain changes through practices like mindfulness, cognitive-behavioral therapy, and affirmations (Hölzel et al., 2011). For instance, one study found that just eight weeks of mindfulness practice led to increased gray matter density in the hippocampus, which is linked to learning and memory, and decreased density in the amygdala, which is involved in stress and fear responses (Hölzel et al., 2011).

This means that your thoughts literally shape your brain, and by choosing new thoughts, you are creating a new mind—one that supports, rather than sabotages, your growth.

How Neuroplasticity Works

Neuroplasticity refers to the brain's incredible ability to form and reorganize synaptic connections, especially in response to learning, experiences, and trauma. This means that the brain is not static but rather constantly adapting and rewiring itself based on the information and stimuli it receives. Every time we think a thought, feel an emotion, or take an action, we are reinforcing a neural pathway, which can either strengthen existing connections or form new ones. Over time, these pathways become automatic, creating what we commonly refer to as our default scripts or mental habits.

However, much of this automatic behavior and thinking is shaped by our past experiences—particularly the ones that were repeated frequently or deeply emotionally charged. For example, if you were repeatedly told as a child that you were not good enough or that failure was to be feared, your brain may have created strong neural pathways that reinforce these beliefs and reactions. These pathways are often unconscious and automatic, leading to limiting beliefs like "*I'm not enough*" or "*I always fail.*"

But the beautiful thing about neuroplasticity is that it works both ways. Just as we have unintentionally built limiting beliefs, we can intentionally rewire our brains to support healing, growth, and confidence. By deliberately engaging in new thoughts, behaviors, and practices, we can forge new mental highways—paths that align with our goals, values, and true potential.

For instance, if you practice self-compassion and positive affirmations regularly, you are literally creating new neural pathways that promote self-worth and resilience. These new connections, formed through repetition, gradually replace the old ones and begin to become your brain's "default" mode, shifting how you think, feel, and react.

The more you engage with these new mental habits, the more your brain adapts, making it easier to embody the positive beliefs and behaviors over time. This process can take time and patience, but the brain's adaptability means that no matter how deep-seated the old scripts may seem, new pathways are always possible to create. It is a powerful reminder that we are not prisoners of our past; we have the ability to rewrite our mental landscape with intention, repetition, and commitment.

Rewriting Through Repetition

Repetition is key to forming new pathways. The more you practice a new belief or behavior, the more the brain begins to favor it over the old script. This means:

- Repeating affirmations such as *"I am worthy"* or *"I am lovable"* creates real physical changes in the brain.
- Practicing gratitude daily wires your brain to notice the positive more than the negative.
- Catching and reframing negative self-talk disrupts old patterns and builds new mental habits.

It is not about instant change, but consistent rewiring. Just as the brain was wired over time through repeated messages and experiences, it must be rewired through intentional practice and emotional engagement.

Emotional Intensity Accelerates Learning

The brain has a remarkable ability to remember what it emotionally feels. This is why powerful experiences—particularly traumatic ones—can leave such lasting marks on our mental scripts. When an event is accompanied by intense emotion, whether positive or negative, the brain takes note and stores that experience deeply, reinforcing the neural pathways associated with it. The stronger the emotion, the more readily the brain encodes the memory, and the more entrenched the associated beliefs and behaviors become (LeDoux, 2000).

This same principle works in our favor when it comes to transformation. Practices that evoke strong emotional responses, such as meditation, visualization, storytelling, or journaling, are particularly effective because they engage both the mind and the emotions. When we pair new thoughts or empowering beliefs with deep emotion, those thoughts are more likely to embed themselves in the brain, forming new neural pathways that are more robust and resilient. Studies in neuroplasticity support this, showing that emotionally charged experiences are more likely to lead to structural changes in the brain (Davidson & McEwen, 2012).

For example, visualization techniques that tap into feelings of joy, confidence, or gratitude can wire the brain to focus on and create those emotions in real life (Tindle et al., 2009). Similarly, journaling about personal experiences in a way that invites emotional expression helps to process and reframe past wounds or limiting beliefs, promoting healing and growth (Pennebaker, 1997).

In fact, research shows that when people use emotion-driven techniques like guided imagery or even creative activities like art and writing, they can accelerate the learning process and reinforce new, positive scripts more quickly. The emotional intensity behind these practices serves as a catalyst for rewiring the brain, making new beliefs feel more authentic and real (Siegel, 2012). When we genuinely feel the emotions associated with the changes we want to make, the brain responds by strengthening those connections, making them part of our default way of thinking and behaving.

This process highlights the crucial role emotions play in shaping our experiences and in the rewiring of our brains. By tapping into the emotional undercurrent of transformation, we make lasting change more powerful and more sustainable.

From Default to Design

Neuroplasticity puts the power back in your hands. You are no longer bound to the past or to automatic responses. With an understanding of how your brain operates, you now have the ability to consciously pause, observe, and choose a new direction. In this process, your brain does not resist change—it adapts, forming new neural pathways that support your intentions. Your thoughts, emotions, and behaviors no longer have to be automatic reactions to past experiences or ingrained patterns; they can become intentional responses to the present moment.

The key to this transformation is awareness. Once you recognize that your thoughts and reactions are learned habits, it becomes easier to interrupt them. Through practices like mindfulness, meditation, or simply taking a pause before reacting, you create space to choose more constructive, empowering responses. This pause allows you to examine your thoughts without becoming emotionally entangled in them, creating an opportunity for new choices to emerge (Siegel, 2010). Over time, your brain, which has been conditioned by repetitive patterns, begins to favor these new pathways, making them more automatic and less reliant on the old scripts that once dominated your behavior.

This process is much like designing a new roadmap. You are no longer stuck following the well-worn paths of negativity, self-doubt, or fear. Instead, you can consciously create a new mental map—one that reflects the person you are becoming rather than the person you were. This is where neuroplasticity meets intention. Every time you choose to act in a new, healthier way, your brain builds new neural circuits, rewiring itself to reflect your evolving thoughts and behaviors.

As you consistently practice this new way of thinking, those neural connections strengthen, making these new pathways your "default." Over time, what started as a conscious effort becomes your natural response. In essence, you are designing your brain, not just relying on default settings dictated by past experiences. Your thoughts become aligned with your intentions, and the new beliefs and behaviors you cultivate eventually form the foundation of your truth.

The power of neuroplasticity means that change is always possible. You are not stuck in a set way of thinking or living. You have the ability to shape your mind, behavior, and, ultimately, your life. The more you practice these new thoughts and behaviors, the more you solidify them in your brain. As a result, they become your new default, guiding you toward a future that is consciously designed by you.

The Power of Conscious Language

Language does not simply reflect reality—it constructs it. The words we use to describe ourselves and the world become the lens through which we interpret experience. This applies both to the internal language of self-talk and the external language we use in our conversations, writing, and expressions.

Research highlights the strong connection between language, thoughts, and behaviors. Negative automatic thoughts often carry cognitive distortions such as overgeneralization, catastrophizing, or labeling (Beck, 2011). By learning to recognize and replace these patterns with more accurate and empowering statements, individuals can enhance both their mental well-being and decision-making abilities.

Examples of Rewritten Language Patterns:

- **From:** "I always mess things up."
  To: "I've made mistakes, but I'm learning and improving every day."
- **From:** "I'll never succeed like them."
  To: "I have my own path, and I'm making steady progress."
- **From:** "I can't do this."
  To: "This is challenging, but I'm capable of figuring it out."

Even changing the phrase *"I have to"* to *"I get to"* can shift your experience. Saying *"I get to go to work today"* transforms obligation into opportunity. This reframing cultivates gratitude, motivation, and a sense of personal empowerment. (Fredrickson, 2009).

Additionally, labeling emotions precisely—known as "affect labeling"—helps regulate those emotions. A 2007 study found that when individuals labeled their emotions (e.g., *"I feel anxious"*), their brain's emotional centers showed decreased activity, and they were more likely to make rational choices (Lieberman et al., 2007).

Words are tools for shaping identity, behavior, and mood. By speaking with awareness and intention, we can literally speak life into our future selves.

The Spiritual and Faith-Based Dimension of Rewriting

While psychology and neuroscience offer powerful tools for transformation, many individuals find their deepest healing and clarity through spirituality and faith. For centuries, spiritual traditions have offered transformative practices—such as confession, affirmation, prayer, meditation, and storytelling—that allow individuals to reshape their internal beliefs and align with higher truths. These practices are not only tools for personal growth but serve as profound methods for rewriting the narratives of our lives, helping to break free from cycles of pain, guilt, and limitation.

In Christian theology, for example, transformation is a central theme: "*Be transformed by the renewing of your mind*" (Romans 12:2, New International Version). This idea of renewing the mind aligns remarkably with modern neuroscience, which also emphasizes the power of thought and intention in reshaping neural pathways. Just as neuroplasticity suggests that the brain's structure can be rewired through focused, intentional practices, the Bible offers the insight that spiritual renewal begins in the mind. This theological concept confirms that transformation is both a spiritual and neurological process—an intertwining of faith and science that creates lasting change.

The Bible also speaks to the power of words, which resonates with the science of language and neuroplasticity. Proverbs 18:21 teaches, "*Life and death are in the power of the tongue,*" emphasizing the importance of how we speak to ourselves and others. Our words are not merely reflections of our thoughts—they actively shape our reality. Research shows that the language we use can directly influence our emotions and behaviors, reinforcing the way we experience and respond to the world around us (Beck, 2011). For example, when individuals engage in self-affirmation and positive self-talk, it helps to reframe their internal narrative, much like the power of prayer or confession, which can align one's beliefs with divine truth.

The connection between spirituality and mental health is also supported by research. Studies show that religious and spiritual practices, such as prayer and meditation, are linked with better mental health, reduced anxiety, and increased emotional resilience (Koenig, 2012). Prayer and meditation, which are common in many spiritual traditions, activate the prefrontal cortex—the brain's center for focus, decision-making, and intention—while simultaneously reducing activity in the limbic system, the area of the brain responsible for stress and reactivity (Newberg & Waldman, 2009). These neurological changes support a more grounded, calm, and intentional sense of self, enabling individuals to move through life's challenges with greater resilience and clarity.

Furthermore, the power of spiritual practices like confession, journaling, and meditation lies in their ability to help individuals confront and release old, limiting beliefs. In the Christian tradition, for example, confession offers a way to acknowledge and release negative patterns while aligning one's thoughts with the truth of God's grace. This act of spiritual surrender—whether through prayer, meditation, or worship—creates a shift in perspective, enabling individuals to rewrite their personal narratives in light of their faith and connection to a higher power.

In this context, faith-based identity reframing becomes a profound tool for transformation. Spiritual narratives offer frameworks for forgiveness, purpose, and redemption—elements that may be missing in purely secular approaches to healing. For example:

- "I am loved unconditionally."
- "I am created with purpose."
- "My past does not define me."
- "There is meaning in my suffering."

These beliefs have the power to transcend trauma, shame, and loss, helping individuals reconnect with hope and personal dignity. Even when scientific methods provide cognitive strategies for change, faith often provides the emotional depth and existential grounding needed for long-term transformation.

Moreover, many spiritual traditions emphasize the importance of community, which provides both support and accountability in the process of rewriting one's story. Being surrounded by a supportive spiritual community reinforces the narrative of connection, encouragement, and grace. This collective support enhances resilience, fostering an environment where individuals feel empowered to embrace their true identities and live with greater purpose.

As Proverbs 23:7 (King James Version) states, *"For as he thinketh in his heart, so is he."* This wisdom speaks to the profound connection between our thoughts and our identity. When we intentionally reshape our thoughts through spiritual practices, such as meditation or prayer, we align our minds with a higher truth, and as a result, we begin to transform not only our beliefs but our very identities. By consciously choosing a new narrative rooted in faith and spiritual truth, we begin to design a life that reflects our deepest values and purpose.

In summary, the fusion of faith, spirituality, and neuroscience offers a powerful approach to rewriting our personal narratives. Just as our thoughts and language shape our reality, our spiritual beliefs and practices can serve as a transformative foundation for growth and healing. By integrating these spiritual principles with the practices of neuroplasticity and language reprogramming, individuals can create lasting change in their lives, grounded in both the science of the brain and the wisdom of spiritual truth.

The Role of Faith-Based Identity Reframing

Spiritual narratives provide powerful frameworks for healing— offering elements of forgiveness, purpose, and redemption that are often absent in purely secular approaches. These beliefs can be deeply transformative, especially when they align with an individual's sense of identity. For instance, embracing the idea that one is unconditionally loved, created with purpose, and that suffering holds meaning can be pivotal in healing. Such beliefs empower individuals to transcend trauma, shame, and loss, reconnecting them with hope and personal dignity.

While cognitive strategies in psychology are valuable, faith often adds a layer of emotional and existential depth that fosters lasting change. It offers a connection to something greater than oneself—an anchor during times of turmoil.

Additionally, many spiritual traditions emphasize the role of community in the healing process. Being part of a faith-based or spiritual group provides vital social support and accountability, reinforcing a narrative of connection, encouragement, and grace. This sense of belonging strengthens the journey toward self-discovery and growth.

Putting It All Together: Becoming the Conscious Author of Your Life

Ultimately, you are the author of your own story. Your thoughts shape your reality, your language defines your identity, and your spirit offers resilience through challenges.

Rewriting your life's narrative is about claiming ownership of your internal world. It requires recognizing outdated scripts, shifting the language you use to describe yourself, and embracing a vision of who you are becoming. With the tools of neuroplasticity, intentional language, and spiritual grounding, you now hold the pen firmly in your hand, ready to write the next chapter of your life.

Key Takeaways

1. **Awareness is the First Step**

   Understanding that the stories we tell ourselves shape our identities, decisions, and actions. Becoming aware of our narratives allows us to recognize the limiting beliefs that may be unconsciously guiding us.

2. **The Power of Language**

   The language we use—internally and externally—has the power to reinforce or change our personal stories. Words can either confine us to old patterns or empower us to create new realities.

3. **Personal Responsibility**

   Rewriting our narrative means owning our life story. It involves acknowledging that we have the power to change our perceptions, beliefs, and, ultimately, the course of our future.

4. **Healing Through Reframing**

   By reframing negative or limiting beliefs, we can transform our mindset and open ourselves up to new possibilities. Rewriting the story is a healing process that allows us to let go of the past and step into a future of empowerment.

5. **Self-Compassion is Key**

   When rewriting our stories, it is essential to be compassionate with ourselves. Understanding that change takes time and practice fosters patience and persistence on this journey.

Reflection Questions

1. What is a recurring narrative you tell yourself about who you are or what you are capable of?

   Where do you think this story came from—early experiences, family, culture, religion, or personal setbacks?

2. How has this internal story shaped your decisions, relationships, or goals?

   Has it held you back, pushed you forward, or created confusion?

3. If you could rewrite this narrative with compassion and intention, what would your new story sound like?

   Try beginning with: "I used to believe..., but now I choose to see myself as..."

4. What language do you need to let go of in order to make space for your conscious story?

   Are there specific words or labels (e.g., "failure," "too much," "not enough") that no longer serve you?

5. What evidence do you have that supports your new narrative?

   Consider past successes, strengths, growth, and resilience that challenge the old script.

6. Who or what reinforces your old story—and who supports your new one?

   Think about the voices in your life (friends, media, environments) and whether they affirm your conscious direction.

7. How can you anchor your new narrative in daily life?

   What affirmations, routines, or reminders can help you stay connected to the story you want to live?

8. If your life were a book, what would you title the next chapter?

   Use this question as a metaphor to envision what is ahead in your consciously written life.

These exercises and reflection questions are designed to help you become aware of the narratives influencing your life, reframe limiting beliefs, and actively rewrite your story in a conscious, empowering way.

✦ Chapter Summary

Chapter 15 explores the intentional process of becoming the author of your own life story. By consciously rewriting your narrative, you gain control over the story that defines your identity, your actions, and your interactions with the world. This chapter integrates three powerful elements—language, neuroscience, and faith—as tools for creating a life story that aligns with your true self and your higher purpose.

Language is the foundation of how we construct meaning, shape our perceptions, and influence the course of our lives. The words we choose in our self-talk, our affirmations, and our external communication hold immense power in altering our mental and emotional landscape. Additionally, neuroscience reveals that the brain is highly malleable—neuroplasticity shows that we can literally rewire our brains through intentional practice, thought, and experience. By consciously choosing to shift limiting beliefs and replace them with empowering thoughts, we can create new neural pathways that support personal growth and transformation.

Furthermore, faith—whether spiritual, religious, or rooted in personal values—provides a sense of purpose and meaning that can guide our narrative rewriting. Faith offers a deep, intrinsic belief in the possibility of transformation and the strength to persevere through challenges. Together, these three elements—

language, neuroscience, and faith—empower you to reclaim your narrative, rewrite old stories that no longer serve you, and create a future filled with potential, authenticity, and purpose.

Chapter 16

The Power of Purpose: *Aligning with Meaningful Direction*

"Efforts and courage are not enough without purpose and direction."
— John F. Kennedy

We all long for a life that matters—one where our daily actions reflect a deeper sense of why we are here. Purpose is not something we find once and for all; it is something we align with, return to, and refine throughout life. It gives our choices context, our pain meaning, and our growth direction. Living with purpose is not about perfection—it is about being intentional. It is the difference between drifting aimlessly and moving forward with clarity, even in the face of uncertainty.

When we live from a place of purpose, we begin to shape a narrative that is not only fulfilling for us but also inspiring for others. Purpose connects us to something larger than ourselves, whether it is a calling, a cause, a community, or a sense of spiritual conviction. It acts as an internal compass, reminding us of who we are and what we stand for when life becomes noisy or uncertain.

In this chapter, we will discuss what purpose is (and what it is not), how to differentiate external expectations from inner direction, and how purpose impacts emotional well-being. We will explore how our values provide the foundation for meaningful direction and examine ways to uncover and sustain a purpose-driven life. This chapter also looks at how purpose can act as an anchor during seasons of transition, doubt, or struggle.

As you explore this chapter, remember: your purpose does not have to be monumental to be meaningful. It simply needs to be authentic to *you*.

The Story Arc of Purpose

The Story Arc of Purpose refers to the evolving journey of discovering, developing, and fulfilling your life's purpose. Purpose isn't static; it's a dynamic narrative shaped by challenges, growth, and milestones that influence how you understand and pursue goals that truly matter to you.

Imagine reading a novel where the main character wanders aimlessly, reacting to events without clear direction or meaning—no mission, no goal, just drifting. Most readers would lose interest quickly. In much the same way, when we lack a sense of purpose in our own lives, we become passive participants in our own story. Purpose gives our lives a narrative arc, weaving together past wounds, present choices, and future hopes into a meaningful whole.

Psychologist Viktor Frankl (1984) famously observed in *Man's Search for Meaning* that people who have a "why" to live can bear almost any "how." His experiences surviving Nazi concentration camps led him to develop logotherapy, which centers on finding meaning even in the most tragic circumstances. This chapter explores how grounding our internal narrative in a sense of purpose can build emotional resilience, improve overall well-being, and reshape the way we perceive life experiences.

The Psychology of Purpose

A growing body of research supports the idea that living with a sense of purpose contributes to greater mental, emotional, and even physical health. Purpose provides a framework for interpreting life's events, especially hardships. According to Hill, Burrow, and Sumner (2013), people with high levels of purpose report significantly higher levels of psychological well-being, life satisfaction, and self-esteem.

Purpose is not always about grand achievements or global impact—it often emerges through everyday moments of service, connection, creativity, or caregiving. Whether one finds purpose in parenting, mentoring, creating, healing, or serving, that clarity of direction has measurable psychological benefits.

A longitudinal study conducted by Hill and Turiano (2014) found that people with a strong sense of purpose lived longer lives, even after controlling for age, sex, race, education, and emotional well-being. Their findings suggest that having a life purpose is as crucial for longevity as not smoking or exercising regularly.

Rewriting the Narrative Through Purpose

Purpose has the power to reframe past pain and reorient our story. Individuals who once saw their trauma as an identity may, through a lens of purpose, see it as fuel for growth or service.

For example:

- A survivor of childhood abuse may find healing by becoming a counselor or advocate for others.
- A person who lost a parent to addiction might use that grief as motivation to lead substance abuse recovery groups.
- Someone who struggled with self-worth could turn that experience into creative expression, inspiring others to see their own value.

This kind of post-traumatic growth is well-documented. Park (2010) explains that finding meaning after trauma leads to more positive emotional outcomes, greater personal strength, and deeper relational connections. Purpose does not erase pain—it transforms it into something meaningful.

The Brain on Purpose: Neurological Benefits

Living with a clear sense of purpose does more than improve emotional well-being—it creates measurable changes in the brain's structure and function. Neuroscience increasingly supports the idea that purpose activates and strengthens areas of the brain involved in planning, motivation, and emotional regulation.

For instance, Ryff et al. (2004) found that individuals with a strong sense of life purpose show elevated levels of dopamine and serotonin—neurotransmitters tied to mood stabilization, reward, and pleasure. These chemical shifts not only reduce the risk of depression and anxiety but also contribute to greater vitality and psychological resilience. A purposeful mindset is also linked to lower cortisol production, the stress hormone that can negatively affect both mental and physical health.

Purposeful living heavily engages the prefrontal cortex, the brain region responsible for executive functions such as goal-setting, decision-making, and self-regulation (Steger, 2012). When guided by meaningful goals, the brain prioritizes long-term vision over short-term gratification—supporting greater discipline, emotional balance, and clarity.

Research in neuroplasticity further demonstrates that consistently aligning behavior with one's core values strengthens neural pathways associated with intentional living and mindful action. Over time, this makes it easier to make empowering choices and harder to fall back into reactive or self-sabotaging habits (Davidson & McEwen, 2012).

Example:

Consider someone recovering from burnout. Initially, their focus may be on simply escaping exhaustion. But as they reconnect with deeper life goals—such as building a meaningful career or nurturing fulfilling relationships—their brain begins to adapt. Instead of chasing external approval, they experience more intrinsic motivation. They find it easier to focus, say no to distractions, and feel fulfilled—even by small, daily tasks—because those actions align with a greater purpose.

Living with purpose, then, is more than a mindset—it is a neurological upgrade. Purpose reorganizes how our brains function. It reduces stress by calming the amygdala (the brain's fear center), activates the prefrontal cortex for better decision-making, and increases dopamine to boost mood and reinforce positive behavior. Ultimately, purpose doesn't just shape how we feel—it transforms how we live, think, and grow.

Faith, Spirituality, and Divine Purpose

Spiritual traditions across the world emphasize the concept of divine purpose. In Christianity, believers are often reminded that their lives are designed with intention: *"For I know the plans I have for you," declares the Lord, "plans to prosper you and not to harm you, plans to give you hope and a future"* (Jeremiah 29:11, NIV). This faith-based view suggests that purpose is not something we create alone, but something we uncover through spiritual alignment.

Spirituality is also strongly associated with psychological resilience and well-being. Kim et al. (2013) found that individuals who report spiritual or religious belief often experience greater hope, optimism, and lower levels of depression, primarily because their faith connects daily events to a larger story.

Spirituality offers people a sense of transcendence—the belief that their lives are part of something bigger than themselves. This belief strengthens emotional stability in the face of adversity and fosters moral and ethical purpose. Faith-based narratives often offer redemptive meaning, teaching that no pain is wasted, and no story is beyond rewriting.

Purpose as a Source of Identity

Purpose functions as a stabilizing force in the formation of personal identity. Rather than being defined by past wounds, societal roles, or external labels, individuals who live with purpose anchor their identity in intentional choice and meaning. This shift empowers people to view themselves not as passive recipients of life's circumstances but as active authors of their life narrative—a concept known as *self-authorship* (Baxter Magolda, 2001).

Purpose provides coherence across time. It connects who we were, who we are, and who we want to become. When individuals pursue goals aligned with deeply held values, they experience increased self-understanding, which fosters both resilience and psychological well-being (McKnight & Kashdan, 2009). It becomes easier to say "no" to distractions and "yes" to what truly matters, reinforcing a strong and evolving sense of self.

In contrast, the absence of purpose often leaves individuals vulnerable to identity diffusion, existential anxiety, and hopelessness—feelings that are strongly correlated with depression and low self-worth (Steger et al., 2008). Without a guiding sense of direction, people may become more susceptible to external validation, societal pressures, and reactive decision-making.

However, when purpose is integrated into one's identity, people tend to:

- Set clearer goals and maintain motivation even in the face of obstacles,
- Establish and enforce healthy boundaries,
- Engage in more pro-social behaviors, such as volunteering, mentoring, and community-building—actions that deepen both self-worth and connection to others (Damon, Menon, & Bronk, 2003).

Example:

Consider a woman who grew up in a chaotic environment and internalized the belief that her identity was defined by dysfunction and survival. In her twenties, she begins volunteering at a shelter for at-risk youth, drawn by a desire to create change. Over time, this calling transforms her view of herself—from someone shaped by trauma to someone who shapes others' healing. This sense of purpose gives her direction, emotional strength, and the confidence to make empowered life decisions. Her identity is no longer limited by her past but expanded by her commitment to something meaningful.

Practical Steps to Align with Purpose

1. **Reflect on Key Life Themes**

   What recurring themes or challenges show up in your life story? These often point to the work you are called to do.

2. **Clarify Your Core Values**

   Identify the values that guide your decisions: compassion, justice, creativity, service, etc.

3. **Explore Through Action**

   Try volunteering, mentoring, writing, or creating. Purpose often reveals itself through doing, not just thinking.

4. **Ask Big Questions**

   "What legacy do I want to leave?" "Who do I want to impact?" "What suffering breaks my heart, and how can I help?"

5. **Reframe the Past**

   Consider how past pain could be viewed as preparation for your purpose.

Purpose as Legacy: Writing Beyond the Present

Living with purpose is not solely about achieving personal goals—it is about creating a lasting impact that transcends the present moment. Legacy, in this sense, is not just what we leave *behind*; it is what we actively *pass forward*. It is the ripple effect of our values, words, and actions—how we influence others in both seen and unseen ways (Haidt, 2006).

When individuals align their daily behaviors with their deeper sense of meaning, they become stewards of transformation— not just for themselves, but for everyone their life touches. A purpose-driven life naturally creates a legacy of wisdom, resilience, and inspiration. This legacy may not take the form of accolades or public recognition; more often, it manifests in quiet, intimate moments: a father teaching his child to apologize with sincerity, a mentor guiding someone through a tough decision, or a friend showing up during a dark hour.

Purpose becomes legacy when it is lived consistently and authentically

It is in the repetition of small, intentional actions—encouraging words, principled decisions, acts of service—that we construct a story with enduring significance. Our identity, when fused with purpose, becomes a living narrative that continues to speak long after our physical presence is gone (McAdams, 2001).

As Viktor Frankl (1984) profoundly stated, *"Life is never made unbearable by circumstances, but only by lack of meaning and purpose."* This insight reflects the deep human need for narrative continuity: the belief that our life story matters and can serve as a source of strength and guidance to others. In owning our story and living it with integrity, we do not just leave a trail—we light a path.

Example:

A retired social worker who spent decades advocating for underrepresented youth may never be featured in a history book. But her legacy lives on in the lives of those she served: a former foster child who became a teacher, inspired by her kindness; a community that learned the value of inclusivity through her tireless outreach. Her purpose—quiet, unwavering, and deeply personal—became a generational inheritance of hope and healing.

Key Takeaways

1. **Purpose Fuels Motivation**

    A clear sense of purpose acts as a powerful motivator, driving us toward our goals with passion and perseverance. It gives our actions meaning and keeps us focused, even during difficult times.

2. **Purpose Is Personal**

    Everyone's purpose is unique to them, shaped by individual values, passions, and experiences. It is important to understand that there is no one-size-fits-all definition of purpose; what is meaningful to one person may differ from another's.

3. **Purpose Enhances Well-Being**

    Research shows that having a sense of purpose is linked to improved mental health, emotional resilience, and overall life satisfaction. It fosters a sense of fulfillment and can even contribute to physical health.

4. **Purpose Is Evolving**

    Our purpose is not a static thing—it can change as we grow and evolve. Periodically reassessing what drives us can help us stay aligned with our values and ensure that our actions are aligned with our most authentic self.

us. Purpose without action remains a distant idea, but when we act in alignment with our values, we create a life of meaning and impact.

5. **The Role of Contribution**

   Many people find purpose through contributing to others—whether through work, relationships, or service. Knowing that we are making a positive difference in the world can deepen our sense of purpose and connection.

6. **Purpose Leads to Fulfillment**

   Living a life aligned with purpose provides a sense of fulfillment that external achievements or material possessions cannot. It brings a deeper sense of satisfaction that is sustainable over time.

These exercises will guide you toward greater clarity and alignment with your purpose, leading to a more meaningful and fulfilling life.

Reflection Questions

1. What does purpose mean to you? How would you describe your personal sense of purpose in a few sentences?
   Take a moment to define what purpose looks and feels like in your life. Let this be a raw and honest reflection.

2. How do your current actions and decisions align with your sense of purpose? Are there areas where you feel

disconnected?

Explore any misalignments between your daily choices and your inner calling. Consider what small adjustments could move you closer to alignment.

3. Reflecting on moments when you felt truly fulfilled, what values were being honored in those experiences? How can you integrate more of those values into your daily life?

   Your values are often the compass pointing toward purpose. Use past experiences to identify patterns that reveal what truly matters to you.

4. What impact do you want to have on the people around you or the world at large? How does your purpose contribute to that vision?

   Think about the legacy you want to leave and how your everyday life can embody that purpose-driven impact.

5. When you look at your life a year from now, what purpose-driven goals or changes would you like to see manifest? How can you start moving toward those goals today?

   Visualize the next chapter of your life as one deeply aligned with meaning. Then identify your next courageous step.

These questions will help you dig deeper into your purpose and assess how aligned your daily actions are with a meaningful direction.

✦ Chapter Summary

Chapter 16 examines the profound impact that purpose and meaning have on shaping our personal narrative and the legacy we leave behind. It reveals that when we align our life stories with a clear sense of purpose, we not only create a more fulfilling present but also cultivate a future that resonates with our deepest values and aspirations. Purpose is the compass that guides us through life's complexities, providing clarity, motivation, and direction as we navigate our personal journeys.

Purpose and meaning are often intertwined with the stories we tell ourselves. When we tap into the narrative of purpose, we gain the ability to reframe past experiences, see challenges as opportunities, and direct our energy toward what truly matters. This chapter highlights the importance of connecting with your unique calling and understanding how your story can contribute to a greater collective narrative, both within your community and the world at large.

The power of purpose extends beyond individual well-being—it impacts relationships, career choices, and the way we engage with society. When you understand the role of purpose in your narrative, you create a life that is not only meaningful but also leaves a legacy of positive influence. By living intentionally, driven by purpose, we shape a story that can inspire others and impact future generations.

Additionally, this chapter introduces the concept of legacy—not just as a final moment, but as the ongoing effect of how we choose to live our lives. Legacy is built on the choices we make every day, and by aligning our actions with our higher purpose, we ensure that our story is one worth remembering.

Through guided exercises, reflective prompts, and personal insights, you will be invited to identify what truly drives you, reshape your narrative to reflect your purpose, and begin to craft the legacy you want to leave behind. This chapter offers you the tools to connect your personal narrative with a greater sense of meaning, and through this alignment, create a life of impact, fulfillment, and lasting purpose.

Chapter 17

Emotional Regulation: *Mastering the Mind's Response*

"You don't have to control your thoughts. You just have to stop letting them control you."

— Dan Millman

Emotional regulation is a crucial skill that allows individuals to manage their emotional responses to life's challenges in a balanced and constructive way. It involves understanding and influencing the way we experience, express, and respond to emotions, helping us navigate difficult situations with greater clarity and resilience. At the core of emotional regulation lies the intricate connection between the brain and body, where our neural and physiological systems work together to shape our emotional experiences. This chapter explores how emotional regulation is not just a mental process but a deeply embodied practice, rooted in both our brain's neural pathways and the autonomic nervous system. By mastering the art of emotional regulation, we can transform our reactions, reduce stress, enhance interpersonal relationships, and cultivate a sense of inner peace and control. Through mindfulness, cognitive reappraisal, and other evidence-based techniques, we can learn to tame our emotional impulses and create a more grounded and purposeful life.

The Brain-Body Connection in Emotional Regulation

Emotional regulation goes beyond being a psychological skill; it is a neurobiological process that reflects the dynamic interaction between the brain and body. The way we manage emotional responses is tied to how the brain interprets stimuli and how the body physiologically reacts to those interpretations (Critchley & Harrison, 2013). Understanding this relationship provides a foundation for developing practical tools to regulate emotions, particularly when dealing with intense experiences such as stress, fear, or anxiety.

1. The Role of the Nervous System

At the center of emotional regulation is the autonomic nervous system (ANS), comprised of two main branches:

- The **sympathetic nervous system (SNS)** initiates the "fight or flight" response in the presence of a threat.
- The **parasympathetic nervous system (PNS)** helps restore balance, bringing the body into a "rest and digest" state.

Optimal emotional health involves the ability to move fluidly between these systems—a trait known as autonomic flexibility (Thayer & Lane, 2000). Individuals with greater flexibility can respond adaptively to stress and recover more efficiently.

2. The Brain's Emotional Control Centers

Key brain structures involved in emotional regulation include:

- The **amygdala**, which detects threat and activates emotional arousal.
- The **prefrontal cortex (PFC)**, particularly the medial and dorsolateral areas, which modulate and inhibit emotional responses (Ochsner & Gross, 2005).
- The **hippocampus**, which supports memory processing and contextual awareness.

Under stress, the amygdala can overpower the regulatory efforts of the PFC, leading to impulsive or reactive behavior. Chronic stress can impair the PFC's ability to regulate the amygdala, reducing emotional control (Arnsten, 2009).

3. Interoception: Listening to the Body

Interoception is the ability to perceive internal bodily sensations such as heart rate, breathing, and tension. This self-awareness plays a critical role in emotion recognition and regulation (Craig, 2009). When individuals become attuned to their bodily states, they are better able to respond to early signs of emotional distress, enhancing self-regulation (Fustos et al., 2013).

4. The Vagus Nerve and Emotional Regulation

The **vagus nerve** is the longest cranial nerve, connecting the brainstem to the heart, lungs, and digestive tract. It is a primary component of the parasympathetic nervous system and helps regulate emotional and physiological states. **Vagal tone**, or the responsiveness of the vagus nerve, is associated with emotional resilience and effective social communication (Porges, 2007).

Practices such as deep breathing, chanting, cold exposure, and yoga can stimulate the vagus nerve and improve vagal tone (Kok & Fredrickson, 2010).

5. Chronic Stress and Dysregulation

Prolonged exposure to stress disrupts the delicate balance between the brain and body, particularly affecting regions responsible for emotional regulation. When the body perceives a threat—real or imagined—it activates the hypothalamic-pituitary-adrenal (HPA) axis, releasing cortisol, the body's primary stress hormone. While short-term cortisol release is adaptive and necessary for survival, chronic activation leads to wear and tear on the brain and body (McEwen, 2007).

Elevated cortisol levels over time impair the function of the prefrontal cortex—the brain's center for rational thinking, decision-making, and impulse control—while simultaneously heightening activity in the amygdala, the brain's fear and threat detection center (Arnsten, 2009; Lupien et al., 2009). This neurobiological shift makes it harder to think clearly, regulate emotions, and respond calmly to stress. Instead, individuals become more reactive, hypervigilant, and emotionally volatile.

The long-term effects of this dysregulation can be profound. Chronic stress is associated with an increased risk of mental health disorders such as anxiety, depression, and post-traumatic stress disorder (PTSD) (Yehuda et al., 2015). Physically, it may also contribute to sleep disturbances, weakened immunity, and cardiovascular problems. Furthermore, individuals with a history of trauma or adverse childhood experiences (ACEs) are particularly vulnerable to stress dysregulation, as their stress response systems may have been shaped early in life to be hypersensitive or overactive (Felitti et al., 1998).

Recognizing and addressing chronic stress is essential for restoring emotional balance. Practices such as mindfulness, breathwork, somatic therapies, and cognitive restructuring can help regulate the nervous system, lower cortisol levels, and rebuild the brain-body connection needed for healthy emotional regulation (Siegel, 2012; van der Kolk, 2014).

Practical Strategies to Strengthen Brain-Body Integration

To improve emotional regulation through the brain-body connection, the following strategies are supported by research:

1. **Mindfulness meditation increases activity in the PFC and reduces amygdala reactivity (Hölzel et al., 2011).**
   Example: A person experiencing chronic anxiety begins a daily 10-minute mindfulness meditation practice using a guided app. Over several weeks, they notice they are less reactive to triggering situations and can pause before responding, thanks to increased prefrontal cortex activity and reduced emotional hijacking by the amygdala.

2. **Breathwork supports vagal regulation and emotional calm (Brown & Gerbarg, 2005).**

   Example: During a stressful workday, an individual uses a 4-7-8 breathing technique (inhale 4 seconds, hold 7, exhale 8) before a meeting. This practice activates the vagus nerve, promoting calm and reducing heart rate, which helps them enter the room more composed and centered.

3. **Movement-based therapies such as yoga or tai chi enhance body awareness and nervous system balance (van der Kolk, 2014).**

   Example: A trauma survivor begins attending weekly trauma-sensitive yoga classes. Over time, they gain a stronger sense of bodily control and safety, which improves their ability to stay grounded in the present moment and reduces episodes of dissociation.

4. **Somatic experiencing and body-based psychotherapy focus on releasing stored trauma in the body (Levine, 2010).**

   Example: In a somatic experiencing session, a client working through childhood trauma is guided to notice subtle physical sensations, such as tightness in their chest or numbness in their legs. As they learn to track and release these sensations safely, they experience emotional relief without needing to retell or relive the trauma story.

5. **Grounding techniques help regulate arousal by shifting attention to the physical present (Ogden et al.,**

2006).

Example: A person with PTSD uses a 5-4-3-2-1 grounding exercise during a panic episode—naming five things they can see, four they can touch, three they can hear, two they can smell, and one they can taste. This sensory-based strategy helps bring their nervous system out of hyperarousal and back into the present.

The Role of the Amygdala

At the core of emotional regulation is the amygdala, a small almond-shaped cluster of nuclei in the brain that plays a key role in processing emotions, especially those linked to survival instincts, such as fear, anxiety, and anger. The amygdala acts as an emotional alarm system, quickly responding to perceived threats by triggering an automatic "fight or flight" response. This rapid reaction is adaptive in dangerous situations, allowing us to respond to immediate threats. However, the challenge arises when the amygdala overreacts in situations that are not actually threatening, leading to unnecessary stress or emotional outbursts.

Example:

Kynzie, a project manager in a fast-paced office environment, finds herself overwhelmed during tight deadlines. She begins to feel anxiety and frustration, which escalate quickly into anger when things do not go according to plan. This emotional surge is largely driven by the amygdala's automatic response to perceived stress. However, by practicing emotional regulation techniques such as mindfulness, she can better manage her emotional reactions and reduce the intensity of these automatic responses.

The Prefrontal Cortex and Down-Regulation

Fortunately, the prefrontal cortex—the part of the brain responsible for reasoning, planning, and decision-making—can help modulate the amygdala's activity. When we practice mindfulness or cognitive reappraisal (the act of reframing a situation to change its emotional impact), we activate the prefrontal cortex. This allows us to reflect on the emotional trigger and down-regulate the amygdala's response, resulting in a calmer and more reasoned reaction. As Ochsner and Gross (2005) suggest, mindfulness and reappraisal practices can significantly reduce the emotional intensity associated with challenging situations by engaging the prefrontal cortex to inhibit the amygdala's impulses.

In Kynzie's case, over time, as she practices mindfulness—such as focusing on her breath when she feels overwhelmed—she strengthens the connection between her prefrontal cortex and amygdala, enabling her to remain calm and think clearly in stressful situations. Her ability to stop and pause before reacting reduces her stress and helps her make more measured decisions.

The Polyvagal Theory and the Role of the Vagus Nerve

The Polyvagal Theory (Porges, 2011) further enriches our understanding of emotional regulation by explaining how the vagus nerve plays a key role in modulating our autonomic nervous system (ANS) responses. The vagus nerve connects the brain to various organs in the body, including the heart and gut. It helps regulate the parasympathetic nervous system, which promotes relaxation and social engagement. When we are in a state of calm and safety, the parasympathetic system is activated, leading to feelings of ease, connection, and a reduced physiological stress response.

In contrast, when we are stressed or in danger, the sympathetic nervous system (responsible for the "fight or flight" response) becomes activated. However, when we engage the parasympathetic system—through practices such as deep breathing, meditation, or physical relaxation techniques—we encourage the vagus nerve to calm our body, which in turn helps regulate emotional responses.

Consider the example of John, a college student who experiences frequent anxiety during exams. When he feels overwhelmed, his heart rate increases, and he becomes mentally scattered. However, through practices such as slow diaphragmatic breathing, he engages the vagus nerve, stimulating the parasympathetic system and helping his body enter a state of calm. As a result, his anxiety diminishes, allowing him to focus on the task at hand. Over time, John's ability to consciously activate this relaxation response improves his emotional regulation and reduces his overall anxiety levels.

The Integration of Brain and Body in Emotional Regulation

The integration of brain and body is vital in emotional regulation. When we consciously use language-based techniques, such as reframing negative thoughts or practicing self-compassion, we are able to down-regulate the amygdala and activate the parasympathetic nervous system, both of which help create a calm emotional state. This not only fosters emotional resilience but also strengthens our interpersonal relationships by allowing us to respond more thoughtfully during social interactions.

For instance, Connie, a teacher who often feels frustrated with her students, learns to practice self-talk to calm herself. When she notices her frustration building, she takes a moment to breathe deeply and says to herself, "*I am in control of my emotions. This situation is temporary, and I can respond with patience.*" By using mindful language, she engages the prefrontal cortex and the vagus nerve, promoting a sense of calm and emotional balance.

Real-Life Example: The Power of Emotional Regulation in Leadership

A well-known example of the brain-body connection in emotional regulation is found in the leadership of Nelson Mandela. Mandela faced immense personal and political pressure during his fight against apartheid in South Africa. However, despite these challenges, he demonstrated remarkable emotional regulation by focusing on maintaining a sense of peace, resilience, and hope. This emotional control likely stemmed from a combination of his mindfulness practices, reframing of negative situations, and understanding of the physiological effects of stress.

Mandela's ability to regulate his emotions was not only key to his personal survival but also critical in leading others toward reconciliation and peace. His leadership serves as an example of how emotional regulation, grounded in both the brain and body, can have profound effects on personal well-being and societal change.

The connection between the brain and body plays a critical role in emotional regulation. By understanding how the amygdala, prefrontal cortex, and vagus nerve interact, we can engage in practices that foster emotional resilience, reduce reactivity, and improve our emotional well-being. Whether through mindfulness, reappraisal, or breathing exercises, the act of consciously regulating our emotions involves both the mind and body. As we strengthen this connection, we enhance our ability to respond to life's challenges with greater clarity and emotional balance.

Listening to Emotions: The Pathway to Awareness

Listening to emotions is an active process that involves being aware of the signals our emotions send and understanding the underlying messages they carry. This practice allows us to respond more intentionally to life's challenges, rather than reacting impulsively. By tuning into our emotions, we can gain insight into our needs, fears, and desires, which enables us to navigate difficult situations with greater clarity and resilience.

The phrase "Name it to tame it," coined by psychiatrist Daniel Siegel, highlights the power of identifying our emotions. By putting feelings into words, we engage the prefrontal cortex—the brain region responsible for rational thinking and decision-making. This act of labeling allows us to pause automatic emotional reactions and create mental space to better understand and manage our responses.

Example: Listening to Emotions in the Workplace

Let us look at a workplace scenario where listening to emotions and using emotional literacy can significantly improve outcomes:

The Situation:

Julia, a project manager at a marketing firm, is leading a team on an important campaign. The deadline is fast approaching, and there's been mounting pressure from her boss to get the work completed. One day, Julia receives an email from a colleague, Steve, about a last-minute change in the project scope that would require extra work from the team. Julia feels a wave of frustration wash over her—she is already overwhelmed, and this additional task seems unreasonable.

Step 1: Identifying the Emotion

Instead of reacting immediately, Julia pauses and takes a moment to name the emotion. She reflects on what she is feeling—frustration—and notes that her frustration comes from the pressure of the deadline and the perception that Steve is adding to her burden without consulting her first.

By naming her emotion (*"I feel frustrated"*), Julia creates a space between the emotion and her reaction. This simple act allows her to step into a more reflective mindset rather than letting the frustration fuel a reactive response.

Step 2: Understanding the Emotion's Source

Julia takes it a step further and asks herself why she feels frustrated. Is it because of Steve's actions, or is it more about her own stress levels and the tight deadline? She realizes that while Steve's email triggered her frustration, the deeper issue is her fear of not meeting the deadline and disappointing her team. She also notices that her frustration is less about Steve personally and more about her struggle to manage multiple tasks under pressure.

Step 3: Regulating the Emotion

With this understanding, Julia is able to regulate her emotional response. Rather than sending an impulsive, irritated reply to Steve, she takes a few minutes to calm down and compose herself. She acknowledges the frustration, but now with clarity about its source, she is better equipped to respond with a level head.

Julia replies to Steve's email with a clear, professional message: *"I understand the need for this change, but given the tight deadline and current workload, I'm concerned about the additional pressure this will put on the team. Can we discuss how we can manage this shift without compromising quality or timelines?"*

Step 4: Better Coping and Problem-Solving

By listening to her emotions, Julia is able to engage in problem-solving rather than reacting emotionally. Her ability to identify her frustration and distinguish it from other emotions like anxiety or anger allows her to stay focused on finding a practical solution, which leads to a more productive and respectful conversation with Steve.

The Outcome:

Steve responds positively, appreciating Julia's professionalism and understanding. They agree to meet and discuss how to redistribute the workload and streamline the project timeline to meet both the new requirements and the existing deadline. Julia's ability to listen to her emotions and use them as a guide for communication strengthens her professional relationships and helps her manage the stress of the project more effectively.

The Impact of Listening to Emotions

In this scenario, listening to emotions helps Julia avoid acting on impulse and instead take a thoughtful, measured approach to a challenging situation. By naming her feelings, she is able to understand the source of her emotional reaction, regulate her response, and approach the problem with clarity and calm. This not only benefits Julia's ability to manage the situation but also enhances her overall emotional resilience.

Key Benefits of Listening to Emotions:

1. **Enhanced Emotional Literacy**: Julia's ability to identify and name her emotions allowed her to understand the root cause of her feelings and separate them from other factors.

2. **Improved Self-Regulation**: By stepping back and observing her emotions, Julia was able to manage her frustration and avoid a knee-jerk reaction.

3. **Better Coping Strategies**: By understanding the source of her emotions, Julia could develop a coping strategy (calming down before responding and finding a solution).

4. **Stronger Relationships**: Julia's ability to communicate thoughtfully rather than react impulsively allowed her to maintain a positive and productive relationship with her colleague, Steve.

5. **Increased Resilience**: By actively engaging with her emotions rather than suppressing them, Julia strengthened

her emotional resilience and was better equipped to handle future challenges.

In summary, listening to emotions not only provides valuable insights into our emotional state but also empowers us to act with intention and clarity. Whether in personal or professional settings, emotional awareness fosters emotional literacy and self-regulation, leading to more effective decision-making, communication, and problem-solving.

Vulnerability and the Power of Emotional Openness

Vulnerability is often misunderstood as weakness, but in truth, it is a core strength of emotional regulation. According to Brown (2012), vulnerability is the birthplace of authenticity, courage, and connection. When we allow ourselves to be vulnerable, we engage with emotions in a more honest and regulated way, making room for healing and intimacy.

Suppressing emotions to avoid vulnerability can have negative psychological outcomes, including increased anxiety, depression, and reduced immune functioning (Gross & Levenson, 1997). In contrast, embracing vulnerability through expressive writing or open conversation has been shown to reduce emotional distress and enhance meaning-making (Pennebaker, 1997).

Scenario: Vulnerability in a Romantic Relationship

The Situation:

Sarah and Mark have been dating for over a year. Recently, Sarah noticed that Mark had been pulling away emotionally. He was distant and less engaged during their conversations, which made Sarah feel confused and rejected. Instead of confronting him directly, she spent weeks holding her feelings inside, telling herself it was probably nothing and that she should not overreact.

1. Initial Emotional Response:

Sarah felt a combination of hurt, confusion, and fear. She was afraid that Mark might be losing interest, but she did not want to bring it up because she did not want to seem "needy" or create unnecessary tension. She was also embarrassed about how vulnerable the situation made her feel, so she tried to avoid confronting her emotions.

2. Choosing Vulnerability:

After a few more weeks of emotional strain, Sarah realized that keeping her feelings inside was not helping her or the relationship. She knew that if she wanted the relationship to grow, she needed to communicate her feelings. She decided to be emotionally open and vulnerable with Mark.

That evening, Sarah sat down with Mark and said, "*I've noticed that lately you've been distant, and I'm feeling really hurt and confused by it. I know I tend to internalize things, but I want to be honest with you about how I'm feeling. I'm afraid that this might mean something's wrong with our relationship, and I just need to understand what's going on.*

3. Mark's Response:

At first, Mark was surprised but also appreciative of Sarah's emotional openness. He admitted that he had been struggling with some personal issues at work and had not known how to express his stress to her. He had been withdrawing because he did not want to burden her with his problems. Hearing Sarah's vulnerability gave him the courage to share what he had been going through.

4. The Outcome:

Because Sarah chose to be vulnerable and openly shared her feelings without assuming blame or hiding her emotions, it created a safe space for Mark to also open up. Their conversation was honest, compassionate, and reassuring. By the end of the talk, they both felt more connected and understood.

Sarah's vulnerability not only helped clarify the situation but also deepened the trust in their relationship. She realized that by being emotionally open, she gave Mark the opportunity to express his emotions and ultimately strengthened their bond. Rather than allowing fear and uncertainty to grow, she took the step to create a more meaningful and authentic connection.

5. Lesson Learned:

This example shows the power of emotional openness in fostering vulnerability. Sarah's willingness to confront her emotions and share them with Mark led to a resolution that brought them closer. Vulnerability allowed her to stop hiding her true feelings and opened the door for deeper communication, helping her build trust, understanding, and emotional intimacy in the relationship.

This real-life example demonstrates how vulnerability in relationships—whether romantic, familial, or even professional—can lead to greater connection and healing. By being emotionally open, we invite others to be vulnerable too, which often leads to mutual understanding and strengthened bonds.

Emotion Scripts and Social Conditioning

Many individuals unconsciously adopt "emotion scripts" from childhood or culture—rules about what feelings are acceptable and how they should be expressed. For example:

- **"Boys don't cry"** teaches emotional suppression.
- **"Good girls don't get angry"** teaches emotional inhibition.
- **"Real men don't show fear"** promotes stoicism and discourages vulnerability.
- **"Keep the peace at all costs"** encourages emotional avoidance, often rooted in family dynamics that avoid conflict.
- **"Strong people don't need help"** reinforces self-reliance at the expense of emotional connection or support.
- **"Don't air your dirty laundry"** implies that emotional struggles should be kept private, leading to silence and shame.
- **"You're too sensitive"** invalidates emotional expression and teaches people to distrust their own feelings.
- **"Faith means always being joyful"** can pressure individuals to suppress grief, doubt, or pain in religious settings.

- **"Black women have to be strong"** reinforces emotional suppression due to cultural survival narratives (hooks, 2000).

These scripts are often passed through family systems, media portrayals, and societal expectations (Thompson, 1994). Over time, they shape internal beliefs about emotional worth and identity, often disconnecting people from their authentic emotional experience. Rewriting these scripts begins with awareness and the permission to feel fully and freely.

When emotional suppression becomes habitual, it may result in:

- **Alexithymia** (difficulty identifying and describing feelings),
- Increased **interpersonal conflict**, and
- Somatic symptoms like tension, fatigue, and chronic pain (Taylor et al., 1997).

Expanding the Language of Emotions

One of the most transformative ways to regulate emotion is to expand our emotional vocabulary. Instead of defaulting to words like "mad" or "sad," learning a broader emotional lexicon (e.g., frustrated, disappointed, disrespected, lonely, nostalgic) creates space for emotional nuance and clarity (Barrett, 2017).

This practice—sometimes called "granular emotional language"—is positively correlated with emotional regulation and psychological resilience. People who can label their emotions with specificity are less likely to be overwhelmed by them (Kashdan et al., 2015).

Example:

You feel upset after a disagreement with a close friend.

1. Traditional Emotion Labeling:

- **Common Emotion**: Angry or upset.

2. Expanding the Language of Emotion:

Instead of just labeling the emotion as "angry," you expand your emotional language and identify different layers of the experience.

- **Anger**: You recognize that you are frustrated, irritated, and feeling a sense of injustice. You identify the exact triggers for your anger—perhaps the conversation felt dismissive or invalidating.
- **Hurt**: You also feel hurt because you care deeply about the relationship and feel as though your friend did not understand your perspective.

- **Disappointment**: There is a sense of disappointment, not just in the disagreement itself but in the way it was handled. You feel let down because you expected a more empathetic response.
- **Vulnerability**: You also realize that anger stems from vulnerability—you might fear that this disagreement could cause a rift in the friendship, which evokes feelings of insecurity about the relationship.
- **Confusion**: You feel confused because you are not entirely sure what happened or why your friend reacted the way they did. This confusion adds to your emotional experience, making it harder to process the situation.

3. Benefits of Expanding Emotional Language:

- **Self-Awareness**: By identifying the layers of emotion, you have a clearer understanding of what is happening inside you. You are no longer just "angry"—you are navigating a complex emotional response.
- **Better Communication**: Instead of saying, "I'm just angry," you might express something more nuanced, like, "I'm feeling hurt and frustrated because I don't think my feelings were heard, and now I'm unsure how to move forward."

- **Empathy**: When you are able to identify the underlying emotions, it may help you approach the situation with more compassion—both toward yourself and toward your friend.

4. Actionable Insight:

This expanded emotional awareness can help you regulate your emotions more effectively. For example, once you realize that part of your anger is rooted in fear of losing the relationship, you may decide to approach the conversation with more vulnerability and openness, rather than reacting out of anger alone.

This example illustrates how expanding your emotional language allows for greater clarity in understanding your feelings, which in turn helps you communicate and process emotions in healthier ways. It can be helpful to explore different emotion wheels or emotion charts to help identify more specific emotions beyond the usual labels.

Using Conscious Language to Reframe Emotional Experience

Language does not just describe our emotions—it shapes and reinforces them. Consider the difference between:

- "I'm drowning in stress" vs. "I'm navigating a difficult time."
- "I'm falling apart" vs. "I'm learning how to cope."

The second versions reflect greater emotional regulation and a stronger sense of personal empowerment. Conscious language reinforces a sense of internal control, promoting adaptive coping strategies and lessening distress (Meichenbaum, 2007).

Developing Emotional Agility

Psychologist Susan David (2016) introduced the term emotional agility to describe the ability to be aware of, accept, and move through emotions in a way that aligns with our values. Emotional agility is not about suppressing discomfort—it is about allowing emotional truth to inform our choices rather than control them.

Those who practice emotional agility:

- Pause to notice what they are feeling,
- Step out of the story briefly to assess its validity,
- Reframe it through the lens of growth, and
- Choose actions that reflect long-term values rather than short-term relief.

Practical Tools for Daily Emotional Regulation

Let us further expand the toolkit for practicing emotional regulation in daily life:

1. **"The STOP Method"**
   - **S**: Stop what you are doing.
   - **T**: Take a breath.
   - **O**: Observe what you are thinking and feeling.
   - **P**: Proceed with intention.

   This technique integrates mindfulness and regulation, providing space for reappraisal (Kabat-Zinn, 1990).

2. **Emotion Tracking**
   - Journaling emotions with specific words and triggers builds awareness over time and reduces impulsivity.

3. **Reframing Inner Dialogue**
   - Replace harsh internal scripts with compassionate and empowering ones (Beck, 2011).

4. **Somatic Check-ins**
   - Ask: "Where do I feel this emotion in my body?" Bringing attention to the physical can

reduce rumination and reconnect mind and body.

Emotional Mastery as the Story We Choose to Tell

To master our emotions is not to mute them but to learn their language—and to speak it with intention. Emotional regulation is the ongoing practice of authorship over our internal world.

It is not about suppressing anger, sadness, or fear; rather, it is about pausing long enough to ask, *"What is this feeling trying to tell me?"*

When we name our emotions with clarity, we reclaim our power to choose our response instead of being swept away by reactivity.

Think of emotional mastery as the art of editing a story in progress. Just as a writer reviews a first draft, notices the emotional tone, and adjusts the language to create deeper meaning, we too can revisit our internal narrative. A difficult day can become a lesson in patience. A moment of fear can transform into a call for courage. Through this reframing, we align our experiences with growth instead of struggle.

Scientific research in neuroscience explains why this technique works. Naming an emotion stimulates the prefrontal cortex, the area of the brain involved in logic and self-control, while calming the amygdala, which triggers our instinctive fight-or-flight reactions. As Siegel famously states, "Name it to tame it" (2012), describing how this process shifts us from impulsive reactions to deliberate reflection, enhancing emotional balance and mental focus.

Emotional regulation, then, becomes a form of storytelling—one in which we are both the narrator and the protagonist. While we cannot always control the events in our lives, we *can* shape how we interpret and respond to them.

This is the essence of conscious living: choosing the meaning we assign to our emotions, moment by moment. In doing so, we not only master our emotions—we transform them into instruments of clarity, connection, and courage.

Key Takeaways

1. **Emotions as Messengers:**
   Emotions are signals that communicate valuable information about our inner world, guiding us to understand our needs, values, and boundaries. Rather than viewing emotions as obstacles, embrace them as helpful

messengers offering insights into how we experience the world around us.

2. **The Role of Emotional Regulation:**

   Emotional regulation involves recognizing, understanding, and managing emotional responses in a healthy and constructive way. It is not about suppressing emotions but about responding to them mindfully, allowing us to navigate life's challenges without being overwhelmed.

3. **The Mind-Body Connection:**

   Emotions are not just mental experiences; they also manifest physically in the body. Understanding the physical sensations that accompany emotions helps us become more attuned to our emotional state and prevents emotional reactions from escalating.

4. **Emotions and Decision-Making:**

   Unregulated emotions can cloud judgment and impair decision-making. Learning to regulate   emotional responses enables clearer thinking, better choices, and more thoughtful actions in both personal and professional contexts.

5. **Mindfulness and Emotional Awareness:**

   Mindfulness practices increase awareness of emotional states, providing space to observe feelings without immediately reacting. This awareness allows for reflection and intentional responses to emotions.

6. **Building Emotional Resilience:**

   Mastering emotional regulation fosters resilience, helping us bounce back from setbacks, manage stress effectively, and maintain balance even during difficult circumstances.

7. **Self-Compassion and Emotional Health:**

   Embracing self-compassion is essential for emotional regulation. By treating ourselves with kindness and understanding, we can better navigate our emotional experiences without judgment.

By mastering emotional regulation, we not only improve our emotional health but also build a foundation for healthier relationships, clearer thinking, and a more fulfilling life.

Reflection Questions

1. What are the most common emotions you experience throughout the day, and how do they typically influence your behavior and decision-making?
   Reflect on how your emotions show up in your daily life and the impact they have on your choices, interactions, and actions.

2. When you feel an intense emotion (e.g., anger, sadness, anxiety), what physical sensations do you notice in your body?

   Reflect on how your body responds to emotions and how this awareness can help you understand your emotional triggers.

3. Can you recall a time when you allowed your emotions to guide you in a positive direction? What did you learn from that experience?

   Think about a situation where your emotions led to a constructive outcome and what insights you gained about emotional awareness and regulation.

4. How do you typically respond to emotions you find challenging or uncomfortable? Are there any patterns or habits you would like to change?

   Reflect on your usual emotional responses and explore whether these habits serve you or if there is room for healthier emotional regulation practices.

These questions are designed to deepen your emotional awareness and encourage thoughtful reflection on how emotions shape your life and responses.

✦ Chapter Summary

Chapter 17 discusses the essential practice of emotional regulation and its profound impact on mental and physical well-being. It emphasizes the importance of mastering the brain-body connection to navigate emotions with clarity, balance, and resilience. By learning to regulate emotions, we reclaim control over our responses to life's challenges, shifting from reactive to intentional action.

Emotional regulation is not about suppressing or ignoring feelings but about understanding and managing them in ways that promote well-being. This chapter reveals how emotional responses often stem from unconscious thought patterns and narratives that can either empower or hinder us. Recognizing these patterns is the first step toward rewriting them, creating a more balanced and centered emotional state.

The chapter further highlights the role of the brain-body connection, demonstrating how mindfulness practices, deep breathing, and body awareness techniques can influence emotional experiences. When we become attuned to bodily sensations and reactions, we gain the ability to interrupt automatic responses, creating space for thoughtful, measured reactions.

Through practical exercises and strategies, Chapter 17 provides tools for enhancing emotional resilience, improving self-regulation, and fostering a healthier, more balanced emotional life. These skills are particularly useful for managing stress, anxiety, and emotional triggers, fostering a sense of empowerment and self-mastery. Stronger emotional regulation leads to more harmonious relationships, better decision-making, and enhanced overall well-being.

Finally, the chapter connects emotional regulation to personal growth. As we learn to manage emotions effectively, we open ourselves to greater self-awareness, personal transformation, and the ability to face challenges with calm and purpose. This chapter empowers you to take charge of your emotional responses, strengthening the mind-body connection to support lasting change and fulfillment.

Chapter 18

Integrating Emotional Regulation into Identity, Connection, and Caregiving

"When we learn to regulate our emotions, we don't just change how we feel—we transform how we live, love, and lead."
— Cassandra Williams

In this chapter, we will uncover the transformative power of emotional regulation and its deep connection to living authentically and building resilience. Our emotional states not only shape our responses to life's challenges but also define the relationships we build with others and ourselves. By learning how to regulate emotions effectively, we can unlock our true potential, cultivating a life aligned with our values and goals.

You will discover the vital role emotional regulation plays in fostering resilience, especially in times of stress and adversity. Through empowered language and mindful reframing of our inner narratives, we gain the ability to shift our perspective and respond to challenges in a way that enhances our strength and emotional well-being.

This chapter will guide you through the process of making micro-shifts—small but impactful changes in how we think, speak, and respond. These shifts accumulate over time, leading to profound growth and transformation. We will also examine the science behind self-talk and its direct connection to building resilience, providing practical tools for cultivating healthier, more empowering inner dialogue.

By the end of this chapter, you will have a deeper understanding of how emotional regulation contributes to resilience and authenticity in your life. You will also be equipped with actionable strategies to reframe your story, empowering yourself to face life with confidence and clarity.

Emotional Regulation and Authentic Living

Authenticity requires alignment between our internal experience and external expression. Yet many people wear masks, suppressing true emotions to gain approval or avoid conflict. Emotional regulation helps bridge that gap—not by silencing emotion but by creating space between stimulus and response, allowing one to choose how to express authentically (Gross, 2015).

For instance, a person who feels anger during a disagreement might pause, breathe, and say, "*I feel disrespected and I'd like to understand where this is coming from,*" rather than lash out or shut down. That expression is both honest and regulated.

Authenticity without regulation can feel like emotional dumping. Regulation without authenticity leads to repression and disconnection. The integration of both allows for vulnerable truth expressed with intention—a hallmark of psychological health (Kernis & Goldman, 2006).

Example:

A team leader receives negative feedback and feels defensive. Instead of reacting with denial or blaming others, she regulates her emotion, reflects, and replies: "*I didn't expect that feedback, and I need some time to reflect. I want to show up better for the team.*" That response is both emotionally honest and constructive.

Resilience Through Emotional Regulation

Resilience is often misunderstood as toughness or emotional invulnerability. In reality, resilience is about flexibility—the ability to bend without breaking. It is not the absence of stress or adversity, but the capacity to recover, adapt, and grow through it. At the heart of resilience lies emotional regulation—the skill of staying grounded, composed, and resourceful even when life feels overwhelming (Tugade & Fredrickson, 2004).

When people encounter stress, their emotional response determines whether they spiral into reactivity or find a path forward. Those with strong emotional regulation can acknowledge difficult emotions without becoming consumed by them. They engage in cognitive reappraisal—the act of reinterpreting a negative event in a way that fosters hope and meaning (Gross & John, 2003). For instance, instead of thinking "*I failed, and I'll never recover,*" they might reframe it as "This was painful, but it's also a chance to learn and grow."

According to research by Bonanno (2004), resilient individuals demonstrate an ability to remain optimistic, emotionally expressive, and socially connected in times of crisis. They tend to recover more quickly from setbacks and are less likely to develop long-term psychological symptoms such as depression or PTSD. Aldao et al. (2010) also found that emotion regulation strategies like acceptance, problem-solving, and positive reappraisal are linked to lower levels of anxiety and more adaptive coping in the face of adversity.

Emotional regulation acts as a protective shield amid life's challenges. When we identify and articulate our feelings, we can prevent overwhelming emotions from spiraling into anxiety or despair. Dr. Dan Siegel's insight—"Name it to tame it"— captures this well: putting emotions into words activates our reasoning brain, dampening the emotional brain's intensity and enabling calmer, more empowered choices (Siegel, 2012).

Real-Life Example:

Take Martha, a young professional who loses her job unexpectedly. Initially, she feels a surge of fear and shame. Without emotional regulation, she might spiral into self-doubt, isolate herself, or make impulsive decisions. But instead, Martha practices mindfulness to observe her feelings, journals to clarify her thoughts, and reframes her experience: *"This is scary, but maybe it's also a chance to redirect my career toward something more fulfilling."* Within weeks, she is networking, exploring new paths, and even reconnecting with joy.

Her bounce-back is not because she avoided emotion—it is because she faced it with intention.

Empowered Language and Resilience

Language does more than communicate—it shapes reality. The words we choose to describe life's challenges directly influence how we perceive them, feel about them, and ultimately respond. Empowered language activates resilience by shifting our mindset from helplessness to a sense of control and possibility. When we reframe adversity with words that reflect strength, growth, and possibility, we change our internal narrative—and that narrative becomes a powerful tool for bouncing back.

Resilience is not just about "toughing it out." It is about how we interpret experiences, and that interpretation often starts with language (Seligman, 2011). Saying *"I'm failing"* invokes shame and finality, while saying *"I'm navigating something difficult"* affirms both the reality of the challenge and your capacity to move through it. Language becomes a bridge between emotion and action—between feeling stuck and finding momentum.

Reframing the Story

Cognitive-behavioral psychology has long shown that our thoughts influence our feelings and behaviors (Beck, 2011). Empowered language helps us reframe negative thoughts, which enhances emotional regulation and decision-making. When we speak in ways that support growth, even amidst pain, we create psychological flexibility—a key component of resilience (Kashdan & Rottenberg, 2010).

Disempowered Language:

- "I can't do this."
- "This always happens to me."
- "I'm not good enough."

Empowered Language:

- "This is tough, but I'm learning."
- "This moment doesn't define me."
- "I've made it through hard things before."

Micro-Shifts that Matter

Empowered language doesn't require sweeping affirmations or forced positivity. It starts with subtle shifts—moment-by-moment reframes that soften inner criticism and strengthen hope.

Example 1: After making a mistake at work

- Instead of: "I always mess things up."
- Try: "I made an error, but I can learn from this and grow stronger."

Example 2: When facing a major life change

- Instead of: "My life is falling apart."
- Try: "Things are uncertain, but I'm finding my way, one step at a time."

Example 3: During emotional overwhelm

- Instead of: "I'm breaking down."
- Try: "I'm feeling a lot right now, and that's okay. I can take a breath and keep going."

The Science of Self-Talk and Resilience

Self-talk is not just an internal monologue—it is a powerful tool that shapes our emotional experiences, mental resilience, and even our physiological responses to stress. The way we speak to ourselves in moments of difficulty determines not only how we cope but also how we heal and grow. Research consistently shows that positive and compassionate self-talk is strongly associated with enhanced emotional regulation, better problem-solving skills, and improved long-term mental health (Neff, 2011).

Rather than bypassing pain with forced positivity, healthy self-talk acknowledges emotional truths while creating space for growth, understanding, and compassion. It is not about pretending everything is okay. It is about saying, *"This is hard, and I'm allowed to feel it—but I am also capable of finding my way through."*

How Self-Talk Influences the Brain and Body

Neurologically, self-talk influences the limbic system (our emotional brain) and the prefrontal cortex (our rational brain), which together play a key role in emotional regulation. When we use empowering language, we activate the prefrontal cortex, which allows us to pause, reflect, and choose a more measured response. In contrast, negative and self-critical inner dialogue can keep us locked in amygdala-driven reactivity, increasing stress hormones like cortisol and reinforcing anxious or depressive loops (Siegel, 2020).

In essence, compassionate self-talk calms the nervous system and invites cognitive clarity, while harsh or judgmental self-talk can dysregulate the system and impair decision-making.

Cognitive Reappraisal: The Power of Reframing

One of the most studied and effective emotion regulation strategies is cognitive reappraisal—the process of changing how we interpret a situation to alter its emotional impact (Gross & John, 2003). This is where empowered language becomes a vital skill.

For example, when facing a setback, someone might think:

- "This proves I'm not good enough."
  That thought triggers shame, hopelessness, and withdrawal.

But with cognitive reappraisal, using empowered self-talk, the same person might reframe the thought as:

- "This is a setback, but it is also feedback. I can use it to grow."
  This interpretation supports resilience, curiosity, and engagement.

Studies have shown that individuals who use cognitive reappraisal are more likely to maintain psychological well-being, have better interpersonal relationships, and experience less anxiety and depression (Troy et al., 2010).

Self-Compassion as a Resilience Strategy

Self-compassion—a core element of empowered self-talk—is not indulgent or weak. In fact, it has been shown to buffer the effects of trauma, reduce shame, and increase motivation (Neff, 2003; Germer & Neff, 2013). People high in self-compassion respond to failure not by giving up, but by reflecting on what they can learn and trying again. This mindset is essential to grit, perseverance, and long-term success.

"You can't hate yourself into growth. But you can speak to yourself with honesty and care—and that's where transformation begins."

Real-Life Example: Rewiring the Narrative

Imagine someone experiencing burnout and exhaustion.

Disempowered Self-Talk:

- "I can't handle this. I'm weak. I should be doing better."

Result: Increased stress, guilt, and disengagement.

Empowered Reappraisal:
- "I'm overwhelmed because I care deeply and have taken on too much. It's okay to rest and reset. My value isn't based on how productive I am."

Result: Emotional regulation, self-compassion, and renewed clarity.

Practical Application: Rewiring Through Repetition

The brain is constantly forming and reinforcing neural pathways—and language helps guide this process. The more often you use empowered self-talk, the more those pathways become your default (Doidge, 2007). This is the neuroscience of neuroplasticity in action. Every time you reframe a negative inner narrative, you are literally rewiring your brain toward resilience and self-trust.

Try This Practice: "Catch and Reframe"

1. **Notice** a moment of negative self-talk (e.g., "I'm messing everything up.")
2. **Pause** and breathe.
3. **Reframe** with a compassionate truth (e.g., "I'm having a hard time, but I'm doing my best with what I know right now.")

Do this consistently, and your brain will begin to default to more empowered, balanced thinking.

Real-Life Application: From Breakdown to Breakthrough

Scenario: After losing a job, someone spirals into self-criticism and fear.

- **Disempowered response**: "I'm a failure. No one will hire me. I'll never recover."
- **Empowered reframe**: "This is incredibly painful, and I'm scared—but I've faced tough transitions before. This may be opening the door to something that aligns better with who I'm becoming."

This simple linguistic shift does not erase grief or difficulty, but it opens the nervous system to possibility, rather than shutting it down with fear (Siegel, 2020). Over time, this practice rewires the brain toward resilience.

Takeaway Affirmations

- "I can feel deeply and still move forward."
- "My words have power. I choose ones that support my strength."
- "This challenge is shaping me, not defining me."
- "Even in uncertainty, I can speak possibility."
- "I am good enough."

Emotional Regulation in Relationships

Emotional regulation plays a central role in the health and longevity of relationships. Whether romantic, familial, or platonic, relationships thrive not through the absence of conflict, but through the presence of emotional awareness, empathy, and clarity.

Regulated individuals are better equipped to navigate disagreement without resorting to blame, defensiveness, or avoidance—key dynamics that can erode trust over time.

Research by Gottman and Silver (2015) underscores the importance of emotional regulation in romantic partnerships. In their longitudinal studies of couples, they found that the ability to stay calm and connected during conflict—rather than escalating into criticism or shutting down—was one of the strongest predictors of marital satisfaction and long-term stability. This ability to regulate, often referred to as "self-soothing," protects partners from emotional flooding, a state in which physiological arousal (like an increased heart rate or tense muscles) impairs rational thought and effective communication.

Emotional flooding can transform genuine feelings into harmful behaviors. For instance:

- **Anger** may morph into attack: *"You always ignore me when I talk!"*
- **Sadness** may become withdrawal: *"You wouldn't understand anyway."*
- **Fear** can turn into control: *"If you walk away, I won't survive."*

Without regulation, these patterns create cycles of disconnection and misunderstanding. But when individuals pause to self-regulate—through breathing, mindfulness, or naming their emotions—they create the space to respond rather than react. The same emotional experiences, reframed with language and compassion, foster closeness and healing:

- *"I feel angry because I don't feel heard. Can we slow down?"*
- *"I'm feeling vulnerable and need some reassurance right now."*
- *"This situation scares me. Can we talk about how we're both feeling?"*

Emotionally intelligent communication starts with attunement—not just to others, but to oneself. According to emotionally focused therapy (EFT) frameworks, when individuals can stay present with their internal emotional states, they are more likely to co-regulate with others, creating secure bonds based on trust and mutual responsiveness (Johnson, 2008).

Ultimately, emotional regulation is not about suppressing feelings but expressing them with intention. It invites us to slow down, connect with ourselves, and speak in a way that deepens rather than damages connection.

Example:

During a heated argument, one partner says, "Let's take a five-minute break so I can calm down and come back to this with a clear head." This act of emotional regulation protects the relationship and models emotional maturity.

Parenting with Emotional Regulation

Emotional regulation is one of the most powerful tools a parent can cultivate—not just for their own well-being, but for shaping the emotional development of their children. Research consistently shows that children internalize emotional patterns not through instruction, but through observation. In other words, kids learn how to feel and respond to emotions by watching how their caregivers react in moments of stress, joy, disappointment, or conflict.

When parents model emotional regulation—pausing to breathe before reacting, using words to express feelings, or calming themselves during conflict—they create an environment of psychological safety. This kind of environment allows children to feel secure enough to explore their own emotional world without fear of punishment or shame. It also fosters resilience, emotional intelligence, and self-awareness.

In contrast, parents who respond with emotional outbursts, chronic irritability, withdrawal, or dismissal may unintentionally teach children that emotions are dangerous, shameful, or invalid. According to Eisenberg et al. (2005), these patterns of emotionally dysregulated parenting are strongly associated with children's difficulties in emotional expression, lower self-worth, and increased anxiety or behavioral challenges.

Regulated parenting does not mean being emotionally perfect—it means being emotionally present. It is about owning your emotional experience, using language to name what is happening, and demonstrating strategies to navigate intense feelings. For example, a parent might say, *"I'm feeling really overwhelmed right now, so I'm going to take a moment to breathe and calm down before we keep talking."* This simple act of transparency models emotional literacy and gives children a real-time example of healthy regulation.

Ultimately, when parents hold space for emotional discomfort—whether it is a toddler's tantrum or a teenager's frustration—they teach children that emotions are not threats to be silenced, but messages to be understood. By staying grounded, responsive, and compassionate, parents lay the foundation for their children's lifelong emotional well-being.

Example:

A child throws a tantrum in a store. An unregulated parent might yell, "*Stop it now, or you're getting punished!*" A regulated parent might say, "*I see you're upset. Let's breathe together. I know you wanted that toy, and it's hard to hear no.*"

This approach builds connection, emotional literacy, and internal regulation skills in children.

Even when a parent loses control, repairing with emotional honesty is powerful. Saying, "*I was really frustrated earlier and I didn't handle that well. I'm sorry,*" models humility and emotional responsibility.

The Interconnected Cycle: Emotional Regulation as the Foundation of Well-Being

Authenticity, resilience, relationships, and parenting are often viewed as distinct pillars of psychological and emotional well-being. However, they are intricately connected through one essential skill: emotional regulation. Rather than operating in isolation, these domains form a dynamic feedback loop in which each supports and reinforces the others. Emotional regulation acts as the central axis, allowing these areas of life to remain balanced, responsive, and growth-oriented (Gross, 2015).

- Authenticity is the capacity to be honest and congruent with your internal experience. It begins with the ability to name and regulate your emotions rather than suppress or distort them. Emotional regulation enables authenticity by providing psychological safety to express feelings without fear of judgment or shame (Brown, 2012).

- That authenticity becomes a resilience asset. When people acknowledge their feelings truthfully, they can respond rather than react. This honesty encourages cognitive flexibility and adaptability, key features of resilience (Tugade & Fredrickson, 2004). In moments of adversity, emotionally regulated individuals are better equipped to process difficult emotions and pivot toward growth.

- Resilience, in turn, plays a crucial role in relationships. It buffers individuals during conflict and prevents emotional flooding. According to Gottman & Silver (2015), couples who regulate their emotions are more likely to repair ruptures effectively, maintain emotional intimacy, and express needs without blame. The same applies to friendships and workplace dynamics— emotionally regulated people foster safer, more responsive interpersonal spaces.

- In parenting, emotional regulation is both modeled and transmitted. Children observe not only how parents handle stress but also how they express or suppress emotions. Parents who can calmly validate their child's feelings while managing their own model emotional intelligence, which research shows is foundational for a child's socio-emotional development (Eisenberg et al., 2005; Siegel & Bryson, 2011).

In essence, a regulated mind creates a regulated life. These domains continuously influence one another—when one strengthens, the others are lifted. For example, a parent who becomes more emotionally aware (authenticity) is better equipped to manage conflict with their child (resilience), which strengthens the parent-child bond (relationship), and reinforces emotionally intelligent parenting.

For Example:

Consider Lisa, a teacher and mother of two, who is learning to manage anxiety through mindfulness and journaling. As she becomes more emotionally attuned (authenticity), she notices patterns of stress that previously led to irritability at home. By practicing deep breathing before reacting (resilience), she begins responding to her children with curiosity rather than criticism. Her relationships become warmer, and her children begin mirroring her calm tone and self-reflection skills. Lisa's growth in one domain has cascaded into all others, forming a loop of mutual reinforcement.

Presence Over Perfection

Importantly, the goal is not emotional perfection but presence—to remain grounded and aware, even when emotions are intense or confusing. Emotional regulation offers the space to pause, reflect, and choose language and behavior that aligns with core values rather than reactivity. As Kabat-Zinn (1994) writes, "You can't stop the waves, but you can learn to surf." Being present allows us to ride life's waves with greater skill and self-compassion.

Practical Integration Tools

1. **Emotion Check-In Rituals**

   Start meetings or family dinners with "one word for how you feel today."

2. **Reframing Journals**

   Write about a difficult experience and practice rewriting it through a lens of regulation and growth.

3. **Mindful Pausing**

   Implement a three-breath rule before responding during tension.

The Regulated Life Is the Empowered Life

To truly live, we must allow ourselves to feel—not just deeply, but wisely. Emotional regulation isn't about suppressing emotions; it's about choosing how we engage with them. Through this mindful approach, authenticity flows more freely, resilience becomes a steady anchor, relationships gain trust and depth, and parenting evolves into a transformative experience.

In the stories we tell through our regulated responses, we do not just change our mood—we shape our reality.

Key Takeaways

1. **Emotional Regulation Is Foundational**

   Emotional regulation is not an isolated skill—it underpins many areas of psychological well-being, including how authentically we live, how resiliently we respond to adversity, how we maintain healthy relationships, and how we parent with intention.

2. **Authenticity Begins with Emotional Awareness**

   Being true to yourself requires recognizing and regulating your emotions so you can act in alignment with your values rather than reacting from unconscious patterns or societal pressures.

3. **Resilience Is Fueled by Regulation**

   The ability to bounce back from setbacks and navigate challenges with adaptability is rooted in the ability to manage intense emotions like fear, frustration, or grief without becoming overwhelmed by them.

4. **Healthy Relationships Require Emotional Attunement**

   Relationships flourish when individuals can express their emotions with clarity and empathy. Emotional regulation supports communication, reduces reactivity, and creates space for mutual respect and understanding.

5. **Emotionally Regulated Parenting Models Security**

   Children learn how to navigate their own emotions by observing how caregivers respond to stress and emotional triggers. Parents who model emotional regulation foster emotional safety, trust, and emotional intelligence in their children.

6. **Integration Creates a Feedback Loop**

Each domain—authenticity, resilience, relationships, and parenting—reinforces the others. Emotional regulation binds them together, creating a life that is more grounded, responsive, and aligned with one's deeper purpose.

7. **Presence Over Perfection**

    The goal is not to never feel difficult emotions, but to be present with them—naming, understanding, and choosing how to respond. This mindful approach to emotional regulation enhances self-awareness, compassion, and growth.

Practical Exercises

1. The "Name It to Tame It" Daily Practice

Each day, pause for 3–5 minutes to identify and name your current emotional state. Write it down using precise emotional vocabulary (e.g., "disappointed" instead of "sad," "overwhelmed" instead of "stressed").

- *Why it works: Naming emotions activates the prefrontal cortex, helping you regulate instead of react.*
- *Link to Integration: Cultivates emotional awareness for authenticity, resilience, and relational clarity.*

2. Emotion–Value Alignment Journaling

At the end of each day, reflect on a situation where your emotional reaction aligned (or did not align) with your core values. Ask:

- *What did I feel?*
- *How did I respond?*
- *Did my response reflect my values?*
- *What would I change next time?*
- *Why it works: Increases alignment between emotions, behavior, and identity.*
- *Link to Integration: Strengthens authenticity and intentional parenting.*

3. Co-Regulation Check-Ins (With Partner or Child)

Schedule regular emotional check-ins with someone close to you (partner, child, friend). Use prompts like:

- *"What's been on your heart lately?"*
- *"How can I support you emotionally today?"*

- *Why it works: Builds trust and models emotional safety.*
- *Link to Integration: Deepens connection and emotional regulation in relationships and parenting.*

4. Resilience Reappraisal Exercise

Write about a recent emotional challenge. Then, reframe it using empowering language:

- *What did this teach me?*
- *How did I grow from it?*
- *What strength did I discover in myself?*
- *Why it works: Trains the brain to find growth in adversity.*
- *Link to Integration: Builds resilience through cognitive reappraisal and emotional regulation.*

5. The Breath + Pause Method

Before responding to emotional triggers, pause and take 3 deep breaths. Ask:

- *What am I feeling?*

- *What's the story I'm telling myself?*
- *What's the most compassionate response I can offer—to myself and others?*
- *Why it works: Activates the parasympathetic nervous system and centers the mind.*
- *Link to Integration: Supports emotional presence in parenting, relationships, and decision-making.*

Reflection Questions

1. How does your current emotional regulation practice support or challenge your ability to live authentically?

• In what ways do you suppress, ignore, or override your emotions to meet expectations?

• How might emotional honesty strengthen your sense of self?

2. Think of a recent challenge—how did your emotional response impact your resilience?

• Did you react or respond?

• What emotional tools did you use (or wish you had used) to navigate that moment?

3. How does your ability to regulate emotions affect your closest relationships?

• Are there patterns of conflict, withdrawal, or emotional flooding?

• How would your relationships shift if you led with emotional clarity and self-awareness?

4.   In what ways do you model emotional regulation for the people who look up to you (children, students, employees, etc.)?
• What lessons about emotions are you consciously or unconsciously   teaching?
• How can you be more intentional in modeling emotional resilience?

5.   What does a "regulated life" look like to you?
• How would it feel in your body, your mind, and your relationships?
• What small daily practices could help you move closer to that vision?

✦ Chapter Summary

Chapter 18 emphasizes the integration of emotional regulation as a core foundation for living authentically, building resilience, and fostering healthier relationships, including the critical role it plays in parenting. This chapter builds on the principles of emotional regulation, illustrating how mastering this skill can empower us to live more intentional, grounded lives, enabling deeper connections with ourselves and others.

At the heart of this chapter is the understanding that emotional regulation is not merely a tool for managing stress but a fundamental practice that shapes our authenticity and personal growth. When we can regulate our emotions effectively, we create space for vulnerability, allowing us to be true to ourselves, express our feelings, and make decisions that align with our values. Emotional regulation empowers us to stay connected with our true essence, free from the distortions of reactive, unchecked emotional responses.

The chapter considers how emotional regulation is the bedrock for resilience, offering the ability to bounce back from adversity with greater strength and flexibility. By cultivating emotional awareness and learning to navigate difficult emotions, we develop the resilience necessary to face life's challenges with a sense of calm and inner strength. This resilience, in turn, fosters a more authentic and empowered self, capable of embracing life's uncertainties with confidence.

In the realm of relationships, emotional regulation is key to creating deeper, more meaningful connections. The ability to stay present and respond thoughtfully, rather than react impulsively, leads to more compassionate and effective communication, improving trust and understanding with others. Healthy emotional regulation promotes empathy, patience, and a greater capacity for forgiveness, allowing relationships to thrive on mutual respect and emotional safety.

Additionally, the chapter explores the transformative impact emotional regulation has on parenting. By modeling emotional regulation, parents can help their children develop the same skills, fostering emotional intelligence, resilience, and a stable sense of self. Emotionally regulated parents are better equipped to respond to their children's needs with patience, understanding, and compassion, creating a nurturing environment for healthy emotional development.

Ultimately, Chapter 18 presents emotional regulation as a crucial skill for holistic growth—one that impacts not only personal development but also our relationships and ability to parent effectively. By mastering emotional regulation, we can create a more balanced, empowered, and connected life, where our actions, decisions, and relationships reflect our true selves. The chapter encourages you to integrate emotional regulation as a lifelong practice, unlocking the potential for greater well-being, authenticity, and resilience.

Chapter 19

The Language of Hope and Vision: Creating Daily Practices to Reinforce New Scripts

"The best way to shape your future is by intentionally creating it through the language you choose and the vision you hold."
— Alice Reed Murphy

In this chapter, we look into how language serves as a powerful tool for shaping our future through hope, vision, and consistent practice. Language is not merely a form of communication but a creative force that influences how we perceive ourselves and the world around us. By choosing hopeful and vision-centered language, such as *"I am becoming"* or *"This challenge is shaping my strength,"* we generate a sense of forward momentum that anchors us in the future we are actively building. Rather than denying pain or struggle, hopeful language emphasizes growth, resilience, and the belief in change (Snyder, 2002). This chapter also emphasizes the importance of daily practices, such as affirmations, journaling, and setting intentions, to reinforce new, empowering scripts. These practices not only help rewire the brain by creating new neural pathways (Doidge, 2007) but also serve as constant reminders of the empowering narrative we are choosing to live. Furthermore, we discuss the process of reframing limiting beliefs, which are often reinforced by negative self-talk. By shifting language patterns from fixed, disempowering beliefs to growth-oriented statements, we can challenge these beliefs and unlock new possibilities for personal growth (Dweck, 2006). This chapter also highlights how societal and familial narratives can shape our internal dialogue, often limiting our potential. By adopting new, empowering language and challenging inherited scripts, we reclaim our power and foster self-compassion (Neff, 2003). Finally, we explore how language is used in therapy and coaching to facilitate positive change, emphasizing the role of language in reprogramming our beliefs and behaviors to create a more fulfilling life (Beck, 2011). Ultimately, this chapter illustrates that the words we choose not only reflect who we are but shape who we are becoming, offering a gateway to transformation.

The Language of Hope and Vision

Language is more than communication—it is a creative force that shapes how we see ourselves and the world. When we speak with hope, we generate a sense of forward momentum, possibility, and belief in change. Vision-based language—phrases like *"I am becoming," "I trust the process,"* or *"This challenge is shaping my strength"*—anchors us in the future we are building, rather than the past we are escaping. Hopeful language is not about denying pain; it is about choosing to narrate life in a way that honors growth and resilience. As Snyder (2002) noted in his work on hope theory, hopeful individuals do not just wish for a better future—they actively create it by imagining pathways forward and believing in their capacity to get there.

Creating Daily Practices to Reinforce New Scripts

Lasting change does not come from one breakthrough—it comes from intentional, repeated actions that reinforce new narratives. Daily practices like morning affirmations, journaling with empowering language, setting intentions, and reflecting on small wins help rewrite your internal script over time. These rituals not only strengthen the neural pathways associated with self-belief and motivation (Doidge, 2007), but also serve as tangible reminders of the story you are consciously choosing to live. Repetition creates familiarity—and familiarity builds identity. When you regularly speak and act in alignment with your desired narrative, you begin to embody it. As with any new language, fluency comes through consistent practice.

The Role of Language in Overcoming Limiting Beliefs

Limiting beliefs are often deeply ingrained, subconscious assumptions we hold about ourselves, others, or the world. These beliefs shape our perceptions and influence our choices, often preventing us from reaching our full potential. For example, a person might believe that they are not intelligent enough to succeed in their career or that they are unworthy of love. These limiting beliefs are perpetuated by the language we use—both internally and externally—which reinforces these negative perceptions.

The language of limiting beliefs tends to be absolute, deterministic, and disempowering. Words such as "*I can't,*" "*I never,*" and "*I'm not good enough*" are common expressions that perpetuate a fixed mindset (Dweck, 2006). This kind of language reinforces the belief that change is impossible, trapping individuals in cycles of fear, avoidance, and self-doubt.

Conversely, the language of empowerment has the potential to disrupt these limiting beliefs and transform them into beliefs that promote growth, possibility, and change. By shifting from fixed language patterns to growth-oriented language, we begin to challenge and reframe these limiting beliefs, opening up new possibilities for growth and success.

The Process of Reframing Limiting Beliefs

Reframing is a powerful tool for recognizing and transforming negative thought patterns into more balanced and supportive perspectives. When we become aware of our limiting beliefs, we can use language to challenge and change them. Reframing involves interpreting a belief or experience from a different perspective, often highlighting positive outcomes or alternative ways of viewing the situation (Beck, 2011).

For example, a person who believes they are not capable of achieving their goals might say, "*I have the ability to learn and grow from every experience.*" This reframed statement acknowledges the potential for learning and personal growth, which is more empowering than the original belief. The reframed language shifts the focus from a fixed mindset to a growth mindset, in which effort and learning lead to success.

Example:

- **Limiting Belief:** "I am terrible with money and will never be able to manage my finances."
- **Reframed Belief:** "I am learning how to manage my finances better every day, and I am improving my financial literacy step by step."

This shift in language does not ignore past failures but instead acknowledges the capacity for change and growth through effort and practice.

The Role of Self-Talk in Overcoming Limiting Beliefs

Self-talk—the internal dialogue we have with ourselves—is a primary source of our limiting beliefs. Negative self-talk typically involves self-criticism, catastrophizing, and labeling ourselves in harsh terms. For example, someone facing a challenging project might think, "*I'll never finish this*" or "*I'm just not good enough for this job.*" These internal statements only perpetuate self-doubt and fear.

In contrast, positive self-talk—using empowering, solution-focused language—helps counteract these limiting beliefs. It involves talking to oneself in a compassionate and encouraging way, emphasizing strengths, abilities, and the potential for growth. Self-compassionate self-talk (Neff, 2011) encourages individuals to view themselves with kindness, even when facing setbacks or challenges, rather than berating themselves for mistakes.

Example:

- **Limiting Belief:** "I always fail when I try something new."

- **Reframed Self-Talk**: "Trying new things helps me learn and grow. I am capable of handling challenges as I move forward."

Research in cognitive psychology and self-affirmation theory (Cohen & Sherman, 2014) suggests that positive self-talk and affirmations help individuals reframe negative beliefs, reduce stress, and enhance their sense of self-efficacy. In practice, using language that affirms one's ability to adapt and overcome challenges strengthens mental resilience and self-confidence.

Shifting Language to Challenge Societal and Family Narratives

The language we use to describe ourselves is often inherited—shaped not just by personal experience but also by the cultural and familial scripts we absorb throughout our lives. Societal norms around gender, race, achievement, and success can subtly encode limiting beliefs into our internal dialogue, reinforcing messages such as *"I must always be strong,"* *"I should never fail,"* or *"My worth depends on what I produce."* These beliefs are frequently mirrored in family narratives, especially in environments where value is placed on perfectionism, control, or self-sacrifice (Hewitt & Flett, 2002; Neff, 2011).

For instance, individuals raised in high-achieving families may internalize a conditional sense of worth based on performance, leading to a narrative like, *"I'm only lovable when I succeed."* This kind of language fosters anxiety, imposter syndrome, and chronic dissatisfaction (Flett & Hewitt, 2002). To shift these patterns, individuals can adopt the language of self-compassion and authenticity, which research shows fosters greater resilience, motivation, and emotional well-being (Neff, 2003). Rewriting the script from *"I must be perfect to be accepted"* to *"I am worthy of love regardless of my performance"* is a powerful act of liberation.

Real-Life Example:

Consider Jeanny, a 32-year-old professional who grew up in a family where achievement was a form of currency. Praise was only given for accomplishments, and vulnerability was seen as weakness. Jeanny's internal narrative became, *"If I slow down, I'll fall behind—and I'll disappoint everyone."* This belief led to burnout and strained relationships. Through therapy and reflective journaling, she began to identify the origins of her self-talk and experiment with new language. She replaced her old script with, *"Rest is not failure. I am allowed to prioritize my well-being,"* and *"My value is not defined by how much I do, but by who I am."* Over time, this shift allowed her to set healthier boundaries and reconnect with her intrinsic worth.

Challenging inherited narratives requires conscious effort and repeated practice. Language reprogramming is not about denial—it is about choosing a vocabulary that empowers rather than restricts. Studies confirm that those who challenge social and familial scripts by reshaping their internal dialogue experience greater psychological flexibility, self-esteem, and autonomy (Chao, 2011; Kashdan & Rottenberg, 2010). In essence, rewriting the words we live by is a radical act of reclaiming one's truth.

Language as a Tool for Empowerment in Therapy and Coaching

In therapeutic settings, language plays a critical role in helping clients reframe their limiting beliefs. Therapists and coaches use language techniques to guide clients in challenging negative self-perceptions and replacing them with more empowering narratives. This approach emphasizes recognizing negative thought patterns and intentionally replacing them with healthier, more constructive self-talk (Beck, 2011). For example, a therapist might help a client identify catastrophic thinking—where the client assumes the worst-case scenario—and replace it with a more balanced and realistic thought. By doing so, the therapist helps the client develop a growth-oriented mindset, one that acknowledges both the difficulties and the opportunities for change.

Example:

- **Client's Limiting Belief**: "If I fail this project, it will be the end of my career."
- **Therapist's Reframing**: "While failing this project might be disappointing, it doesn't define your career. Every successful person has encountered setbacks, and these are opportunities for learning and growth."

Therapists may also encourage clients to use affirmative language by reframing negative statements into positive ones. This language shift allows individuals to focus on their strengths and their capacity to overcome obstacles, rather than being trapped by limiting beliefs.

Language as the Gateway to Transformation

Language is not just a tool for communication—it is the lens through which we interpret reality and define our sense of self. The stories we tell ourselves shape our identities, influence our behaviors, and determine the trajectory of our lives (Pennebaker & Seagal, 1999). Overcoming limiting beliefs, therefore, requires more than just noticing negative thoughts; it involves intentionally reshaping the very words and phrases we use to make meaning of our experiences.

When we say, *"I'm just not good at relationships"* or *"I always mess things up,"* we are not merely stating facts—we are reinforcing narratives that limit growth and possibility. These phrases become cognitive scripts that the brain repeats, embedding them more deeply into our belief system (Beck, 2011). But when we choose to reframe these beliefs using empowering language—such as, *"I am learning how to show up more authentically in relationships,"* or *"Mistakes are part of my growth journey"*—we begin to rewrite the mental programs that once kept us stuck.

The process of reframing focuses on recognizing the link between our thoughts, emotions, and behaviors. Research demonstrates that transforming negative self-talk can significantly alleviate symptoms of anxiety and depression while fostering a greater sense of personal empowerment and control. (Beck, 2011; Hofmann et al., 2012). Empowering language activates parts of the brain associated with hope, motivation, and future planning, helping us envision and move toward a more fulfilling life (Snyder, 2002).

Real-Life Example:

Jason, a 28-year-old nurse, had internalized the belief that he was "too sensitive to succeed." Raised in a household where emotional expression was devalued, he often felt ashamed of his deep feelings. This belief undermined his confidence both at work and in relationships. Through journaling and therapy,

Jason began to reframe his story—from *"I'm too sensitive"* to *"My sensitivity is a strength; it helps me connect, create, and care."* As he embraced this new narrative, he experienced a boost in self-esteem and started advocating for himself more confidently in both personal and professional spaces.

Language is a gateway to transformation because it offers us a way to move from unconscious programming to conscious creation. When we adopt the language of self-compassion, growth, and purpose, we not only challenge outdated narratives but actively build new neural pathways that support healing and expansion (Doidge, 2007). In this way, the words we choose do not just reflect who we are—they shape who we are becoming.

Key Takeaways

1. **The Power of Language in Shaping Our Reality**
   Language plays a critical role in defining our perceptions and shaping our beliefs. The words we use, both internally and externally, have the power to reinforce limiting narratives or create empowering ones. The shift from negative, fixed language to positive, growth-oriented language can significantly transform our emotional and psychological landscape.

2. **Hope and Vision as Tools for Change**

   The language of hope and vision allows us to look beyond our current circumstances and envision a future filled with possibilities. By adopting language that emphasizes potential, growth, and transformation, we can reframe our understanding of challenges and opportunities, fostering a sense of control and empowerment.

3. **Reframing Limiting Beliefs**

   Shifting our language from statements of limitation (e.g., "I can't do this" or "I'm not good enough") to empowering affirmations (e.g., "I am learning and growing" or "I have the ability to adapt") rewrites the mental scripts that have kept us stuck. This practice of reframing enables us to break free from outdated and restrictive narratives, opening the door to new possibilities.

4. **Creating Consistent Daily Practices**

   Reinforcing new, empowering scripts requires daily intentional practice. Just as old narratives were developed through repetition, new stories are reinforced by consistently using language that reflects our goals, aspirations, and values. Daily practices, such as affirmations, journaling, and mindfulness, can help solidify these new narratives and make them a part of our ongoing dialogue.

5. **The Importance of Self-Compassion and Growth-Oriented Language**

   The language of self-compassion and growth emphasizes the importance of accepting oneself in the process of change. Rather than criticizing or judging ourselves for past mistakes, we are encouraged to use language that acknowledges our humanity, celebrates our progress, and motivates us to keep going. This compassionate approach fosters a healthier relationship with ourselves and our development.

6. **Building a Resilient Mindset**

   By consistently using language that reflects hope, vision, and possibility, we cultivate a resilient mindset. This mindset helps us navigate challenges with optimism and perseverance, knowing that setbacks are not failures but opportunities for growth and learning.

7. **Impact on Relationships and Well-Being**

   The language we use not only affects our own experience but also influences how we relate to others. By speaking with hope, clarity, and empathy, we strengthen our relationships and foster an environment of support and mutual growth.

These key takeaways emphasize the importance of intentional language use in creating lasting change and fostering a mindset of hope, resilience, and growth.

Reflection Questions

1. How do the words you use to describe yourself shape your sense of self-worth and identity?

    • Reflect on any limiting beliefs you have internalized and how they may be influencing your life choices.

2. In what areas of your life do you notice a gap between your current narrative and the future you want to create?

    • What language shifts can you make to align your inner script with the future you envision?

3. What empowering affirmations can you start using daily to reinforce your new narrative?

    • Consider how these affirmations can support your growth and how you can integrate them into your routine.

4. How can you reframe past experiences where you felt stuck or powerless?

    • Reflect on a challenging moment in your life and rewrite the narrative using language of growth, resilience, or empowerment.

5. How has societal or family language influenced the way you view success, failure, and self-worth?

    • Are there narratives that you have inherited from others that need to be redefined in a way that aligns with your authentic self?

6. What practices or rituals can you implement in your daily life to consistently reinforce the language of hope, empowerment, and vision?

　• Think about journaling, meditation, or other practices that might support your new narrative.

7. When you face challenges, what language do you use to describe your emotions and reactions?

　• How can you transform negative or limiting language into more positive, resilient, or compassionate statements?

8. How do you want your story to change over the next year?

　• Reflect on the kind of person you want to become and the language you can use to start shifting your trajectory today.

9. In what ways do you see the power of language transforming your relationships, both with yourself and others?

　• How might changing your language influence your communication and emotional connections with others?

10. What small steps can you take today to begin rewriting your story in a way that reflects your fullest potential?

　• Consider actionable steps you can take to begin integrating this new language of hope and vision into your life right now.

These reflection questions encourage deep self-awareness and intentionality, helping readers connect with their personal narratives and identify the language they can use to create meaningful change.

✦ Chapter Summary

Chapter 19 centers on the profound role that hope and vision play in reshaping our personal narratives and reinforcing the new scripts we create for ourselves. By harnessing the transformative power of language, this chapter explores how we can intentionally cultivate hope and a future-oriented vision aligned with our highest potential—fostering empowerment, resilience, and lasting change.

The chapter opens by examining the essential link between language and mindset. Our words shape not only how we see ourselves but also how we interpret the world and what we believe is possible. Through mindful language practices, we can reframe limiting beliefs, develop positive self-talk, and articulate a future that is both uplifting and attainable. Speaking life into our hopes and goals generates the energy, confidence, and momentum needed to pursue them.

A key theme in this chapter is integrating hope and vision into daily life. Rather than treating them as abstract ideals, we're encouraged to ground them in practical routines—such as affirmations, visualization, and intentional speech. These tools help rewire the subconscious mind and reinforce our new internal scripts through repetition and emotional engagement.

By committing to daily practices, we strengthen our ability to stay focused and resilient—even in the face of setbacks. Hope becomes more than a fleeting emotion; it becomes an active, guiding force that fuels forward movement. The chapter emphasizes that hope requires intention and discipline—it's not passive, but something we consciously nurture. When our language and vision align, we begin to see opportunities instead of limitations, empowering us to act with clarity and confidence.

The power of vision is also explored as a driver of aligned action. A clear, compelling vision of who we want to become helps us make decisions that support our purpose. Vision brings direction, motivation, and a sense of coherence to our journey—even when challenges arise.

Finally, Chapter 19 underscores the importance of consistency in rewriting our internal scripts. Just as our old beliefs were formed through repeated messages, our new ones must be reinforced with equal persistence. By consistently using the language of hope and vision, we begin to transform our inner world—and by extension, our outer reality.

This chapter invites readers to embrace daily practices that anchor hope, vision, and intentional language into the rhythm of everyday life. In doing so, we lay the foundation for personal growth and lasting transformation, while strengthening our belief in our ability to shape the story we want to live.

Chapter 20

The Language of Healing: How Words Awaken the Body's Power to Restore Itself

"The body achieves what the mind believes." – Napoleon Hill

The power of language extends far beyond shaping identity and relationships—it plays a vital role in how the body heals. For centuries, spiritual traditions, shamans, and holistic healers have spoken of the body's innate ability to repair itself through focused intention, prayer, and spoken affirmations. Today, modern science is beginning to validate what ancient wisdom has long known: the words we use can influence not only our mental and emotional states, but also our physical health.

In this chapter, we explore the profound connection between language and the body's natural healing processes. You will discover how the thoughts you think and the words you speak—both silently and aloud—can impact your emotional well-being, nervous system, and overall vitality. As we unpack how language interacts with biological systems like the immune response and cellular communication, it becomes clear that healing is not only physical—it is also deeply psychological and energetic.

We will examine fascinating research on the placebo and nocebo effects, revealing how belief and expectation—shaped by internal dialogue—can either accelerate or impede recovery. You will learn how affirmations, visualization, and compassionate self-talk can reduce stress, regulate your physiology, and invite your body back into a state of balance and healing.

Blending ancient healing traditions with modern scientific insights, this chapter will guide you in becoming more intentional with your words. Whether you are navigating illness, emotional wounds, or simply seeking deeper vitality, you will find practical tools to reframe your inner narrative, cultivate hope, and create a supportive internal environment for healing. Through exercises, reflection prompts, and inspiring stories, you will learn how to speak to yourself—and your body—with language that nurtures resilience, restoration, and holistic well-being.

The Healing Power of Belief

The placebo effect is perhaps the most widely studied phenomenon illustrating the body's ability to heal in response to belief. Patients given sugar pills, inactive injections, or fake surgeries often experience real improvements when they believe they are receiving effective treatment (Benedetti, 2009). This effect is not "just in the mind"; it triggers measurable physiological changes—such as increased dopamine, reduced pain perception, and improved immune response.

Language plays a central role in this process. Words of hope, expectation, and encouragement can activate healing pathways in the brain. In contrast, words of fear and hopelessness may exacerbate symptoms or even delay healing (Kaptchuk et al., 2010).

The Hidden Messages in Water

Dr. Masaru Emoto's work in *The Hidden Messages in Water* offers a poetic, though controversial, lens into the relationship between language, intention, and healing. Emoto exposed water samples to various words, prayers, and music, then froze and photographed the resulting ice crystals. Positive words like "love" and "gratitude" formed beautiful, intricate patterns, while negative expressions such as "hate" or "you make me sick" produced distorted, chaotic crystals (Emoto, 2004).

Though Emoto's methodology has been critiqued by the scientific community for lack of rigor, his work has deeply inspired holistic practitioners, particularly because the human body is composed of more than 70% water. If our words can change water, what might they be doing to us?

"Water is the mirror that can show us what we cannot see. It is the blueprint for our reality." — Masaru Emoto

Personal story:

I was deeply struck when I first learned about Dr. Emoto's water experiments. I was fascinated by how the water crystals changed their formations based on the words that were repeatedly spoken to them, as well as the effects words had on his rice experiment. After trying the rice experiment myself, I was able to replicate his results. While I already understood that words have the power to heal or cause harm, seeing it demonstrated through clear and practical research was truly remarkable.

Words and the Nervous System

Neuroscience increasingly supports the profound influence of language on the nervous system. At the heart of this relationship lies the Polyvagal Theory, developed by Dr. Stephen Porges. This theory identifies the vagus nerve—the longest cranial nerve in the body—as a key regulator of the autonomic nervous system. The vagus nerve governs vital functions such as heart rate, digestion, immune response, and even facial expression and vocal tone (Porges, 2011).

When we feel safe, this nerve activates the parasympathetic nervous system, often called the "rest and digest" or "rest and restore" mode, promoting deep healing and emotional regulation.

Words are among the most powerful tools we have to create this felt sense of safety. Calming language, loving affirmations, and gentle tone of voice can down-regulate the stress response—lowering cortisol levels, reducing inflammation, and slowing the heartbeat. In contrast, harsh, critical, or threatening language—even self-directed—can signal danger, activating the sympathetic nervous system and triggering fight, flight, or freeze responses (Siegel, 2012).

This is particularly relevant in the context of trauma recovery. Survivors of trauma often remain in a state of heightened alertness, where the nervous system is stuck in defense mode. Through co-regulation with a trusted person, such as a therapist or loved one, and through repetitive use of safe, soothing language, individuals can begin to rewire their nervous system. This process, often referred to as neuroception, allows the brain to subconsciously detect cues of safety through language, facial expressions, and tone (Dana, 2018).

When we practice positive self-talk, repeat healing affirmations, or engage in mindful inner dialogue, we are not just encouraging ourselves mentally—we are helping our body transition into a state where healing can occur. Words like *"I am safe now," "My body knows how to heal,"* or *"I am supported"* can actually lead to increased vagal tone, which is associated with greater emotional resilience, faster recovery from illness, and improved overall health.

Language is a bridge between mind and body. It has the power to regulate our biology, shift our emotional state, and create the internal safety required for physical and emotional healing to take root.

Real-Life Example: Joe Dispenza

Dr. Joe Dispenza, a chiropractor and neuroscientific researcher, became widely known not only for his recovery story but for the scientific insights it inspired. In 1986, Dispenza was hit by an SUV while competing in a triathlon, fracturing six vertebrae in his spine. Medical experts insisted that spinal fusion surgery was his only option for walking again. Dispenza refused the procedure and instead chose to use the power of his mind—specifically, focused intention, meditation, and affirming language—to initiate healing.

For two hours a day, he visualized the reconstruction of his spinal column. He described entering a meditative state and mentally building his spine, vertebra by vertebra. During this time, he also practiced intentional language, repeating thoughts and affirmations such as "My body is healing," and "I am whole again." After about nine weeks of mental rehearsal and inward focus, he began to regain mobility. Within ten weeks, he was walking. Within twelve weeks, he was back to work, fully recovered—without surgery (Dispenza, 2014).

This remarkable recovery inspired Dispenza to devote his life to studying the intersection of neuroscience, quantum physics, and mind-body medicine. One of his central findings is that thoughts produce measurable biological changes in the brain. Every time we think a thought; we fire a neural circuit. Repeating that thought strengthens the neural pathway—a concept known as Hebbian learning, summarized by the phrase: "neurons that fire together, wire together" (Hebb, 1949).

Dispenza asserts that the language we use—internally and externally—guides what circuits we strengthen. If we consistently say or think, "I'm broken," we reinforce pathways of limitation, illness, and fear. In contrast, language that expresses empowerment—"I am healing," "My body knows what to do," "I am free"—can literally rewire the brain,

405

opening new neuro-pathways that support wellness, coherence, and vitality (Dispenza, 2014).

In his workshops and books, Dispenza also references heart-brain coherence, a state in which the heart and brain rhythms are synchronized. Through focused thought, visualization, breathwork, and uplifting emotional language (like gratitude and compassion), individuals can enter this state. It is associated with enhanced immune response, improved gene expression, and autonomic nervous system regulation (McCraty et al., 2009).

Dispenza's story and subsequent research underscore a powerful truth: "Our words don't just reflect our state—they shape it." When language is aligned with healing intention, it becomes a biological catalyst.

Summary of Dr. Joe Dispenza's Findings:

- Focused thought + intentional language = activation of new neural circuits
- Repetition of healing phrases supports **neuroplasticity**, allowing the brain to rewire around new beliefs
- Emotional states (gratitude, hope, joy) coupled with words enhance **heart-brain coherence**
- Positive internal dialogue affects **gene expression, stress hormones, and immune response**

- Visualization and affirmations can alter the **neurological and energetic signature** of the body, leading to physical healing

Healing Through Conscious Language: Teachings from Thought Leaders

Throughout modern history, a number of spiritual teachers and metaphysical authors have explored the power of language and belief to create, heal, and transform reality. Their teachings align with emerging neuroscience and psychophysiology, affirming that how we speak to ourselves has the power to reshape our lives—emotionally, physically, and energetically.

Neville Goddard: "Assume the Feeling of the Wish Fulfilled"

Neville Goddard (1905–1972), a mystic and author, taught that our inner speech creates our external world. His core message was that imagination, when combined with feeling and belief, manifests into physical experience. According to Goddard, we are always speaking inwardly—often unconsciously—and this inner conversation forms the foundation of our reality.

"Change your conception of yourself and you will automatically change the world in which you live" (Goddard, 1944).

In his book *The Power of Awareness*, Goddard explains that healing occurs when one adopts the assumption of already being well, reinforcing this state through repetition and belief. His method involved affirming in present-tense, emotionally charged language—"I am whole," "I am healed," "It is done"—while visualizing the desired outcome. He insisted that this internal dialogue sends instructions to the subconscious mind, which then organizes reality to match.

Example Practice:

A person struggling with illness might repeat nightly before sleep: *"I am now completely healed. My body is in perfect health."* According to Goddard, the key lies in speaking **as if** the healing has already occurred.

Dr. Wayne Dyer: "You'll See It When You Believe It"

Dr. Wayne Dyer (1940–2015), often called the "father of motivation," echoed similar themes with a psychological and spiritual blend. He taught that words are tools of co-creation, and that what we say repeatedly becomes not only a belief but a lived reality.

Dyer emphasized the importance of conscious self-talk and often said, *"Don't say what you don't want to manifest."* He encouraged replacing phrases like *"I'm always sick,"* or *"I never get better*" with affirmative, empowering language that aligns with the desired outcome.

He often shared his own morning ritual of beginning each day with the phrase: *"I am healthy. I am abundant. I am at peace."* He believed that language, spoken with emotional conviction, could change energy fields and bring the body into harmony.

Louise Hay: "Every Thought We Think is Creating Our Future"

Louise Hay (1926–2017), founder of Hay House Publishing and author of *You Can Heal Your Life*, taught that the body responds to mental patterns, and physical illness often reflects unresolved emotional or psychological issues.

Hay created detailed lists matching physical ailments with metaphysical causes. For example:

- **Back pain** = lack of support
- **Throat issues** = inability to speak your truth
- **Digestive problems** = difficulty "digesting" life experiences

She developed the use of mirror work—repeating affirmations while looking into a mirror—as a method of reprogramming the subconscious mind. A foundational affirmation of hers:

"I am willing to release the pattern in my consciousness that has created this condition. I am healthy, whole, and complete."

Many people reported healing from chronic illness, anxiety, and trauma through her techniques of affirmative language, emotional release, and radical self-love.

Dr. Joseph Murphy: "The Subconscious Accepts What You Repeat"

Dr. Joseph Murphy (1898–1981), author of *The Power of Your Subconscious Mind*, was among the first to popularize the idea that repetitive self-suggestion has the power to shape reality by influencing the subconscious mind.

Murphy taught that the subconscious is neutral and obedient: it accepts what is repeatedly impressed upon it through emotion-laden words and visualization, whether positive or negative.

"Your subconscious mind does not argue with you. It accepts what your conscious mind believes" (Murphy, 1963).

He often recommended affirmations like:

- "Every cell of my body is radiant with health."
- "Divine order governs my life. I am at peace."

Murphy's writings emphasized that spoken words, combined with faith and repetition, could rewire neural patterns, support healing, and attract opportunities.

Practical Tools for Healing with Language

You can use language as a tool for self-repair by:

- **Speaking to your body with love**: Say aloud or write affirmations like, "My body is wise and knows how to heal."
- **Guided imagery**: Narrate a story where light, energy, or warmth is moving through your body to restore each cell.
- **Releasing language**: Let go of phrases like "I'm broken" or "I'll never get better." Replace them with empowering alternatives.
- **Prayer and intention**: Use faith-based language to align your healing with a higher purpose.

Key Takeaways

1. **Language influences the nervous system:**

   Gentle, affirming language can activate the parasympathetic nervous system, supporting physical and emotional healing.

2. **The subconscious mind responds to repeated language:**

   Consistent, emotionally charged affirmations can reprogram deeply embedded beliefs and influence physical well-being.

3. **Self-talk shapes biological response:**

   Words we speak to ourselves influence neurochemical activity and immune function.

4. **Visualization and belief enhance healing:**

   Focused imagery and belief-based language (as shown in Joe Dispenza's recovery) engage neuroplasticity and the body's natural healing mechanisms.

5. **Metaphysical pioneers taught language as medicine:**

   Neville Goddard, Louise Hay, Wayne Dyer, and Joseph Murphy each emphasized that words have the power to transform physical reality.

6. **Emotion + Language = Transformation:**

   It's not just the words, but the emotional energy behind them that imprints the subconscious and initiates healing.

7. **The body listens to your thoughts**:

   What you habitually think and say becomes an internal script that the body often obeys.

8. **Present-tense affirmations are most effective**:

   Speaking as if the healing is already done activates belief and aligns internal states with desired outcomes.

9. **Repetition builds new neural pathways**:

   Neuroplasticity confirms that repeated, conscious language reshapes the brain and behavior.

10. **Intentional language is a form of self-care**:

    Speaking to oneself with compassion, hope, and affirmation fosters not only healing but deep inner safety.

Reflection Questions

1. What kinds of messages do you regularly send to your body through your thoughts and words?

2. Have you ever experienced a physical or emotional shift after changing your internal language?

3. Which of the metaphysical teachings (Goddard, Dyer, Hay, Murphy) resonate most with you, and why?

4. How might your healing process change if you began to speak to your body like it was a trusted friend?

5. What is one phrase you have been telling yourself that might be limiting your healing or growth?

6. How can you turn that phrase into a healing affirmation that supports your desired outcome?

7. What emotions do you feel when you say healing affirmations aloud? How do they affect your body?

8. How could incorporating visualization with language strengthen your healing journey?

9. In what ways have you been unconsciously affirming limitations or illness?

10. What would your self-talk sound like if you fully believed in your body's ability to heal?

✦Chapter Summary

Chapter 20 dives into a powerful intersection of language, the nervous system, and the body's innate ability to heal. Scientific insights like Polyvagal Theory and neuroplasticity show how gentle, supportive language activates the body's healing systems by promoting feelings of safety and calm. Through the real-life story of Dr. Joe Dispenza, we see how visualization and self-directed thought can influence biological repair and transformation.

The teachings of Neville Goddard, Dr. Wayne Dyer, Louise Hay, and Dr. Joseph Murphy expand this understanding by offering timeless practices in using affirmations, present-tense language, and self-concept to influence reality and support healing. These thinkers emphasized that what we repeatedly say—especially with emotion—becomes a command to the subconscious mind and, by extension, to the body.

Ultimately, this chapter reinforces the idea that language is a powerful healing tool—one that is always accessible, always shaping, and capable of creating meaningful change from the inside out.

Conclusion: Rewriting Your Story for a Life of Empowerment and Fulfillment

As we reach the end of this journey, it is crucial to remember that the most transformative tool we possess lies not in the world around us, but within us—and it is found in the language we choose. The stories we tell ourselves shape how we experience life. They have the power to either confine us to a small, limiting existence or to set us free to live fully and authentically. By making the conscious choice to use language that empowers rather than diminishes, we can rewrite the scripts that have held us back, replacing them with ones that encourage growth, healing, and fulfillment.

Rewriting your story is not an overnight process. It requires patience, self-compassion, and consistent effort. But the rewards are profound: deeper authenticity, unshakable resilience, and a life filled with joy and possibility. As you move forward, always remember that your narrative is not static. Every new day is a fresh opportunity to challenge the old stories and embrace the ones you are creating right now.

You are the author of your life, and with each word you choose, you have the power to reshape your future. The story you are living today is only the beginning—through the language of empowerment, your journey toward a more fulfilling, purposeful life is only just starting. Embrace it fully. You hold the pen.

Ready to Go Deeper?

Transform Insight into Action with the Companion Journal

You've taken the first step by exploring the stories that shape your life. Now it's time to **put pen to paper and begin the process of rewriting your script** — one reflection at a time.

Introducing the companion guide:

Rewriting Your Script: *A Guided Companion Journal to Mind Scripts* **by Alice Reed Murphy**

Designed as a powerful extension of this book, this journal offers:

- ❖ **Bonus reflection prompts** aligned with each chapter
- ❖ **Lined pages** for free writing and deep self-exploration
- ❖ **Visualization space** to draw, sketch, or map your thoughts
- ❖ **Inspiring quotes** to encourage and ground your growth
- ❖ **A clean**, minimalist design that creates space to think and feel

"Awareness is the first step, but transformation happens when you begin to engage."

Whether you're journaling daily or working through a chapter each week, this tool will help you **clarify your inner voice, uncover limiting scripts, and rewrite your story with intention.**

Available on Amazon – just search for:

Rewriting Your Script: *A Guided Companion Journal to Mind Scripts* **by Alice Reed Murphy**

or visit: www.jolcc.com

"Keep your thoughts positive because your thoughts become your words. Keep your words positive because your words become your behavior. Keep your behavior positive because your behavior becomes your habits. Keep your habits positive because your habits become your values. Keep your values positive because your values become your destiny."

— Mahatma Gandhi

References

Adler, A. (1930). *The Individual Psychology of Alfred Adler: A Systematic Presentation in Selections from His Writings*. Basic Books.

Adler, A. (1930). The case of the neurotic child. *Journal of Individual Psychology, 2*(1), 35-42.

Aldao, A., Nolen-Hoeksema, S., & Schweizer, S. (2010). Emotion-regulation strategies across psychopathology: A meta-analytic review. *Clinical Psychology Review, 30*(2), 217–237.

Ainsworth, M. D. (1978). *Patterns of attachment: A psychological study of the strange situation*. Hillsdale, NJ: Lawrence Erlbaum Associates.

Ainsworth, M. D. S. (1979). *Infant–mother attachment*. American Psychologist, 34(10), 932–937.

Ainsworth, M. D. S., Blehar, M. C., Waters, E., & Wall, S. (1978). *Patterns of attachment: A psychological study of the strange situation*. Hillsdale, NJ: Lawrence Erlbaum Associates.

Arnsten, A. F. (2009). Stress signalling pathways that impair prefrontal cortex structure and function. *Nature Reviews Neuroscience, 10*(6), 410–422.

Asch, S. E. (1951). Effects of group pressure upon the modification and distortion of judgments. In H. Guetzkow (Ed.), *Groups, leadership, and men* (pp. 177-190). Pittsburgh, PA: Carnegie Press.

Barrett, L. F. (2017). *How emotions are made: The secret life of the brain*. Houghton Mifflin Harcourt.

Baumrind, D. (1991). The influence of parenting style on adolescent competence and substance use. *Journal of Early Adolescence, 11*(1), 56-95.

Baumeister, R. F., & Leary, M. R. (1995). The need to belong: Desire for interpersonal attachments as a fundamental human motivation. *Psychological Bulletin, 117*(3), 497-529.

Baxter Magolda, M. B. (2001). *Making their own way: Narratives for transforming higher education to promote self-development.* Stylus Publishing.

Beck, A. T. (1976). *Cognitive therapy and the emotional disorders.* New York, NY: International Universities Press.

Beck, A. T. (2011). *Cognitive therapy: A development in theory and practice.* HarperCollins.

Beck, J. S. (2011). *Cognitive behavior therapy: Basics and beyond* (2nd ed.). Guilford Press.

Begley, S. (2007). *Train your mind, change your brain: How a new science reveals our extraordinary potential to transform ourselves.* Ballantine Books.

Bem, S. L. (1981). Gender schema theory: A cognitive account of sex typing. *Psychological Review, 88*(4), 354–364.

Bem, S. L. (1993). *The lenses of gender: Transforming the debate on sexual inequality.* Yale University Press.

Benedetti, F. (2009). *Placebo effects: Understanding the mechanisms in health and disease.* Oxford University Press.

Bonanno, G. A. (2004). Loss, trauma, and human resilience. *American Psychologist, 59*(1), 20–28.

Bowlby, J. (1969). *Attachment and loss: Vol. 1. Attachment.* New York, NY: Basic Books.

Bowlby, J. (1969). *Attachment and loss: Volume I. Attachment.* London: Hogarth Press.

Bowlby, J. (1980). *Attachment and Loss: Vol. 3. Loss: Sadness and depression.* New York: Basic Books.

Bargh, J. A., & Chartrand, T. L. (1999). The unbearable automaticity of being. *American Psychologist, 54*(7), 462–479.

Brown, B. (2015). *Daring greatly: How the courage to be vulnerable transforms the way we live, love, parent, and lead.* New York, NY: Gotham Books.

Brown, B. (2010). *The Gifts of Imperfection: Let Go of Who You Think You're Supposed to Be and Embrace Who You Are.* Hazelden Publishing.

Brown, R. P., & Gerbarg, P. L. (2005). Sudarshan Kriya Yogic breathing in the treatment of stress, anxiety, and depression: Part II—Clinical applications and guidelines. *Journal of Alternative and Complementary Medicine, 11*(4), 711–717.

Chao, R. K. (2011). Parenting and child development in the Chinese cultural context. In M. H. Bornstein (Ed.), *Handbook of parenting: Volume 4: Social conditions and applied parenting* (2nd ed., pp. 137–163). Lawrence Erlbaum Associates.

Chao, R. K. (2011). Parenting and the internalization of culture: Cultural influences on parental socialization of emotion regulation. *Child Development Perspectives, 5*(2), 82–88.

Chapman, G. (1995). *The 5 love languages: The secret to love that lasts.* Chicago, IL: Northfield Publishing.

Chou, H. T. G., & Edge, N. (2012). "They are happier and having better lives than I am": The impact of using Facebook on perceptions of others' lives. *Cyberpsychology, Behavior, and Social Networking, 15*(2), 117–121.

Clance, P. R., & Imes, S. A. (1978). The imposter phenomenon in high achieving women: Dynamics and therapeutic intervention. *Psychotherapy: Theory, Research & Practice, 15*(3), 241-247.

Craig, A. D. (2009). How do you feel—now? The anterior insula and human awareness. *Nature Reviews Neuroscience, 10*(1), 59–70. https://doi.org/10.1038/nrn2555

Cohen, G. L., & Sherman, D. K. (2014). The psychology of change: Self-affirmation and social psychological intervention. *Annual Review of Psychology, 65*, 333–371.

Corrigan, P. W., & Watson, A. C. (2002). Understanding the impact of stigma on people with mental illness. *World Psychiatry, 1*(1), 16–20.

Critchley, H. D., & Harrison, N. A. (2013). Visceral influences on brain and behavior. *Neuron, 77*(4), 624–638. https://doi.org/10.1016/j.neuron.2013.02.008

Damon, W., Menon, J., & Bronk, K. C. (2003). The development of purpose during adolescence. *Applied Developmental Science, 7*(3), 119–128.

Davidson, R. J., & McEwen, B. S. (2012). Social influences on neuroplasticity: Stress and interventions to promote well-being. *Nature Neuroscience, 15*(5), 689–695.

Dispenza, J. (2014). *You are the placebo: Making your mind matter.* Hay House.

Doidge, N. (2007). *The brain that changes itself: Stories of personal triumph from the frontiers of brain science.* New York, NY: Viking.

Duke, M. P., Lazarus, A., & Fivush, R. (2008). Knowledge of family history as a clinically useful index of psychological functioning. *Emory Center for Myth and Ritual in American Life.*

Duke, M. P., Lazarus, A., & Fivush, R. (2008). The power of family stories: Developmental benefits of knowing one's family history. *Emory Center for Myth and Ritual in American Life.*

Dunkel, C. S., & Langenbucher, J. W. (2004). Birth order, family environment, and personality development. *Journal of Individual Psychology, 60*(3), 359–374.

Dweck, C. S. (2006). *Mindset: The new psychology of success.* Random House.

Dyer, W. W. (1990). *You'll see it when you believe it: The way to your personal transformation.* HarperCollins.

Eckstein, D. (2000). Empirical studies indicating significant birth-order-related personality differences. *Journal of Individual Psychology, 56*(4), 481–494.

Eisenberg, N., Cumberland, A., & Spinrad, T. L. (2005). Parental socialization of emotion. *Psychological Inquiry, 16*(2–3), 98–102.

Eisenberg, N., Spinrad, T. L., & Eggum, N. D. (2010). Emotion-related self-regulation and its relation to children's maladjustment. *Annual Review of Clinical Psychology, 6,* 495–525.

Emoto, M. (2004). *The hidden messages in water.* Atria Books.

Enright, R. D. (2001). *Forgiveness is a choice: A step-by-step process for resolving anger and restoring hope.* American Psychological Association.

Enright, R. D. (2001). The psychology of interpersonal forgiveness. In M. McCullough, K. Pargament, & C. Thoresen (Eds.), *Forgiveness: Theory, research, and practice* (pp. 46–65). Guilford Press.

Ephesians 2:10, New International Version (NIV). BibleGateway.

Erikson, E. H. (1968). *Identity: Youth and crisis.* W. W. Norton.

Falbo, T. (1991). *The Only Child: A Psychological Evaluation.* W. H. Freeman.

Falbo, T., & Polit, D. F. (1986). Quantitative review of the only child literature: Research evidence and theory development. *Psychological Bulletin, 100*(2), 176–189.

Fardouly, J., Diedrichs, P. C., Vartanian, L. R., & Halliwell, E. (2015). Social comparisons on social media: The impact of Facebook on young women's body image concerns and mood. *Body Image, 13*, 38–45.

Felitti, V. J., Anda, R. F., Nordenberg, D., Williamson, D. F., Spitz, A. M., Edwards, V., ... & Marks, J. S. (1998). Relationship of childhood abuse and household dysfunction to many of the leading causes of death in adults. *American Journal of Preventive Medicine, 14*(4), 245–258.

Festinger, L. (1954). A theory of social comparison processes. *Human Relations, 7*(2), 117–140.

Flett, G. L., & Hewitt, P. L. (2002). *Perfectionism: Theory, research, and treatment.* American Psychological Association.

Frankl, V. E. (1984). *Man's search for meaning.* Washington Square Press.

Fredrickson, B. L. (2009). *Positivity: Groundbreaking research to release your inner optimist and thrive.* Crown.

426

Freire, P. (1970). *Pedagogy of the oppressed.* Herder and Herder.

Fustos, J., Gramann, K., Herbert, B. M., & Pollatos, O. (2013). On the embodiment of emotion regulation: Interoceptive awareness facilitates reappraisal. *Social Cognitive and Affective Neuroscience, 8*(8), 911–917.

Gerbner, G., Gross, L., Morgan, M., & Signorielli, N. (1986). Living with television: The dynamics of the cultivation process. In J. Bryant & D. Zillmann (Eds.), *Perspectives on Media Effects* (pp. 17–40). Hillsdale, NJ: Lawrence Erlbaum Associates.

Gilbert, D. T. (2006). *Stumbling on happiness.* New York, NY: Vintage Books.

Gilbert, P. (2006). Emotion regulation: A biopsychosocial perspective. *Clinical Psychology & Psychotherapy, 13*(1), 13–20.

Gilbert, P. (2006). The evolution of the social brain. In J. T. Cacioppo & G. G. Berntson (Eds.), *Social neuroscience: Key readings* (pp. 117–138). MIT Press.

Goddard, N. (1944). *The power of awareness.* DeVorss & Company.

Gottman, J. M., & Silver, N. (2015). *The seven principles for making marriage work.* New York, NY: Three Rivers Press.

Gottman, J. M., & Silver, N. (2015). *The seven principles for making marriage work: A practical guide from the country's foremost relationship expert.* Harmony.

Grabe, S., Ward, L. M., & Hyde, J. S. (2008). The role of the media in body image concerns among women: A meta-analysis. *Psychological Bulletin, 134*(3), 460–476.

Gross, J. J. (2015). Emotion regulation: Current status and future prospects. *Psychological Inquiry, 26*(1), 1–26.

Gross, J. J., & John, O. P. (2003). Individual differences in two emotion regulation processes: Implications for affect, relationships, and well-being. *Journal of Personality and Social Psychology, 85*(2), 348–362.

Hammack, P. L., & Pilecki, A. (2012). Narrative as a root metaphor for political psychology. *Political Psychology, 33*(1), 75–103.

Haidt, J. (2006). *The happiness hypothesis: Finding modern truth in ancient wisdom.* Basic Books.

Harris, R. (2009). *The happiness trap: How to stop struggling and start living.* Boston, MA: Trumpeter.

Hay, L. L. (1984). *You can heal your life.* Hay House.

Hebb, D. O. (1949). *The organization of behavior: A neuropsychological theory.* Wiley.

Hewitt, P. L., & Flett, G. L. (2002). Perfectionism and depression: A review of the literature. *Journal of Abnormal Psychology, 111*(3), 363–380.

Helms, J. E. (1995). An update of Helms's White and People of Color racial identity models. In J. G. Ponterotto, J. M. Casas, L. A. Suzuki, & C. M. Alexander (Eds.), *Handbook of Multicultural Counseling* (pp. 181–198). Sage Publications.

Hill, P. L., Burrow, A. L., & Sumner, R. (2013). Addressing important questions in the field of purpose. *Journal of Positive Psychology, 8*(6), 556–564.

Hill, P. L., & Turiano, N. A. (2014). Purpose in life as a predictor of mortality across adulthood. *Psychological Science, 25*(7), 1482–1486.

Hochschild, A. R. (2012). *The managed heart: Commercialization of human feeling.* University of California Press.

Hofmann, S. G., Asnaani, A., Vonk, I. J., Sawyer, A. T., & Fang, A. (2012). The efficacy of cognitive behavioral therapy: A review of meta-analyses. *Cognitive Therapy and Research, 36*(5), 427–440.

Hölzel, B. K., Carmody, J., Vangel, M., Congleton, C., Yerramsetti, S. M., Gard, T., & Lazar, S. W. (2011). Mindfulness practice leads to increases in regional brain gray matter density. *Psychiatry Research: Neuroimaging, 191*(1), 36–43.

Hölzel, B. K., Lazar, S. W., Gard, T., Schuman-Olivier, Z., Vago, D. R., & Ott, U. (2011). How does mindfulness meditation work? Proposing mechanisms of action from a conceptual and neural perspective. *Perspectives on Psychological Science, 6*(6), 537–559.

hooks, b. (2000). *All about love: New visions.* William Morrow.

Johnson, S. M. (2008). *Hold me tight: Seven conversations for a lifetime of love.* Little, Brown Spark.

Kabat-Zinn, J. (1990). *Full catastrophe living: Using the wisdom of your body and mind to face stress, pain, and illness.* New York, NY: Delta.

Kabat-Zinn, J. (1994). *Wherever you go, there you are: Mindfulness meditation in everyday life.* Hyperion.

Kahneman, D. (2011). *Thinking, fast and slow.* Farrar, Straus and Giroux.

Kaptchuk, T. J., Miller, F. G., & Kelley, J. M. (2010). Placebo effects in medicine. *New England Journal of Medicine*, 363(21), 2038–2040.

Kasser, T. (2002). *The high price of materialism.* MIT Press.

Kashdan, T. B., & McKnight, P. E. (2009). Origins of purpose in life: Refining our understanding of a life well lived. *Psicothema, 21*(1), 289–297.

Kashdan, T. B., & Rottenberg, J. (2010). Psychological flexibility as a fundamental aspect of health. *Clinical Psychology Review, 30*(7), 865–878.

Kernis, M. H., & Goldman, B. M. (2006). A multicomponent conceptualization of authenticity: Theory and research. *Advances in Experimental Social Psychology, 38*, 283–357.

Kilbourne, J. (1999). *Can't buy my love: How advertising changes the way we think and feel.* Simon and Schuster.

Kim, E. S., Sun, J. K., Park, N., & Peterson, C. (2013). Purpose in life and reduced incidence of stroke in older adults: 'The Health and Retirement Study.' *Journal of Psychosomatic Research, 74*(5), 427–432.

Kochanska, G., Barry, R. A., Aksan, N., & Boldt, L. J. (2001). Effortful control in early childhood: Continuity and change, antecedents, and implications for social development. *Developmental Psychology, 37*(5), 682–700.

Koenig, H. G. (2012). Religion, spirituality, and health: The research and clinical implications. *ISRN Psychiatry, 2012*, 278730.

Kok, B. E., & Fredrickson, B. L. (2010). Upward spirals of the heart: Autonomic flexibility, as indexed by vagal tone, reciprocally and prospectively predicts positive emotions and social connectedness. *Biological Psychology, 85*(3), 432–436.

Kross, E., & Ayduk, O. (2011). Making meaning out of negative experiences by self-distancing. *Current Directions in Psychological Science, 20*(3), 187–191.

Langer, E. J. (2009). *Mindfulness.* Cambridge, MA: Perseus Books.

Langer, E. J. (1997). *The power of mindful learning.* Addison-Wesley.

LeDoux, J. E. (2000). *Emotion circuits in the brain.* Annual Review of Neuroscience, 23(1), 155–184. https://doi.org/10.1146/annurev.neuro.23.1.155

Leman, K. (2009). *The Birth Order Book: Why You Are the Way You Are.* Revell.

Levine, P. A. (2010). *In an unspoken voice: How the body releases trauma and restores goodness.* North Atlantic Books.

Lieberman, M. D., Inagaki, T. K., Tabibnia, G., & Crockett, M. J. (2007). Subjective responses to emotional stimuli during labeling, reappraisal, and distraction. *Emotion, 7*(4), 468–480. Lupien, S. J., McEwen, B. S., Gunnar, M. R., & Heim, C. (2009). Effects of stress throughout the lifespan on the brain, behaviour and cognition. *Nature Reviews Neuroscience, 10*(6), 434–445.

Lipton, B. H. (2005). *The biology of belief: Unleashing the power of consciousness, matter & miracles.* Mountain of Love/Elite Books.

Lupien, S. J., McEwen, B. S., Gunnar, M. R., & Heim, C. (2009). Effects of stress throughout the lifespan on the brain, behaviour and cognition. *Nature Reviews Neuroscience, 10*(6), 434–445.

Markus, H. (1977). Self-schemata and processing information about the self. *Journal of Personality and Social Psychology, 35*(2), 63–78.

Markus, H. R., & Kitayama, S. (1991). Culture and the self: Implications for cognition, emotion, and motivation. *Psychological Review, 98*(2), 224–253.

McAdams, D. P. (2001). The psychology of life stories. *Review of General Psychology, 5*(2), 100–122.

McCraty, R., Atkinson, M., Tomasino, D., & Bradley, R. T. (2009). The coherent heart: Heart-brain interactions, psychophysiological coherence, and the emergence of system-wide order. *Integral Review*, 5(2), 10–115.

McEwen, B. S. (2007). Physiology and neurobiology of stress and adaptation: Central role of the brain. *Physiological Reviews, 87*(3), 873–904.

McKnight, P. E., & Kashdan, T. B. (2009). Purpose in life as a system that creates and sustains health and well-being: An integrative, testable theory. *Review of General Psychology, 13*(3), 242–251.

Meichenbaum, D. (1977). *Cognitive-behavior modification: An integrative approach*. New York, NY: Plenum Press.

Merton, R. K. (1948). The self-fulfilling prophecy. *The Antioch Review, 8*(2), 193–210.

Murphy, J. (1963). *The power of your subconscious mind*. Prentice-Hall.

Neff, K. D. (2003). Self-compassion: An alternative conceptualization of a healthy attitude toward oneself. *Self and Identity, 2*(2), 85–101.

Neff, K. D. (2011). *Self-compassion: The proven power of being kind to yourself*. William Morrow.

Neff, K. D. (2003). The development and validation of a scale to measure self-compassion. *Self and Identity, 2*(3), 223–250.

Newberg, A., & Waldman, M. R. (2009). *How God changes your brain: Breakthrough findings from a leading neuroscientist*. Ballantine Books.

Nolen-Hoeksema, S. (2000). The role of rumination in depressive disorders and mixed anxiety/depressive symptoms. *Journal of Abnormal Psychology, 109*(3), 504–511.

Ochsner, K. N., & Gross, J. J. (2005). The cognitive control of emotion. *Trends in Cognitive Sciences, 9*(5), 242–249.

Ogden, P., Minton, K., & Pain, C. (2006). *Trauma and the body: A sensorimotor approach to psychotherapy*. W. W. Norton & Company.

Park, C. L. (2010). Making sense of the meaning literature: An integrative review of meaning making and its effects on adjustment to stressful life events. *Psychological Bulletin, 136*(2), 257–301.

Pennebaker, J. W. (1997). *Writing about emotional experiences as a therapeutic process*. Psychological Science, 8(3), 162–166.

Pennebaker, J. W., & Chung, C. K. (2011). Expressive writing: Connections to physical and mental health. In H. S. Friedman (Ed.), *The Oxford handbook of health psychology* (pp. 417–437). Oxford University Press.

Pennebaker, J. W., & Seagal, J. D. (1999). Forming a story: The health benefits of narrative. *Journal of Clinical Psychology, 55*(10), 1243–1254.

Perloff, R. M. (2014). Social media effects on young women's body image concerns: Theoretical perspectives and an agenda for research. *Sex Roles, 71*(11–12), 363–377.

Phinney, J. S. (1990). Ethnic identity in adolescents and adults: Review of research. *Psychological Bulletin, 108*(3), 499–514.

Polletta, F. (2006). *It was like a fever: Storytelling in protest and politics*. University of Chicago Press.

Porges, S. W. (2007). The polyvagal perspective. *Biological Psychology, 74*(2), 116–143.

Porges, S. W. (2011). *The polyvagal theory: Neurophysiological foundations of emotions, attachment, communication, and self-regulation.* Norton & Company.

Pyszczynski, T., Greenberg, J., & Solomon, S. (1999). A dual-process model of defense against conscious and unconscious death-related thoughts: An extension of terror management theory. *Psychological Review, 106*(4), 835–845.

Romans 12:2, New International Version (NIV). BibleGateway.

Rosenberg, M. B. (2003). *Nonviolent communication: A language of life.* Encinitas, CA: PuddleDancer Press.

Rosenthal, R., & Jacobson, L. (1968). *Pygmalion in the classroom: Teacher expectation and pupils' intellectual development.* New York: Holt, Rinehart & Winston.

Ryff, C. D., Singer, B., & Dienberg Love, G. (2004). Positive health: Connecting well-being with biology. *Philosophical Transactions of the Royal Society B: Biological Sciences, 359*(1449), 1383–1394.

Ryff, C. D., & Singer, B. H. (2008). Know thyself and become what you are: A eudaimonic approach to psychological well-being. *Journal of Happiness Studies, 9*(1), 13–39.

Schank, R. C., & Abelson, R. P. (1977). *Scripts, Plans, Goals, and Understanding: An Inquiry into Human Knowledge Structures.* Lawrence Erlbaum Associates.

Schwartz, R. C. (1995). *Internal family systems therapy.* New York, NY: Guilford Press.

Segerstrom, S. C., & Miller, G. E. (2004). Psychological stress and the human immune system: A meta-analytic study of 30 years of inquiry. *Psychological Bulletin*, 130(4), 601–630.

Siegel, D. J. (2012). *The developing mind: How relationships and the brain interact to shape who we are* (2nd ed.). Guilford Press.

Siegel, D. J. (2010). *The mindful therapist: A clinician's guide to mindsight and neural integration.* W. W. Norton & Company.

Siegel, D. J. (2012). *The whole-brain child: 12 revolutionary strategies to nurture your child's developing mind.* Bantam.

Siegel, D. J., & Bryson, T. P. (2011). *The whole-brain child: 12 revolutionary strategies to nurture your child's developing mind.* Delacorte Press.

Seligman, M. E. P. (1998). *Learned optimism: How to change your mind and your life.* New York, NY: Pocket Books.

Seligman, M. E. P. (2011). *Flourish: A visionary new understanding of happiness and well-being.* Free Press.

Seligman, M. E. P. (2011). *Learned optimism: How to change your mind and your life.* New York, NY: Vintage Books.

Snyder, C. R. (2002). Hope theory: Rainbows in the mind. *Psychological Inquiry, 13*(4), 249–275.

Steger, M. F. (2012). Making meaning in life. *Psychological Inquiry, 23*(4), 381–385.

Steger, M. F., Oishi, S., & Kashdan, T. B. (2008). Meaning in life across the life span: Levels and correlates of meaning in life from emerging adulthood to older adulthood. *The Journal of Positive Psychology, 4*(1), 43–52.

Snyder, C. R. (2002). *Hope theory: Rainbows in the mind.* Psychological Inquiry, 13(4), 249-275.

Tajfel, H., & Turner, J. C. (1986). The social identity theory of intergroup behavior. In S. Worchel & W. G. Austin (Eds.), *Psychology of intergroup relations* (pp. 7–24). Nelson-Hall.

Taylor, G. J., Bagby, R. M., & Parker, J. D. A. (1997). *Disorders of affect regulation: Alexithymia in medical and psychiatric illness.* Cambridge University Press.

Taylor, S. E., Pham, L. B., Rivkin, I. D., & Armor, D. A. (1998). Harnessing the imagination: Mental simulation, self-regulation, and coping. *American Psychologist, 53*(4), 429–439.

Thayer, J. F., & Lane, R. D. (2000). A model of neurovisceral integration in emotion regulation and dysregulation. *Journal of Affective Disorders, 61*(3), 201–216.

The Holy Bible, New International Version (NIV), Psalm 139:14, Matthew 23:11.

Thompson, R. A. (1994). Emotion regulation: A theme in search of definition. In N. A. Fox (Ed.), *The development of emotion regulation: Biological and behavioral considerations* (Vol. 59, pp. 25–52). *Monographs of the Society for Research in Child Development.*

Tiggemann, M., & Slater, A. (2014). NetGirls: The Internet, Facebook, and body image concern in adolescent girls. *International Journal of Eating Disorders, 47*(6), 630–633.

Tindle, H. A., Newberg, A. B., & Shahar, M. (2009). *Mind-body interactions in health and disease: The influence of emotions on health and well-being.* Journal of Alternative and Complementary Medicine, 15(6), 677–688.

Toussaint, L., & Cheadle, A. (2009). Forgiveness and health: An exploration of research and practical applications. *The Journal of Positive Psychology, 4*(3), 118–132.

Toussaint, L., & Cheadle, A. (2009). Forgiveness and health: An empirical review of the impact of forgiveness on physical health outcomes. *Journal of Behavioral Medicine, 32*(4), 241–257.

Tugade, M. M., & Fredrickson, B. L. (2004). Resilient individuals use positive emotions to bounce back from negative emotional experiences. *Journal of Personality and Social Psychology, 86*(2), 320–333.

Twenge, J. M., & Campbell, W. K. (2009). *The narcissism epidemic: Living in the age of entitlement.* Free Press.

van der Kolk, B. A. (2014). *The body keeps the score: Brain, mind, and body in the healing of trauma.* Viking.

White, M., & Epston, D. (1990). *Narrative means to therapeutic ends.* Norton.

Winnicott, D. W. (1965). *The maturational processes and the facilitating environment.* International Universities Press.

Wood, A. M., & Joseph, S. (2010). The absence of positive psychological (eudemonic) well-being as a risk factor for depression: A ten-year cohort study. *Journal of Affective Disorders, 122*(3), 213–217.

Yehuda, R., Daskalakis, N. P., Desarnaud, F., Makotkine, I., Lehrner, A., Koch, E., ... & Meaney, M. J. (2015). Epigenetic biomarkers as predictors and correlates of symptom improvement following psychotherapy in combat veterans with PTSD. *Frontiers in Psychiatry, 6*, 111.

Yehuda, R., Halligan, S. L., & Grossman, R. (2001). Childhood trauma and risk for PTSD: Relation to intergenerational effects of trauma. *Journal of Clinical Psychology, 57*(8), 1373-1383.